Is lesbian Identity Obsolete?

This cross-disciplinary book engages with the provocation, "Is lesbian identity obsolete?". In this volume, researchers offer diverse perspectives on the question of lesbian identity past, present, and future. This eclectic, multidisciplinary compilation composed of chapters and shorter commentaries helps readers understand the roots of conflict and current tensions between the queer and the trans movements and the lesbian community.

Using a historical lens, authors examine the 1970s lesbian communities' practices of racial and trans inclusion and exclusion. Several contributions from across the social sciences utilize qualitative and quantitative methods to illuminate the shifting meaning of lesbian identity today. These contributions help explain why some cis and trans women and nonbinary folx come to either be attached to or disavow lesbian identification. An additional set of chapters engage in theoretical analysis to explore the fraught relationship between queer theory and lesbian thought and the importance of lesbian theory in the formation of transgender scholarship. This collection's eclectic engagement with the question of lesbian identity's obsoleteness helps draw an ethical blueprint for a more sustainable, inclusive, and coalitional future for lesbian communities and identities.

This book will be of great value to students, researchers, and scholars in the fields of Sociology, Psychology, and Anthropology including Gay and Lesbian studies as well as the intersectionality of gender and sexuality. The chapters in this book were originally published in the *Journal of Lesbian Studies*.

Ella Ben Hagai is Assistant Professor of Psychology at California State University, Fullerton, USA. Trained in Psychology and Anthropology, her research focuses on processes that lead individuals who are members of different social groups (e.g., class, ethnic, and religious) to develop a shared political consciousness that supports equal distribution of resources across groups. Her theoretical work examines the intersections between trans* and queer theory and recent psychological research on gender and sexuality.

T0391570

Is lesbian Identity Obsolete?

In Conversation with Queer and Trans Perspectives

Edited by
Ella Ben Hagai

Routledge
Taylor & Francis Group

LONDON AND NEW YORK

First published 2023
by Routledge
4 Park Square, Milton Park, Abingdon, Oxon, OX14 4RN

and by Routledge
605 Third Avenue, New York, NY 10158

Routledge is an imprint of the Taylor & Francis Group, an informa business

Introduction © 2023 Ella Ben Hagai
Chapters 1–9 and 11–15 © 2023 Taylor & Francis
Chapter 10 © 2021 Lexi Webster. Originally published as Open Access.

British Library Cataloguing-in-Publication Data
A catalogue record for this book is available from the British Library

ISBN13: 978-1-032-44253-2 (hbk)
ISBN13: 978-1-032-44255-6 (pbk)
ISBN13: 978-1-003-37123-6 (ebk)

DOI: 10.4324/9781003371236

Typeset in Minion Pro
by codeMantra

Publisher's Note
The publisher accepts responsibility for any inconsistencies that may have arisen during the conversion of this book from journal articles to book chapters, namely the inclusion of journal terminology.

Disclaimer
Every effort has been made to contact copyright holders for their permission to reprint material in this book. The publishers would be grateful to hear from any copyright holder who is not here acknowledged and will undertake to rectify any errors or omissions in future editions of this book.

Contents

Citation information   vii
Notes on contributors   ix

Introduction: Is lesbian identity obsolete? In conversation with queer and trans
perspectives   1
Ella Ben Hagai

1 Shifting inclusions: Identities and spaces of political lesbianism in Montreal
   from 1970 to 2020   5
   Tara Chanady

2 "I was returning to see if the ghosts were still astirring": Southern lesbian
   reflexivity as social movement in *Feminary* (1979–1982)   17
   Sarah Heying

3 Between mother and daughter: Brown erotics and sacred notes   32
   Sara Shroff

4 The institutionalization of queer theory: Where has lesbian criticism gone?   40
   Maite Escudero-Alías

5 "*Somos contra la 'queer-ificación'*"/"We reject the queer-ification of lesbianism":
   Lesbian political identity and anti-queer politics among Mexican lesbians and
   queer Chicanas-Latinas   56
   Stacy I. Macias

6 Women who prefer "lesbian" to "queer": Generational continuity and discontinuity   72
   Jessica Megarry, Catherine Orian Weiss, Meagan Tyler and Kate Farhall

7 Comparing conceptions of gender, sexuality and lesbian identity between baby
   boomers and millennials   92
   Ella Ben Hagai, Rachelle Annechino and Tamar Antin

8 Lesbian, feminist, TERF: A queer attack on feminist studies   111
   Carly Thomsen and Laurie Essig

9 *"Lezibian/mulezi"*: Adoption of "globalized" lesbian identity and secondary self-labels among same-sex attracted women in Harare 129
Nelson Muparamoto

10 "Erase/rewind": How transgender Twitter discourses challenge and (re)politicize lesbian identities 146
Lexi Webster

11 Toward a historiography of the lesbian transsexual, or the TERF's nightmare 164
Jules Gill-Peterson

12 Learning butch: Tracing lesbian and trans becoming in the classroom 179
L. Helton

13 Lesbian vitality: A provocation 190
Julie R. Enszer

14 Is lesbian identity obsolete? Some (limited) answers and further questions from a unique philology of human behavioral science perspective 197
Charlotte Chucky Tate

15 Willful lives: Self-determination in lesbian and trans feminisms 214
Kathryn J. Perkins

Index 219

Citation Information

The following chapters were originally published in various volumes and issues of the *Journal of Lesbian Studies*. When citing this material, please use the original page numbering for each article, as follows:

Chapter 1

Shifting inclusions: Identities and spaces of political lesbianism in Montreal from 1970 to 2020
Tara Chanady
Journal of Lesbian Studies, volume 26, issue 2 (2022) pp. 121–132

Chapter 2

"I was returning to see if the ghosts were still astirring": Southern lesbian reflexivity as social movement in Feminary *(1979–1982)*
Sarah Heying
Journal of Lesbian Studies, volume 26, issue 1 (2022) pp. 12–26

Chapter 3

Between mother and daughter: Brown erotics and sacred notes
Sara Shroff
Journal of Lesbian Studies, volume 26, issue 1 (2022) pp. 45–52

Chapter 4

The institutionalization of queer theory: Where has lesbian criticism gone?
Maite Escudero-Alías
Journal of Lesbian Studies, volume 26, issue 3 (2022) pp. 253–268

Chapter 5

"Somos contra la 'queer-ificacíon'"/"We reject the queer-ification of lesbianism": Lesbian political identity and anti-queer politics among Mexican lesbians and queer Chicanas-Latinas
Stacy I. Macias
Journal of Lesbian Studies, volume 26, issue 1 (2022) pp. 73–88

Chapter 6

Women who prefer "lesbian" to "queer": Generational continuity and discontinuity
Jessica Megarry, Catherine Orian Weiss, Meagan Tyler and Kate Farhall
Journal of Lesbian Studies, volume 26, issue 1 (2022) pp. 53–72

Chapter 7

Comparing conceptions of gender, sexuality and lesbian identity between baby boomers and millennials
Ella Ben Hagai, Rachelle Annechino and Tamar Antin
Journal of Lesbian Studies, volume 26, issue 3 (2022) pp. 216–234

Chapter 8

Lesbian, feminist, TERF: A queer attack on feminist studies
Carly Thomsen and Laurie Essig
Journal of Lesbian Studies, volume 26, issue 1 (2022) pp. 27–44

Chapter 9

"Lezibian/mulezi": Adoption of "globalized" lesbian identity and secondary self-labels among same-sex attracted women in Harare
Nelson Muparamotoa
Journal of Lesbian Studies, volume 26, issue 3 (2022) pp. 269–285

Chapter 10

"Erase/rewind": How transgender Twitter discourses challenge and (re)politicize lesbian identities
Lexi Webster
Journal of Lesbian Studies, volume 26, issue 2 (2022) pp. 174–191

Chapter 11

Toward a historiography of the lesbian transsexual, or the TERF's nightmare
Jules Gill-Peterson
Journal of Lesbian Studies, volume 26, issue 2 (2022) pp. 133–147

Chapter 12

Learning butch: Tracing lesbian and trans becoming in the classroom
L. Helton
Journal of Lesbian Studies, volume 26, issue 2 (2022) pp. 148–158

Chapter 13

Lesbian vitality: A provocation
Julie R. Enszer
Journal of Lesbian Studies, volume 26, issue 1 (2022) pp. 113–119

Chapter 14

Is lesbian identity obsolete? Some (limited) answers and further questions from a unique philology of human behavioral science perspective
Charlotte Chucky Tate
Journal of Lesbian Studies, volume 26, issue 3 (2022) pp. 199–215

Chapter 15

Willful lives: Self-determination in lesbian and trans feminisms
Kathryn J. Perkins
Journal of Lesbian Studies, volume 26, issue 2 (2022) pp. 194–198

For any permission-related enquiries please visit:
http://www.tandfonline.com/page/help/permissions

Notes on Contributors

Rachelle Annechino is Researcher at the Critical Public Health Research Group at Prevention Research Center, Berkeley, USA.

Tamar Antin is Director at the Center for Critical Public Health, USA. Her work focuses on the role of stigma in public health practice and policymaking. Her research has examined health inequities by considering the intersections between health-related stigma (e.g., the stigma of being a smoker) and other social identity stigmas (e.g. ethnicity, social class, and/or gender).

Tara Chanady is Research Advisor at Université de Montreal's Centre for Public Health Research, Canada. As a lesbian concerned with visibility and equity, her lectures, publications, and university courses aim to critically examine discourses and norms around gender and sexuality.

Kate Farhall is Researcher in the Centre for People, Organisation and Work at RMIT University, Melbourne, Australia. Her work focuses on using critical feminist analyses to address gender inequality in a range of contexts, with a particular focus on questions of sexuality and violence against women. Her primary research examines how non-metropolitan experiences and geographies impact the intersection of domestic and family violence and work.

Julie R. Enszer, PhD, is Scholar and Poet. She edits and publishes *Sinister Wisdom*, a multicultural lesbian literary and art journal.

Maite Escudero-Alías is Senior Lecturer in the Department of English and German Philology at the University of Zaragoza, Spain, where she teaches English and Irish literature. Her research focuses on lesbian criticism and queer theory, on which she has published widely in journals such as *Journal of Gender Studies, Journal of Lesbian Studies, The Journal of Popular Culture, and Journal of International Women's Studies.*

Laurie Essig is Professor of Gender, Sexuality, & Feminist Studies at Middlebury College, USA. She has written for a variety of publications including the *New York Times, The Washington Post,* the *Conversation,* and *Lesbian Studies.*

Jules Gill-Peterson is Associate Professor of History at Johns Hopkins University, Baltimore, USA. She is General Co-Editor of *TSQ: Transgender Studies Quarterly.*

Ella Ben Hagai is Assistant Professor of Psychology at California State University, Fullerton, USA. Trained in Psychology and Anthropology, her research focuses on processes that lead individuals who are members of different social groups (e.g., class, ethnic, and religious) to develop a shared political consciousness that supports equal distribution of resources across groups. Her theoretical work examines the intersections between trans* and queer theory and recent psychological research on gender and sexuality.

L. Helton is Doctoral Student in English Education program at Teachers College at Columbia University, USA. Her research focuses on queer pedagogy and intersections between queer studies and English education.

Sarah Heying is PhD Candidate in English and Gender Studies at the University of Mississippi, USA, where she researches lesbian and trans literature that invokes the site of the U.S. South to negotiate the intersections between gender, sexuality, race, and legacies of reproductive dispossession.

Stacy I. Macias is Associate Professor in the Department of Women's, Gender, and Sexuality Studies at California State University, Long Beach, USA.

Jessica Megarry is Lecturer in Political Science in the School of Social and Political Sciences at the University of Melbourne, Australia. Her research interests include women's political communication, feminist activism, and digital politics.

Nelson Muparamoto is Postdoctoral Fellow at the WITS Center for Diversity Studies at the University of the Witwatersrand, Johannesburg, South Africa, and Lecturer at the University of Zimbabwe in the Department of Demography, Settlement and Development, Harare, Zimbabwe. Nelson is Diversity and Social Inclusion Advocate and works closely with marginalized communities in Zimbabwe in advocacy for social justice and social inclusion.

Kathryn J. Perkins is Assistant Professor of Political Science and Affiliate Faculty in Women's, Gender, and Sexuality Studies at California State University, Long Beach, USA. Her research in public law and feminist legal theory focuses on queer and trans jurisprudence and politics.

Sara Shroff is 2019–2021 inaugural Postdoctoral Fellow at the Mark S. Bonham Center for Sexual Diversity Studies at the University of Toronto, Canada. She is Assistant Professor at Lahore University of Management Sciences, Pakistan, where she holds a joint appointment in gender and sexuality studies and political science.

Charlotte Tate, PhD, is Behavioral Scientist and Full Professor working in a Psychology Department. Her primary research interests are in gender identity (trans-integrated), sexual orientation (asexual-integrated), and U.S. ethnic identity (mixed-integrated).

Carly Thomsen is Assistant Professor of Gender, Sexuality, & Feminist Studies at Middlebury College, USA. Her work on LGBTQ activism, queer rurality, reproductive justice, intersectionality, and feminist pedagogy is published in various journals, including: *Signs: A Journal of Women in Culture and Society*; *Hypatia: A Journal of Feminist Philosophy*; *Feminist Studies*; *Feminist Formations*; and *Atlantis: Critical Studies in Gender, Culture, and Social Justice*.

Meagan Tyler is Senior Lecturer, based in the Centre for People, Organisation and Work (CPOW), at RMIT University in Melbourne, Australia. Her research interests center on the politics of women's sexuality, men's violence against women, and the political economy of the sex industry. She has also written on the gendered power dynamics of disasters and emergency management.

Lexi Webster is Deputy Director of Digital Humanities at the University of Southampton, UK. Her research focuses primarily on corpus-driven critical discourse studies, focusing on the implications that identity construction/s and cognitive models have for actors, institutions, and social structures.

Catherine Orian Weiss teaches in the School of Global, Urban and Social Studies at RMIT University, Melbourne, Australia. She writes on feminist and anti-racist theory, with a particular interest in connections between care and sexuality in the context of migration. She has also written on the effects of the COVID-19 pandemic on the prevention of violence against women.

Introduction "Is lesbian identity obsolete?" In conversation with queer and trans perspectives

Ella Ben Hagai

The collection of articles featured in this book provides an in-depth and multifaceted analysis of debates important to the lesbian community on queer and transgender inclusions. The articles selected for this edited volume were published in the *Journal of Lesbian Studies* as part of a triple-issue conversation on the question, *"Is Lesbian Identity Obsolete?"* This provocation drew submissions that engaged deeply with the past, the present, and the future of lesbian identity (Ben Hagai & Seymour, 2022). This book brings together submissions that, in tandem, provide a panoramic view of two debates important to lesbian, queer, and trans people today. First is the complex relationship between queer and lesbian theory and identity, and second is trans inclusion in the lesbian community. The research and analysis presented in this book serves as an antidote for the contemporary moment where social media-driven scholarship and popular media promote polarization between lesbian, queer, and transgender identities. Instead, scholarship highlighted in this book provides a nuanced, multidisciplinary, and in-depth analysis of lesbian identity and theory and its impact and interdependence with queer activism and queer and transgender communities.

This volume begins with submissions that examine archives and interviews with lesbian feminists who were activists at the peak of the political lesbian movements in the 1970s. Research from different parts of the world, including the United States South and Montreal, Canada, explores ways in which separatist women-loving women communities were able to develop an independent culture for lesbian women. For instance, in *Shifting inclusions: Identities and spaces of political lesbianism in Montreal from 1970 to 2020*, Chanady (2022) highlights the liberation lesbian women felt and the rich culture they developed in separatist spaces. In *"I was returning to see if the ghosts were still astir-ring": Southern lesbian reflexivity as social movement in Feminary (1979–1982)*, Heying (2022) shows the reflexive and sophisticated manner members of the collective engaged in to understand identity differences among its members. In *Between mother and daughter: Brown erotics and sacred notes*, Shroff (2022) describes the impact of political lesbian theorizations on her own relationship with her mother growing up in Pakistan.

Lesbian and Queer theories and activism

Many lesbians, especially those who were part of the feminist revolution of the 1970s, understand the emergence of queer identity and theory as a form of erasure. In *The institutionalization of queer theory: Where has lesbian criticism gone?* Escudero-Alías (2022) examines the ways in which important contributions made by lesbian theorists, such as Audre Lord, were ignored, coopted, or even erased by queer theorization. The tension between queer and lesbian identity is theoretical; it emerges in meetings of transnational activists. In *"Somos contra la 'queer-ificacíon'"/"We reject the queer-ification of lesbianism"*, Macias (2022) describes the meeting of Chicana and Latinx queer Los Angeles-based activists in Mexico City to organize in solidarity with lesbian activists there. Soon tensions emerge between these two groups over differences in identities (i.e., queer vs. lesbian) as well as political goals. In *Women who prefer "lesbian" to "queer": Generational continuity and discontinuity*, Megarry (2022) and her colleagues survey lesbian women who reject queer identification common among many emerging adults. Their analysis of hundreds of lesbian women's responses suggests that an important reason why lesbian identity continues to be used is due to the desire by many young women to connect with women of past generations through shared collective lesbian identity.

Lesbian communities and Transgender inclusion

Another set of contributions to this book examine the tensions between lesbian identity and transgender inclusion. In *Comparing conceptions of gender, sexuality and lesbian identity between baby boomers and millennials*, Ben Hagai (2022) and her colleagues analyze in-depth interviews with sexual minority women and nonbinary people of different generations. Their analysis suggests that older lesbians were more likely to understand gender as an oppressive category imposed by patriarchy. In contrast, participants under 30 were more likely to see gender as based on an internal identification. Because gender was based on an internal identification, it was fluid and unstable. These differences in the understanding of gender identification serve as the basis of misunderstandings and conflict between cis and trans women and nonbinary folks. In *Lesbian, feminist, TERF: A queer attack on feminist studies*, Thomsen and Essig (2022) describe the ways in which the "diversity inc" apparatus that is used to market products, organizations, and educational institutions works through a neoliberal logic in which some identities are valued and centered over others. When lesbian feminist professors critically examine the intersectionality of gender identities, they become the target of diversity managers because of their supposed "transphobia".

In spite of the schism between transgender and lesbian identity, scholarly work included in this special issue underlines the hybridity and interdependence between lesbian and transgender identities. In *"Lezibian/mulezi":*

Adoption of "globalized" lesbian identity and secondary self-labels among same sex attracted women in Harare, Muparamoto (2022) reveals how the ways in which butch lesbians understand themselves in Harare, Zimbabwe echoes at times how nonbinary gender identities are understood in the United States. In *"Erase/rewind": How transgender Twitter discourses challenge and (re)politicize lesbian identities*, Webster (2022) illustrates how contemporary Twitter discourse invokes language rooted in the lesbian community's culture of understanding one another through culturally specific communication strategies. In *Toward a historiography of the lesbian transsexual, or the TERF's nightmare*, Gill-Peterson (2022) employs archival case study research to show how transwomen were embedded in lesbian relationships and community networks as early as the 1940s. The hybridity and interdependence of trans identities are deeply connected with lesbian identities on a particularly personal level for Helton (2022), who in *Learning butch: Tracing lesbian and trans becoming in the classroom* discusses their personal transition as they taught high school. Although they do not identify as a woman, Helton feels at home in transgender identity. In *Lesbian vitality: A provocation*, Enszer (2022) discusses the important lesbian publication *Sinister Wisdom* in which trans lesbians have contributed their voices to create an eclectic and sustainable lesbian community.

The interdependences between trans and lesbian identity are also theorized in contributions from across the social sciences. In *Is lesbian identity obsolete? Some (limited) answers and further questions from a unique philology of human behavioral science perspective*, Tate (2022) reflects on the possible changes in lesbian identities with the inclusion of people who transition in and out of lesbian identity. In *Willful lives: Self-determination in lesbian and trans feminisms*, Perkins (2022) highlight the affinities between political lesbian theorization such as the work of Monique Wittig (1980) and emerging trans feminist scholarship on gender self-determination.

In a time of growing polarization and tensions in the LGBTQ+ community, this eclectic, multidisciplinary compilation composed of chapters and shorter commentaries helps readers understand the roots of contemporary conflict and tensions, as well as the layers of hybridity and interconnection between lesbian, queer, and trans identities and theories.

References

Ben Hagai, E., Annechino, R., & Antin, T. (2022). Comparing conceptions of gender, sexuality and lesbian identity between baby boomers and millennials. *Journal of Lesbian Studies*, 26(3), 216–234. https://doi.org/10.1080/10894160.2021.1972915

Ben Hagai, E. B., & Seymour, N. (2022). Is lesbian identity obsolete? *Journal of Lesbian Studies*, 26(1), 1–11. https://doi.org/10.1080/10894160.2021.2005231

Chanady, T. (2022). Shifting inclusions: Identities and spaces of political lesbianism in Montreal from 1970 to 2020. *Journal of Lesbian Studies*, 26(2), 121–132. https://doi.org/10.1080/10894160.2021.1975357

Enszer, J. R. (2022). Lesbian vitality: A provocation. *Journal of Lesbian Studies*, 26(1), 113–119. https://doi.org/10.1080/10894160.2021.1953720

Escudero-Alías, M. (2022). The institutionalization of queer theory: Where has lesbian criticism gone? *Journal of Lesbian Studies*, 26(3), 253–268. https://doi.org/10.1080/10894160.2021.2003515

Gill-Peterson, J. (2022). Toward a historiography of the lesbian transsexual, or the TERF's nightmare. *Journal of Lesbian Studies*, 26(2), 133–147. https://doi.org/10.1080/10894160.2021.1979726

Helton, L. (2022). Learning butch: Tracing lesbian and trans becoming in the classroom. *Journal of Lesbian Studies*, 26(2), 148–158. https://doi.org/10.1080/10894160.2021.1976058

Heying, S. (2022). "I was returning to see if the ghosts were still astirring": Southern lesbian reflexivity as social movement in Feminary (1979–1982). *Journal of Lesbian Studies*, 26(1), 12–26. https://doi.org/10.1080/10894160.2021.1954307

Macias, S. I. (2022). "Somos contra la 'queer-ificacíon'"/"We reject the queer-ification of lesbianism": Lesbian political identity and anti-queer politics among Mexican lesbians and queer Chicanas-Latinas. *Journal of Lesbian Studies*, 26(1), 73–88.

Megarry, J., Weiss, C. O., Tyler, M., & Farhall, K. (2022). Women who prefer "lesbian" to "queer": Generational continuity and discontinuity. *Journal of Lesbian Studies*, 26(1), 53–72. https://doi.org/10.1080/10894160.2021.1950271

Muparamoto, N. (2022). "*Lezibian/mulezi*": Adoption of "globalized" lesbian identity and secondary self-labels among same-sex attracted women in Harare. *Journal of Lesbian Studies*, 26(3), 269–285. https://doi.org/10.1080/10894160.2021.2006868

Perkins, K. J. (2022). Willful lives: Self-determination in lesbian and trans feminisms. *Journal of Lesbian Studies*, 26(2), 194–198. https://doi.org/10.1080/10894160.2021.1997073

Shroff, S. (2022). Between mother and daughter: Brown erotics and sacred notes. *Journal of Lesbian Studies*, 26(1), 45–52. https://doi.org/10.1080/10894160.2021.1960617

Tate, C. C. (2022). Is lesbian identity obsolete? Some (limited) answers and further questions from a unique philology of human behavioral science perspective. *Journal of Lesbian Studies*, 26(3), 199–215. https://doi.org/10.1080/10894160.2021.2000561

Thomsen, C., & Essig, L. (2022). Lesbian, feminist, TERF: A queer attack on feminist studies. *Journal of Lesbian Studies*, 26(1), 27–44. https://doi.org/10.1080/10894160.2021.1950270

Webster, L. (2022). "Erase/rewind": How transgender Twitter discourses challenge and (re)politicize lesbian identities. *Journal of Lesbian Studies*, 26(2), 174–191. https://doi.org/10.1080/10894160.2021.1978369

Wittig, M. (1980). The straight mind. *Feminist Issues*, 1(1), 103–111.

Shifting inclusions: Identities and spaces of political lesbianism in Montreal from 1970 to 2020

Tara Chanady

ABSTRACT

This article addresses current tensions around identity and spatial boundaries within Montreal's lesbian and sexual diversity networks, underlining generational and linguistic questions framing identity politics. Based on phenomenological walking interviews (Kusenbach, 2003; Collie, 2013) with 21 variously identified women in Montreal, I posit the participants' situated experiences as valuable horizons of perception to understand sociocultural transformations (Lee, 2015; Weiss et al., 2019). For the purpose of this piece, I look at political lesbianism's history in Montreal from the 1970s to today through the lens of two self-identified political lesbians, exploring what it means politically for once-exclusive "lesbian-only" or "women-only" spaces to move forward in a context of shifting inclusions within lesbo-queer communities.

Tensions around discourses and spaces cans run high within lesbo-queer communities, as some argue for the importance of defending lesbian identities (c.f. Wittig, 1980; Rich, 1980), while others argue for a rethinking of gender and sexuality outside of categorisations (c.f. Butler, 1990). In the specific Montreal context, these discussions also entail generational and linguistic issues as the history of political lesbianism is rooted in older Francophone lesbian communities. Throughout the 1970s and 1980s, various members of these communities deployed a strategic approach to creating visibility with limited resources in a predominantly Anglophone context. This historical background is key in understanding current tensions with the popularity of queer discourses within Montreal lesbian spaces, which are for some perceived as an importation from the Anglophone context (Laprade, 2014) and are more popular among a privileged youth (Podmore, 2019).

My doctoral thesis explores the meanings attached to lesbian, bi, pan, queer, and fluid positionalities by articulating the relation between identification and space[1] (Longhurst & Johnston, 2009; Browne & Ferreira, 2015) through a phenomenological perspective, meaning an attention to the subject's perspective and interpretation of their own experiences within a specific context (Ahmed,

2006; Lee, 2017; Hansen, 2019; Guilmette, 2019). Through phenomenological walking interviews (Kusenbach, 2003; Collie, 2013) conducted in 2019 with 21 variously identified women[2] in Montreal, I posit the participants' situated experiences as valuable horizons of perceptions to understand sociocultural transformations (Lee, 2015; Weiss et al., 2019). The interviewees were chosen from my own network as well as through a mouth-to-ear technique, with the goal of having as many diversified points of views as possible, while also considering the impact of my own positionality during the interview and subsequent analysis. My analysis examined where and how we walked during the interviews in relation to the shared stories and expressed feelings (Jones et al., 2008; Clark & Emmel, 2010; Evans & Jones, 2011; Jones & Garde-Hansen, 2012), as well as visual material submitted by the participants after the interview. The walking interview experience sometimes led to the exploration of community spaces and identity politics (such as in the case presented in this article), and at other times leaned toward wandering and a queer conceptualization of gender and sexuality. The latter points toward a viewpoint common among younger interviewees: that identity-based spaces are no longer as necessary in a 'queer friendly' city; they desire to « exist in the city as I please without thinking about boundaries » (Monia, 32 years old).

While I am myself positioned as a young lesbian concerned with the inclusion of gender and sexual fluidity, I have been progressively made aware of my own shortcomings concerning generational gaps throughout my research. This article thus aims to address the feared erasure of lesbian political, social, and spatial history as organizations, networks, and discourses more generally have transformed to become more inclusive. This leads me to explore what it means politically for once exclusive "lesbian-only" or "women-only" spaces to move forward. For the purpose of this article, I draw on one particular interview with self-identified political lesbians Thérèse and Marta, a couple in their 70s who were an active part of the École Gilford, a cultural and meeting center for lesbians in Montreal in the 1980s. I first present a brief history of political lesbianism in Montreal, with a subsequent focus on the École Gilford's "lesbian-only policy." This contextualization allows me to address current tensions around identity and spatial boundaries within lesbian and sexual diversity networks, underlining generational and linguistic questions framing identity politics, in the hopes of fostering more fruitful dialogues within lesbo-queer communities.

Political lesbianism in Montreal: A short history

Political lesbianism has generally been understood as a standpoint outside of heteronormativity to reflect on and to criticize sexist power relations, most often paralleled by exclusive female-female relations in the personal realm (Rich, 1980; Wittig, 1980). Political lesbianism can also be defined in relation to physical space, as shown by lesbian geographies (Valentine, 1993a, 1993b, 1996; Browne & Ferreira, 2015) which look at the frameworks, infrastructures and geographies/spatialities, as well as everyday encounters, imaginaries, and practices through which politics is exercised. These writings underline how exclusive spaces were fundamental for creating the potential and real conditions for lesbian empowerment and emancipation in the late twentieth century.

The emergence of a radical and separatist strategy in the 1970s and 1980s in Quebec also revolved around the creation and liberation of a lesbian identity (Lamoureux, 1998, p. 182). Many academic and activist interpretations of lesbian identities draw on classical American and French thinkers such as Adrienne Rich (1980) and Monique Wittig (1980), as well as contemporary French authors (Revillard, 2002; Chartrain & Chetcuti, 2009; Chetcuti, 2010; Falquet, 2010, 2016; Cattan & Clerval, 2011), Quebecer lesbian scholars centering their thinking within the Québécois national context (Turcotte, 1998; Hildebrand, 1998; Chamberland, 1996, 2009; Chamberland & Julie, 2015; Demczuk & Remiggi, 1998; Lamoureux, 1998, 2009, 2014; Goyette, 2014; Podmore, 2001, 2019). As Line Chamberland depicts in the historical monograph *Lesbian Memories* (1996), which is based on interviews with lesbians living in Montreal from 1950 to 1972, the development of lesbian cultural and language codes took place in the shadows before gaining momentum through the feminist movement in the 1970s (Chamberland, 1996, pp. 191–195). The first women's associations emerged during the 1970s, particularly in English-speaking communities which had more resources, such as McGill University (Hildebrand, 1998, p. 211). The Montreal Gay Women conferences which took place in 1974 and 1975 were intended to be bilingual but took place almost exclusively in English (Hildebrand, 1998, p. 217). The rise of linguistic nationalism within Quebec encouraged the development of relations with French associations overseas, as well as the development of resources accessible to a population that did not speak English.[3] Linguistic differences still mark lesbian and queer networks today, with several participants in my research associating the "lesbian" designation with French and the "queer" designation with English. While it is important to nuance this association ("lesbian" is for example used by the popular Québécois networks *lezpreadtheword* and *the l nights* to which I will come back to in the conclusion), a geographical division contributes to this distinction – Montreal's Gay Village in the francophone Center-Sud neighborhood is marked by expressions of "mainstream gay-lesbian identities" (Laprade, 2014), whereas the more hip, English-speaking Mile-End neighborhood is home to most queer-identified bars and artistic venues (Podmore, 2019). Lesbian-identified spaces, however, remain marginal in comparison to gay spaces, now almost non-existent following the *Golden Age* of lesbian bars in the 1980s and the development of lesbian nights in the Gay Village in the 1990s (Podmore, 2006)

When asked to walk through the most significant places in their experiences as lesbians, Thérèse (72) and her partner of 30 years Marta (77) take me on a tour of the former École Gilford center in the Plateau Mont-Royal neighborhood, now a residential building, which used to be home to many 1980s lesbian bars as well. Established in an old elementary school, the collective brought together various groups of women and activities, including artists, workshops, a coffee-shop, and a printed journal, all run independently through fund-raising and donations. This community, social and political gathering center for lesbian women hosted the majority of its activities between 1982 to 1984 and gathered up to 400 women at a time during its most popular events (Boisvert & Boutet, 1998). The collective that founded Gilford also founded the still-existing *Journées de Visibilité Lesbienne*, the longest-running lesbian event to date in Montreal.[4] This space of "possibilities" was meant for lesbians to challenge each other by discussing political and social issues with each other in a safe environment (Boisvert & Boutet, 1998, p. 320). However, as the only lesbian-only political space in Montreal (a few bars also maintained this policy in the 1980s), many political tensions surrounding inclusion explain its short history and demise, as conflicting thoughts also arose regarding what was meant by "lesbian" (Turcotte, 1998, p. 363).

Lastly, being a woman, a lesbian, and working-class positioned several of these women in a triple marginality, due to the already-inferior socioeconomical status of women (particularly Francophone women due to the important wage gap between Francophones and Anglophones (Albouy, 2008) and the stigma surrounding women who want to live outside of the patriarchal system (which presents, for example, difficulties in finding a job). But while poverty can create a feeling of helplessness, it "can also, as was the case in Gilford, create a desire for invention and action" (Boisvert & Boutet, 1998, p. 322). The socioeconomic and patriarchal conditions generated tools for particular struggles, such as the collectively-financed magazine *Amazones d'aujourd'hui, lesbiennes d'aujourd'hui (Yesterday's Amazons, Today's lesbians)*. The establishment of an informal economy network was organized with limited resources, necessitating a lot of free labor, and the investment of significant personal, social, and political time, Thérèse and Marta expressed pride in this community approach—which included a pay-what-you-can policy at the coffee shop, free workshops, and fundraising through beer-selling events and garage sales of objects found in the basement of the École Gilford.

Exclusive spaces and identities: For lesbians only

The precarity of the members of the community led some women to adopt a very radical approach to identity, arguing that it is important to center struggles and demands around a cohesive sense of identity. As Thérèse mentions "being lesbian is a choice, I made that choice to stand outside of patriarchy." The collective feeling of sharing and claiming a lesbian positionality (in its social, political and cultural dimensions) is, and was, for her essential to articulate demands and organize resistance (Turcotte, 1998). On the contrary, many other interviewees such as Lox, 35 years old, consider identifications restrictive: "I don't like to put myself in a box and say that I am just that, I try not to limit myself. If tomorrow I wanna change, I give myself the chance to do that."

As we walk around the old residential building of the former École Gilford, Thérèse recalls the politics surrounding the collective's magazine *Amazones d'hier, lesbiennes d'aujourd'hui*, which she is currently digitizing to create archives. As I will later see in the documents she sends me, the magazine cover declares, *Pour lesbiennes seulement,* meaning "For lesbians only," a strategy similar to many other circles and publications during political lesbianism's development in North America, although centered on specific linguistic issues. Thérèse explains that it was essential for this knowledge and resistance tool to circulate strictly amongst lesbian-identified women. This positioning work takes place in a protected and exclusive space – the subtitle of the magazine, for lesbians only, expressing a radical gesture, a refusal to share, to reveal oneself in an oppressive system.

Cover of the printed magazine *Amazones d'hier, lesbiennes d'aujourd'hui* (1983)

Keeping ideas in "the community" is still an important issue for women such as Thérèse, who expresses concerns about the current distribution of the digital journal despite later collective discussions about the importance to circulate it more widely, notably to generate more lesbian knowledge within academia

> "For a while, it was important that it was only between us. Because there were lesbians who didn't want to write for a larger audience, who didn't want to be out of the community, there were girls who spoke because it was for lesbians only. It was important to come together and continue our analysis".

The lesbian identity and strategic sense of belonging is thus mobilized as a tool for social transformation, securing borders to create a safe space for some who feel violated by heteronormative social structures As some former members of the École Gilford point out, "it was not about convincing a heterosexual audience of the oppression and injustices we experienced, nor about justifying our existence. Rather, it was about building a dialogue between lesbians and exploring together the meaning of this identity." As we discuss the current ramifications of this history, Marta and Thérèse express frustration at the lack of women-only spaces nowadays. For Marta, the disappearance of lesbian bars is partly caused by a generational desensitization: "it does not matter for them, young people say they are not lesbians… so the need to be with others … it does not exist there." This echoes their fear of an erasure of lesbian political and social history which they keep bringing up during our walk, pointing to the challenges of memory transmission in a heteronormative context that does not validate the production of lesbian knowledge. This sometimes comes into conflict with other queer identified lesbians, who mobilize a different politic approach by arguing for a general rupture of gender boundaries instead of securing borders around identities.[5]

Rethinking boundaries in 2021 – conflicting mediations

The boundaries of exclusive safe spaces have indeed been up for discussion within lesbian and queer communities. Some assert that women-only spaces are necessary to feel safe and to avoid harassment and objectification such as Aisha, 34 years old and Maria, 35 years old who also feel strongly about their political lesbian identification. Although I look at generational tensions in this article, it is certainly worthy to note that some younger generation lesbians also argue for political lesbianism and exclusive spaces, albeit in a changing context. However, the queer critique is most present amongst the discourses of 20 and 30 years old who notably insist on the problematic exclusions of bisexual women as well as transand gender non-conforming people (which was also the case of the École Gilford, as Thérèse explains). Roxane, 30 years old, mentions: "In a few lesbian environments, I would say that there is queerphobia and transphobia that go together. It sucks, but every time I go to the Journée de Visibilité Lesbienne, there have been negative comments about transpeople or about non-binary people, or biphobi[a]. That's what I like less about the term lesbian, sometimes I position myself less as a lesbian, but more as a queer woman or as a gouine [dyke]. Lesbophia does exists, but phobia against pansexuality too".

Many organizations and networks such as the *Journées de visibilité lesbienne* have thus faced much backlash and have tried in response to transform, such as by offering more workshops and conferences by and for variously identified members of sexual and gender-diverse communities. Lively discussions have also taken place around the replacement of the term "lesbian" by "women of sexual diversity" within the Réseau des lesbiennes du Québec (RLQ), another organization which has struggled to be inclusive while addressing lesbian invisibility. However, for Marta and Thérèse, these attempts at inclusiveness result in an invisibilization of lesbians, who have always been on the fringes of the non-heterosexual community – a fear which points to the lack of resources which must be shared within minority communities (Voirol, 2005).

Thérèse evokes the loss of the feeling of being safe and understood:

"At the RLQ we felt that we were among ourselves, among lesbians. Now it's not the same. We have to integrate other diversities. I think that takes a political dimension away from what it means to be a lesbian, for me to be a lesbian is to be outside of heterosexuality. In the groups that I meet, queer, trans, we don't talk about that at all, this political dimension doesn't exist anymore, we are still in a society that is terrible towards women and lesbians, and it doesn't seem to anger a lot of people. The word lesbian is in one workshop, the rest is queer and gay, and [in] a lot of trans workshops, there's nothing more about lesbians".

For Thérèse and Marta, the emphasis on a feeling of belonging around a cohesive sense of identity contrasts with the queer perspective which emphasizes the individuality, peculiarity, and uniqueness of each human being outside of fixed categories (Hansen, 2019). Thérèse and Marta explicitly consider this deconstruction as a form of depoliticization, with Thérèse emphasizing that "we no longer have a movement, people want to have personal freedom." The material and structural realities of lesbian women are, according to her, denigrated by the positioning of sexuality and gender as an effect of discourse that can be deconstructed.

Having always been outside the norm, neither fully accepted in non-heterosexual communities, nor comfortable in a heteronormative and sexist system, Thérèse and Marta once again find themselves outside the norm in the face of a new generation with changing concerns and issues, many of whom reject the lesbian label due to its history of bisexual and transexclusion. The frustrations the couple evoke are telling of the contextual nature of identity, and of the fact that sociocultural transformations constantly challenge horizons of perception (Lee, 2017, p. 318) – thus the importance of intersectional thinking within lesbian communities which can bring a better understanding of intersecting and not hierarchical oppressions (Tremblay & Podmore, 2015). Their defensive positioning reflects a need to claim the validity of their identity as a political tool: a conflicting mediation with the emergence of new issues and conceptualizations of sexual diversity. Indeed, the social and cultural discourses around identities fluctuate despite the sometimes stubborn will to preserve them, generating tensions in the defense of a coherent vision of identity fighting against the elements that disturb its meaning (Lee, 2017, p. 320). As critical phenomenology points out, contextual changes lead to perceptual disorientation, while the feeling of being a misfit is renewed in different forms (Al-Saji, 2015; Guilmette, 2019; Garland-Thompson, 2019).

Conclusion – Lesbian resignifications across time and space

Lesbian identities in Montreal are rooted in many linguistic, national, class-related, and generational peculiarities, whereas a queer approach to identity and sexuality amongst women developed in the 1990s within artistic, anglophone and sometimes more privileged circles in Montreal (see Boudoir and Meow Mix events as of 1997). These are important to recognize in order to grasp the current tensions within lesbo-queer communities, which receive little attention in an academic context. Montreal is a particularity interesting ground to explore, as this so-called "queer city" is complicated by many dynamics, notably racial and immigrational ones which I address in my thesis. Certainly, this article only offers a short vignette of the tensions and discussions within lesbian communities, as many different interpretations of lesbian identities are produced and reproduced throughout the city. A telling example of lesbian resignification can be seen with the popular online network lezspreadtheword (lstw), which has produced the only Quebecer lesbian webseries (*Feminin/Feminin*), as well as bimonthly social gatherings since 2012 (lesbian gatherings are also produced by *the l nights* and many other smaller networks). Many of these popular networks, such as *lstw* and *the l nights*, signifies the term "lesbian" as a hip and desirable identification by focusing on parties and esthetics, leaving aside a political association with radical politics. Between a young and urban festive commodity and a landmark identity with political potential, lesbian identity will keep being resignified across various social and economical networks. Virtual spaces have also taken up a significant place within Montreal lesbian culture, fostering many different networks with specific interests instead of limited spaces where social and political tensions can run higher, such as was the case with École Gilford.

Bridging lesbian and queer approaches to foster more inclusive and in-depth dialogue has been a main focus of my work. The originality of my approach lies in my phenomenological walking interview methodology, which allows me to delve in an embodied manner in the interviewee's perspective, while examining my own positionality in these narratives. Occupying the same space as the participant allows a more intimate relation to build, while also triggering certain emotions and memories – this was often the case when revisiting old buildings and remembering sounds and smells (Jones & Garde-Hansen, 2012). The ways in which we walked also illustrated a different approach to sexuality, as some brought me to very specific spaces (a lesbian history walking tour) and others preferred to aimlessly wander, leaning toward a queer approach to identity and boundaries (Carrera Suárez 2015). It also allowed new insights to emerge, notably as some newly migrated participants preferred to stay in their appartements, bringing forward a discussion on the costly and overall whiteness aspects of lgbtq+spaces in the city. Finally, by mobilizing the phenomenological approach with the literature on geography of sexuality, I position sexual orientation not as a producer of a universal experience, but rather as guiding differences and alterities (Al-Saji, 2015; Guilmette, 2019; Lee, 2017; Alcoff, 2019). Exploring the relationship between sexual orientation and space thus allows me to grasp the particularities of lesbian and queer experiences and identifications without essentializing them. I strongly believe that furthering phenomenological perspectives will pave the way to a renewal of lesbian theories and epistemologies that can reconcile current tensions.

Notes

1. *Des désirs qui orientent : une analyse phénoménologique des identifications lezbiqueer dans l'espace montréalais,* PhD Thesis, Université de Montréal, 2021.
2. The 21 participants variably identified as cis, trans, intersex, agender or non-binary (all also used feminine pronouns and the woman designation at the time of the research); are between 24 and 80 years old; anglophone and francophone; born in Montreal, refugee or immigrant.
3. The Coop-femmes network in 1977 can be understood as the first French-speaking feminist-lesbian association in Montreal (Hildebrand, 1998, p. 226).
4. The inclusion of genderfluid people, trans women and bisexual and sexually fluid women has been at the center of many eventful discussions within Montreal associations. The *Réseau des lesbiennes du Québec,* who now organises les *Journées de Visibilité lesbiennes,* has recently actively promoted the inclusion of variously identified women:

«*The Quebec Lesbian Network* includes all sexually diverse women (women who identify as lesbian, queer, bisexual, trans, pansexual, fluid sexuality, radical lesbian, political, feminist, etc)». (https://rlq-qln.ca/en/, December 2020). The use of the term lesbian to describe events for sexually diverse women has created tensions amongst many networks as underlined by Maria, 30 years old, when describing the complaints of anglophone queer and non-binary participants during a LesbianSpeedDating (LSQ) event at the Notre-Dame-des-Quilles bars in 2018.

5.   This point is addressed in depth on my thesis by looking at queer-identified lesbians discourses and spaces, which I unfortunately cannot expand upon in this piece.

Disclosure statement

The authors report no conflicts of interest. The authors alone are responsible for the content and writing of the paper.

Funding

Fonds de Recherche du Québec-Société et Culture.

References

Ahmed, S. (2006). *Queer phenomenology*. Duke University Press.

Albouy, D. (2008). The Wage Gap between Francophones and Anglophones: A Canadian Perspective, 1970-2000. *Canadian Journal of Economics/Revue Canadienne D'économique*, *41*(4), 1211–1238. Retrieved August 13, 2021, from http://www.jstor.org/stable/25478322https://doi.org/10.1111/j.1540-5982.2008.00501.x

Al-Saji, A. (2015). A phenomenology of hesitation: Interrupting racializing habits of seeing. In E. Lee (dir.), *Living alterities: Phenomenology, embodiement and race* (pp. 133–172). Suny Press.

Alcoff, A. M. (2019). Public self/lived subjectivity. In G. Weiss, A. V. Murphy, & G. Salamon (Eds.), *50 Key concepts in critical phenomenology* (pp. 269–274). Northwestern University Press.

Boisvert, S., & Boutet, D. (1998). Le projet Gilford: Mémoires vives d'une pratique artistique et politique. In I. Demczuk, F. W. Remiggi (dirs.), *Sortir de l'ombre. Histoires des communautés lesbienne et gaie de Montréal* (pp. 313–336). VLB.

Browne, K., & Ferreira, E. (2015). *Lesbian Geographies: Gender, Place and Power*. Routledge.

Butler, J. (1990/2006). *Gender Trouble: Feminism and the Subversion of Identity*. Routledge.

Carrera Suárez, I. (2015). The stranger Flâneuse and the aesthetics of pedestrianism. *Interventions*, *17*(6), 853–865. https://doi.org/10.1080/1369801X.2014.998259

Cattan, N., & Clerval, A. (2011). Un droit à la ville? Réseaux virtuels et centralités éphémères des lesbiennes à Paris. *Justice spatiale-Spatial Justice*, *3*, 1–19.

Chamberland, L. (1996). *Mémoires Lesbiennes*. Remue-ménage.

Chamberland, L. (2009). *Diversité sexuelle et constructions de genre*. Presses de l'Université de Québec.

Chamberland, L., & Julie, P. (2015). Entering the urban frame: Early lesbian activism and public space in Montréal. *Journal of Lesbian Studies, 19* (2), 192–211.

Chartrain, C., & Chetcuti, N. (2009). Lesbianisme: Théories, politiques et expériences sociales. *Genre, sexualité & société, 1.*

Chetcuti, N. (2010). *Se dire Lesbienne: Vie en couple, sexualité et représentation de soi.* Payot.

Clark, A., & Emmel, N. (2010). Using walking interviews. *ESRC National Center for Research Methods, Realities Toolkit #13,* 1–6.

Collie, N. (2013). Walking in the city: Urban space, stories, and gender. *Gender Forum,* 5.

Demczuk, I., & F. W. Remiggi. (1998). *Sortir de l'ombre. Histoires des communautés lesbienne et gaie de Montréal.* VLB.

Evans, J., & Jones, P. (2011). The walking interview: Methodology, mobility and place. *Applied Geography, 31* (2), 849–858. https://doi.org/10.1016/j.apgeog.2010.09.005

Falquet, J. (2010). Rompre le tabou de l'hétérosexualité, en finir avec la différence des sexes: Les apports du lesbianisme comme mouvement social et théorie politique. *Genre, Sexualité & Société, 1.*

Falquet, J. (2016). La combinatoire straight. Race, classe, sexe et économie politique: Analyses matérialistes et décoloniales. *Cahiers du Genre, HS4*(3), 73–96. https://doi.org/10.3917/cdge.hs04.0073

Jones, P., Bunce, G., Evans, J., Gibbs, H., & Hein, J. R. (2008). Exploring space and place with walking interviews. *Journal of Research Practice, 4* (2).

Jones, O., & Garde-Hansen, J. (2012). *Geography and memory: Explorations in identity, place and becoming.* Palgrave Macmillan.

Garland-Thompson, R. (2019). Misfitting. In G. Weiss, A. V. Murphy, & G. Salamon (Eds.), *50 Key concepts in critical phenomenology* (pp. 225–230). Northwestern University Press.

Guilmette, L. (2019). Queer orientations. In G. Weiss, A. V. Murphy, & G. Salamon (Eds.), *50 Key concepts in critical phenomenology* (pp. 275–282). Northwestern University Press.

Goyette, E. (2014). L'invisibilité lesbienne dans la sphère publique (médiatique): Pratiques et enjeux d'une identité proto-politique. *Commposite, 17*(2).

Hansen, S. (2019). Queer performativity. In G. Weiss, A. V. Murphy, & G. Salamon (Eds.), *50 Key concepts in critical phenomenology* (pp. 283–288). Northwestern University Press.

Hildebrand, A. (1998). Genèse d'une communauté lesbienne: Un récit des années 1970. In I. Demczuk and F. W. Remiggi (Eds.), *Sortir de l'ombre. Histoires des communautés lesbienne et gaie de Montréal* (pp. 205–233). VLB.

Kusenbach, M. (2003). Street phenomenology: The go-along as ethnographic research tool. *Ethnography, 4*(3), 455–485. https://doi.org/10.1177/146613810343007

Lamoureux, D. (1998). La question lesbienne dans le féminisme montréalais: Un chassé-croisé. In I. Demczuk and F. W. Remiggi (Eds.), *Sortir de l'ombre. Histoires des communautés lesbienne et gaie de Montréal* (pp. 167–186). VLB.

Lamoureux, D. (2009). Reno(r/m)mer « la » lesbienne ou quand les lesbiennes étaient féministes. *Genre, Sexualité et Société, 1.* https://doi.org/10.4000/gss.635

Lamoureux, D. (2014). Dissonances identitaires. *Politique et Sociétés, 33*(1), 61–75. https://doi.org/10.7202/1025587ar

Laprade, B. (2014). Queer in Québec: Étude de la réception du mouvement queer dans les journaux québécois. *Cygne Noir, 2,* 1–20.

Lee, E. (2015). *Living Alterities: Phenomenology, Embodiement and Race.* Suny Press.

Lee, E. (2017). Identity-in-difference to avoid indifference. In H. Fielding, & D. Olkowski (Eds.), *Feminist Phenomelogy Futures* (pp. 313–327). Indiana University Press.

Longhurst, L., & Johnston, R. (2009). *Space, place and Gender: Geographies of sexuality.* Rowman & Littlefield Publishers.

Podmore, J. (2001). Lesbians in the Crowd: Gender, sexuality and visibility along Montréal's Boul. St-Laurent. *Gender, Place and Culture, 8* (4), 333–355. https://doi.org/10.1080/09663690120111591

Podmore, J. (2006). Gone 'underground'? Lesbian visibility and the consolidation of queer space in Montréal. *Social & Cultural Geography, 7*(4), 595–625. https://doi.org/10.1080/14649360600825737

Podmore, J. (2019). Au-delà du Village gai, Le Mile-End: Habitus d'une jeunesse distinctement queer à Montréal. In H. Bélanger & D. Lapointe (dirs.) *Les approches critiques: Quelles perspectives pour les études urbaines, régionales et territoriales?* (pp. 73–94). Presses de l'Université du Quebec.

Revillard, A. (2002). L'identité lesbienne entre nature et construction. *Revue du MAUSS, 19*(1), 168–182. https://doi.org/10.3917/rdm.019.0168

Rich, A. (1980). Compulsory heterosexuality and lesbian existence. *Signs. Women: Sex and Sexuality, 5*(4), 631–660.

Turcotte, L. (1998). Itinéraire d'un courant politique: Le lesbianisme radical au Québec. In I. Demczuk and F. W. Remiggi, *Sortir de l'ombre. Histoires des communautés lesbienne et gaie de Montréal* (pp. 363–398). VLB.

Tremblay, M., & Podmore, J. (2015). Depuis toujours intersectionelles: Relecture des mouvements lesbiens à Montréal, de 1970 aux années. *Recherches Féministes, 28*(2), 101–120. https://doi.org/10.7202/1034177ar

Valentine, G. (1993a). (Hetero)sexing space: Lesbian perceptions and experiences of everyday spaces. *Environment and Planning, Society and Space, 11*, 394–413.

Valentine, G. (1993b). Negotiating and managing multiple identities: Lesbian time-space strategies. *Transactions of the Institute of British Geographers, 18*(2), 237–248. https://doi.org/10.2307/622365

Valentine, G. (1996). (Re)negotiating the 'Heterosexual Street': Lesbian productions of space. In D. N. Duncan (dir.) *Body space: Destabilising geographies of gender and sexualities* (pp. 146–155). Routledge.

Voirol, O. (2005). Les luttes pour la visibilité: Esquisse d'une problématique. *Réseaux, 129–130*(1), 89–121.

Weiss, G., Murphy, A. V., & Salamon, G. (2019). *50 key concepts in critical phenomelogy.* Northwestern University Press.

Wittig, M. (1980). The straight mind. *Feminist Issues, 1*(1), 103–111. https://doi.org/10.1007/BF02685561

"I was returning to see if the ghosts were still astirring": Southern lesbian reflexivity as social movement in *Feminary* (1979–1982)*

Sarah Heying

ABSTRACT

This article examines an instructive moment in the archive of *Feminary*, a periodical that began in 1969 as a local feminist newsletter for the Triangle region of North Carolina. In 1979, the editorial collective announced a shift in focus toward "a feminist journal for the South emphasizing the lesbian vision." I argue that through this turn, the Feminary Collective experiments with *lesbian* and *southern* as discursive laboratories for shaping what I refer to as backward-onward community-for-mation—a praxis that requires confronting and acknowledging historical specificity and experiential limits while also imagining new possibilities for social movement. Instead of framing *southernness* and *lesbianism* as fixed identities, the Collective treats them as multivalent, slippery markers that resist closure, produce ambivalence, and contain vast relational and political potential. Moreover, this article discusses the Collective's configuration of the U.S. South as a spatial and temporal avenue for confronting the experiential and institutionalized afterlives of slavery and for critiquing the white-washed classism of literary conventions. The article's methodology includes close readings of material from the Collective's nationally-circulated journal, as well as discussions of excerpts from the oral histories of two former members of the Collective, one of which was conducted for the purposes of this project.

We can read tension surrounding the descriptor *lesbian* adjacently to that of *southern* in that both affinities frequently connote temporal displacement (e.g. backward or old-fashioned values) or exclusionary practices (e.g. segregation, separatism, and essentialism). Just as widespread associations of southernness with legacies of racial violence cannot be conscionably discounted, the entanglement of some expressions of lesbianism with *Trans Exclusionary Radical Feminists* (TERFS) leaves many women-loving-women wondering how to speak to their specific experiences and desires without drawing a line in the sand. Yet I also sense that for many people uncomfortable with *lesbian*, including many queer-identifying people, the identity

---

* Title comes from Anita Cornwell's (1982) story, "Backward Journey," from *Feminary*, 12(1).

serves as a bucket into which they dump unchecked misogyny, just as the South can serve in other contexts as a convenient space to offload unchecked elitism and racism. *Southern* and *lesbian* have not only been co-opted by mechanisms of capitalist branding and biopolitical control (like all widely-recognizable identity categories), but they have also become public dumping-grounds for the psychic excess of the histories of violence that we have barely begun to face. In an effort to work through some of the baggage of southern lesbian identity politics, this article engages with the following question: Is it possible to productively and responsibly collect around such heavy-laden language without rehearsing or ignoring our most violent practices and histories?

Such questions are not new to lesbian communities, yet in the historical amnesia surrounding lesbian feminism from the 1970s and 1980s, a number of valuable interventions have been overlooked. This article examines a particularly instructive moment in the archive of *Feminary*, a periodical that began in 1969 as a local feminist newsletter for the Triangle region (Chapel Hill, Durham, and Raleigh) of North Carolina. After struggling for a decade to define their mission and scope, in 1979 the editorial collective announced a shift in focus toward "a feminist journal for the South emphasizing the lesbian vision." In their redirection, *Feminary* uses *lesbian* and *southern* as discursive laboratories for experimenting with technologies of affiliation; rather than wielding these terms as identifiable fixed identities, the Collective treats them as multivalent markers that resist closure and contain vast relational and political potential. Even more unique to them, The Feminary Collective sought to confront the constellations of ambivalence that accompany living as a lesbian in the South, and they were adamant about building a body of literature that reflected on the ways in which southern lesbian ambivalence intersects with other social positions, especially race and class. To work toward these goals, the Collective pursued a praxis what I refer to as backward-onward community-formation, which requires confronting and acknowledging historical specificity and experiential limits while also imagining new possibilities for social movement.

This is not to say that all members of the Collective remember their work primarily in terms of social justice. In a personal interview, Deborah Jamieson (2019)—a Black lesbian, lifelong southerner, mother of two,[1] and a member of the Collective during the particular incarnation that concerns this article—describes her memories more in terms of her emotional connection to an accepting community:

> Child, I've had two strokes and some mini-strokes. So when you ask me, what do I remember.... [Laughs]. [...] I lost some memories, but I still have the emotional part, even though I might have lost some of the actual doings and sayings. [...]

For us, for me, and for Lalenja [her daughter, who also attended some meetings], Feminary was not just a magazine that put out. It wasn't just that. It wasn't just these women who came together and decided on one line and put this thing together. It was women who loved women who loved each other, who was respectful. And respected other women and their choices and their beliefs. And though I may not agree with you—or as my baby would say, I might be problematic with some of the stuff you believe [laughs]—still, there's room for all at the table. (p. 21)

Throughout our conversation, it was clear that Jamieson's emotion-based memories centered on feelings of acceptance and respect not only for her perspectives as a Black woman and as a mother, but as a whole and complex human being. Notably, these memories of wholeness also hold temporal connotations for Jamieson: "Feminary, in essence, was not just a collective for me. It was a time for me. Because in Feminary, all parts of my life were entwined. Not entangled, but entwined with" (p. 17). This experience with Feminary speaks to how the Collective's praxis of looking backward-onward made possible multitemporal states of being that continued long after the journal stopped printing and the interpersonal relationships dissolved. Later in the interview, Jamieson speaks of Feminary's temporality in both present- and future-tense, simultaneously moving between individual and collective experiences: "It's woven into our [both Jamieson's and her daughter's] lives, still affecting us. [...] It will always, always, always be with me. Those women will always be part of my sisterhood. They will. I don't care if I never see them again" (pg. 34). Jamieson elucidates a type of kinship that extends across various spaces and timelines, allowing one's whole self to exist in all its multiplicities, contradictions, and impermanent states of being. This vision of lesbian collectivity works against gate-keeping-via-definition and works toward living, breathing articulations of affiliation.

The Feminary Collective's archive has much to teach us about treating lesbianism and southernness as multitemporal articulations of collective being, and I suggest that academic elitism, racism, and misogyny—along with a pervading fear of accusations of essentialism—have prevented us from taking seriously such regenerative modes of kinship found throughout lesbian feminism from the seventies and eighties. Though Feminary was a nationally-circulated journal whose Collective boasted well-known members Minnie Bruce Pratt and Mab Segrest, there was for a long time a dearth of related scholarship on this visionary group of women. Until about 2014, the only in-depth studies were two articles published in an issue of the North Carolina Literary Review (Powell, 2000; Wynn, 2000) and a Duke University Master's student's thesis (Gilbert, 1993). This gap in scholarship is gradually closing thanks to more recent work from Keira V. Williams (2020), Jaime Harker (2018), Julie Enszer (2015), and Jaime Cantrell (2015), yet there is still much more to be said about the Collective's radical imaginings of subjectivity. The Feminary Collective resisted mono-lithic notions of southern lesbianism, working to express the heterogeneous yet interrelated ways southern lesbians reckon with their sexualities within a diverse and complicated region. While previous issues of *Feminary* explored explicitly lesbian content, vol. 10, no. 1 (1979) marked the turn toward a particular sexual orientation. The turn also came as the first nationally circulated lesbian magazines were printing their final issues: *The Ladder* in 1972, followed by *Amazon Quarterly* in 1975, and then *The Lesbian Tide* in 1980. Harriet Desmoines and Charlotte Nicholson were in the process of transitioning *Sinister Wisdom* from a national journal based in North Carolina to one based in Massachusetts, with Adrienne Rich and Michelle Cliff taking the helm.[2] It only took a few more years for *Feminary* to change hands and move to San Francisco for its two final issues as a nationally-circulated magazine with an international perspective, a "lesbian feminist magazine of politics, passion and hope" (1985).[3] I am more interested in the journal's moment as a regional project with a largely literary focus during a period when, as now, regionalism appeared to many a hopelessly parochial approach to community-formation, just as lesbianism might currently appear to many a hopelessly limited identity category. Rather than abandoning language that carries such sticky associations I suggest we look toward the more transformative, generative, and produc-tively ambivalent articulations of backward-onward-looking subjectivities for strategies to create usable networks of affiliation that can extend across time and space.

Before *Feminary* found its new focus as a regional lesbian journal, it served any and all feminists in the Triangle community as the *Female Liberation Newsletter of Durham-Chapel Hill* (1970), meaning the journal was more geographically localized in scope yet socially, politically, and ideologically broad. The Collective had struggled for quite some time to elucidate their purpose and audience,[4] and by vol. 9, no. 1 (1978), they decided to test out a special issue on Lesbian Community.[5] Writing on behalf of the Collective, Mab Segrest (1978) explains that "we are working to keep our 'borders' open to any women who want to join us for mutual nurturance, in mutual strength," lesbian-identified or not. "Also," she con-tinues, "the lesbian community serves as a laboratory for relationships between and among all women since it is not only lesbians who have lived and worked in isolation from another" (p. 2). This perception of lesbianism as a relational laboratory rather than identity category suggests that the Collective sought to position inclusive methods of communal care at the core of lesbian identity. Two issues later, *Feminary* vol. 10, no. 1 (1979) fully embraced this lesbian vision and extended it beyond the politically progressive Triangle and into the politically fraught region known as the South. A productive tension between competing politics, desires, and perspectives is an essential component of Feminary's lesbian vision, with the hopes of challenging both ideological purity (as seen in some versions of lesbian separatism) and racist, classist nostalgia (as seen in some versions of southern pride).

Much as lesbianism does not signal an essential, stable meaning—and few lesbian feminist thinkers ever argued for one—the Feminary Collective made clear that while the term *southern* was useful in providing language through which people could process the specificities of their shared experiences, *the South* hardly existed as a distinct region with definable cultural practices. Their goal was not to define *southernness*, but to "explore how (lesbian) lives fit into a region about which we have great ambivalences" and to "explore how this Southern experience fits into the American pattern" (p. 4). The parentheses surrounding *lesbian* recall an image of overlapping circles of community—lesbians within and outside of the South, within and outside of the United States—and are useful for imagining contingent, ever-evolving subjectivities. One particularly illustrative poem from vol. 12, no. 1 (1982)—the "Maps" issue—makes clear the complex ambivalence that inevitably arises from treating identity as contingent. In "Adversity," Flying Thunder Cloud (1982) questions the possible masochistic underpinnings of choosing to living in the South as a "Blackdyke." The speaker, a native New Yorker, is "happy/proud/to be living/in the South" (p. 107) because it is where she experienced her sexual awakening. However, she is also intimately familiar with the keen sting of oppression that is sometimes intensified in the region depending on one's social position, and she often feels "someplace/way out of the concern/of many of/[her] paler skinned 'sisters'" (p. 108). The pages of *Feminary* are full of intersectional, ambivalent expressions of subjectivity such as this, and the Collective clearly valued any work that could destabilize monolithic assumptions about what it means to identify with lesbian southernness.

As feminist politics became increasingly transnational in scope by the late 1970s, the Feminary Collective paused to consider how the acts of looking backward and thinking provincially are equally as important as imagining global communities of the future. For Feminarians, great opportunity lay in what Jaime Harker (2018) refers to as a simultaneous deconstruction and construction of the South that worked to dismantle "a toxic, nostalgic South" while also envisioning the possibility of "a just and inclusive one" (p. 78). The Collective's project required a delicate balance of remaining aware of popular associations with the South and working toward more expansive and complex articulations. If Kraft-Ebbing, Havelock, and other social scientists popularized the term *lesbianism* as a container for women's sexual deviance—a container with its own associations of imagined geographic boundaries—then perhaps the Civil War and its aftermath popularized an imagined South as a container for the newly formed nation's moral, economic, political, and social deviance. Widespread imaginings of the South as backward have as much to do with a perceived cultural divide as they do with a perceived temporal divide. Feminarians reconfigured this backwardness into backward-onwardness: a praxis of reflection in service of movement toward a more equitable future.

Central to this praxis is the principle that creation does not end with publication but continues within a framework of communal reflection and nurturance—which involves challenging each other's and our own creations as much as we offer our support. Like many feminist periodicals from the 1970s and 80s, *Feminary* frequently published retrospective notes, responses, and critiques alongside poems, essays, stories, and reviews. Often, pieces involved the writers' relationships to the creations of other important women in their lives, such as the excerpt from Kady Van Deurs's autobiography that opens *Feminary*, vol. 10, no. 1 (1979). In the final scene, Van Deurs reflects upon her inheritance from her grandmother Kate—an inheritance that includes her name, "four forties of submarginal swamp land in Alabama," and an urge to account for her life through writing. Her grandmother, it turns out, had also tried to leave Van Deurs all of her unpublished poetry: "I wrote back and said, 'Kate, being a writer myself I know how important it is that your writing should fall into the right hands, and I hate your poetry'" (p. 11). This statement could be read as an expression of tough love, and it could also be read as indicative of the desire of a young writer to break away from the "bad poetry" of her white southern lineage. Throughout the excerpt, Van Deurs writes of feeling a sense of responsibility to "go back to the South and Do Something," and she reflects on an unproductive conversation with her mother about "the guilt that white southerners feel" (pp. 10–11). However, even though the excerpt ends with the recollection of the response Van Deurs wrote to her grandmother about her poetry, she ultimately memorializes her grandmother with direct quotations from the one poem of hers that she could remember in full (a short eulogy to her dead dog), plus a line from another. The closing lines of the excerpt are telling of Van Deurs's more complex sense of ambivalence: "In another poem, she [Van Deurs's grand-mother] managed to say, somehow, 'Before you kill yourself, pick up your pen and write.' Kate did not kill herself until she was 92" (p. 11). Though Van Deurs carries with her a strong urge to destroy attachments to her white southern legacy, she also recognizes the complicated humanity of those attachments, which are often upheld through deep emotional con-nection. Kristen Hogan (2016) refers to this commitment to honest con-frontations with legacies of racialized violence as a feminist politics of accountability, in which many feminist bookwomen worked to build a shared dialogue for the difficult and sincere conversations they needed to have in order to uphold their commitments to anti-racist work within the overwhelmingly white women's movement. For Van Deurs and the Feminary Collective, a feminist politics of accountability entailed reflecting on one's individual complicity within legacies of southern white supremacy for the sake of working toward a more just lesbian South.

Identity: skin, blood, heart, and S/place[6]

By vol. 10, no. 3 (1980), the Feminarians had stopped writing their editorial, "Collective Comments," from a group perspective. "We have decided that printing a collective 'statement' in each issue is much too impersonal," writes Minnie Bruce Pratt (1980). "It makes us sound like a stone-faced corporation—and there are only six of us—and it gives you no idea of what we do and feel in getting the magazine out" (p. 4). This acknowledgment that jointly-endorsed comments could be read as corporatization might seem a surprising turn for a feminist collective, yet the implication is that the cultivation of a group identity should never be mistaken for branding or uniformity. The individual gestates within, along, and outside the group, pulling from available patterns and conversations to create a distinct interpretation and articulation of, in this case, southern lesbian feminism. The Feminary Collective's insistence on naming the humanity of social movement encourages a type of collectivity that does not assume a completely unified front, but rather allows for diverse, amorphous, and sometimes contradictory constellations of ethics, approaches, and interpretations. As Deborah Jamieson notes in her interview, the Collective created space for the various threads of a person's experiences and convictions to become "entwined with" one another, generating a feeling of wholeness that does not erase complexity (pg. 17).

In "Identity: Skin Blood Heart," Pratt (1991b) compares her journey toward understanding her white southern lesbianism—and understanding identity more generally—to the image of an interlocking, expanding circle:

> So this is one gain for me as I change: I learn a way of looking at the world that is more accurate, complex, multilayered, multidimensioned, more truthful. To see the world of overlapping circles, like movement on the mill pond after a fish has jumped, instead of the courthouse square with me at the middle, even if I am on the ground. (p. 33)

This image that describes self as becoming is not one of an ameba that shape-shifts, but is instead one of expansion and increasing connection to the world outside the self—a centrifugal movement that Pratt refers to as living "on the edge at [her] skin" (p. 35). Importantly, this expansion still remains grounded within and cognizant of the self's history and limitations. By contrast, she offers a counterexample of living at the edge of skin in "Books in the Closet, in the Attic, Boxes, Secrets," (1991a) a later essay in the same collection that reflects on her college training in New Criticism:

> We bent ourselves to a closer and closer examination of words, making of writing a world in itself, applying what we understood of the New Criticism by escaping into art, into the story, into the poem. We shut out the feelings, thoughts, and histories of people who lived in another dimension of the world than ours. (p. 157)

Pratt's call for reading practices that peer beyond the text itself might seem commonsensical now, but this approach was counterto the methodologies that had swept through U.S. American academies from the 1940s through the 1970s. For New Critics, a text was a self-contained, self-referential object in which meaning could be discerned through a careful and close analysis of formalistic elements like rhyme, structure, characterization, or irony. The New Critical movement took its name from *The New Criticism* (1941), a collection of essays by John Crowe Ransom, a key member of another southern collective: the Southern Agrarians. The Agrarians (1930) championed a romanticized version of the South that placed itself in opposition to the "American or prevailing way" (p. xli). That "American way" privileged the industrialization and secular cultures of urban areas over the rural agricultural economies and religious communities of the South. Their manifesto, *I'll Take My Stand: The South and the Agrarian Tradition* (Twelve Southerners, 1930), contains scant reference to Jim Crow laws, and the one essay that grapples with slavery in-depth paints the institution as one forced upon the region by outside agitators. As PhD students at the University of North Carolina and Duke University, both Pratt and Segrest would have been educated under New Criticism and its Agrarian influence, and so to reject its practices was to reject their institutional training and instead forge their own contextually-based reading practices that recognized literature as part of social movement.

To reclaim a genealogy of southern literature that paid mind to historical and social forces of influence, Pratt and Segrest looked outside the white southern Agrarianism that had come to define much of the literature of the so-called Southern Renaissance of the 1920s and 30 s. In "Lines I Dare," an essay from her collection *My Mama's Dead Squirrel*, Mab Segrest (1985) references slave narratives as a more direct influence on southern lesbian writing than Agrarian literature. In addressing the question, "Is there (southern) writing after Faulkner?," Segrest responds,

Obviously, there is. But it is not a literature, like Faulkner's, that establishes a mythic county unto itself, a "postage stamp of native soil." It is rather in the tradition of liberation as Black poet June Jordan explains it: "the movement into self-love, self-respect, and self-determination is the movement now galvanizing the true, the unarguable majority of human beings everywhere." (p. 103)

These liberatory traditions of literature strive for something more than representation of the human condition: they aim for movement, action, and change. While Faulkner's characters undoubtedly express ambivalence about the South, it is an ambivalence that often manifests in his white characters as self-destructive shame and emotional blockage. The Feminary Collective, on the other hand, sought to channel the transformative energy of ambivalence into action. In her study of Pratt's work, Tara McPherson (2003) refers to such uses of ambivalence as *strategy* rather than *sign* or *symptom*: "Here, ambivalence becomes a conscious tactic, a skillful maneuver that underwrites a refreshing mobility and new affective modes" (p. 231). For the Collective, this meant mobilizing literature for the purposes of confronting and transforming legacies of white supremacist violence.

This is precarious business, however, when spearheaded by a group whose core membership consisted of mostly white women.[7] In her oral history, Pratt (2005) acknowledges a significant mistake in gatekeeping that the Collective made in their ambition to create a southern journal. A woman who was "Native Choctaw or Creek" and living in Oklahoma submitted her work, and the Collective turned it down because they deemed her non-southern, disregarding the history of the forced displacement of Choctaw and Creek people from the region, and despite the fact that they published many works of displaced black women. "We were so focused on issues around racism against African American people, we made mistakes around other stuff," explained Pratt. "[...] And we reevaluated ourselves and did a whole issue about what does it mean to be Southern in these different ways, and including Native voices and redrawing the map" (p. 41). The "Maps" issue, vol. 12, no. 1 (1982), was the Collective's mostly clearly-defined effort at mobilizing ambivalence. The series of maps throughout the issue are redrawn again and again, often overlaid with text and image, in what Jaime Harker (2018) refers to as a transformation of a "seemingly known quantity" (p. 79). These continual reconfigurations of space and collective identity exemplify the transformational potential of backward-onward reflexivity, in which labeling, naming, and drawing boundaries around collectives are necessarily imprecise and impermanent actions—actions that do not privilege closure, certainty, or other forms of symbolic stasis.

Despite the Collective's missteps, their work addressing the violent racism of the South's color line, which at the time had only recently been deemed unlawful and was (still is) overtly and implicitly maintained, might be some of the most nuanced to come out of the Women in Print Movement. In her survey of periodicals from the WIP Movement, Agatha Beins (2017) notes that many publications—particularly those edited by white women—relied upon images of women of color to boost the perceived radicalism and intersectionality of the movement. Mainstream media and New Left discourses tended to trivialize women's liberation in a variety of ways, one of which was to label it as a racist movement. Several periodicals sought to speak back, and one method of doing so was by signaling inclusivity and anti-racist politics through images of revolutionary black women and, because of many feminists' involvement in anti-war organizing, women from South Vietnam (pp. 121–122). Beins discusses how these visualizations of a radical Other implied to many a site of ideological purity sought by U.S. feminists in which women of color "disproportionately bear the weight of revolution" (p. 135). Many of these images were recycled from a repository of copyright-free illustrations, meaning the same depictions of Sojourner Truth and South Vietnamese women holding guns appeared across a number of publications. This repetition of visual rhetoric in service of unspoken narrative builds a sense of what Nicole Fleetwood (2011) calls *iconicity*, or "the ways in which singular images or signs come to represent a whole host of historical occurrences and processes" and indicate a "desire to have the cultural product solve the very problem that it represents" (pp. 2–3). *Feminary*, on the other hand, did not pull from this same repository; they used original artwork submissions for all of their graphics. Moreover, their depictions of southern lesbians did not rely upon a stable reference of meaning with prepackaged semiotic stickiness but instead depicted as transformational figures-in-process that challenged reading practices of closure. Their images signal social movement, but not self-referential solution.

The cover art of vol. 11, no. 1&2 (Sneddon, 1980, Figure 1) communicates this point most clearly with its rendering of an ink-drawn figure overlaying a photograph of a dilapidated cabin under trees. The figure, whom I will refer to with feminine pronouns given the journal's audience, stares directly into the reader's eyes, her arms held defiantly akimbo, and the sign posted on the building behind her declares the issue's theme: "Disobedience." Her translucence blends body with landscape and architecture, blurring the distinction between internal and external identification. The photograph is filtered red, the color of rage.

It is only upon examining the masthead that a reader will realize that the cabin behind the figure formerly housed enslaved people, and turning to the back cover (Figure 2) further complicates the front cover's image of rebellion. Unlike the figure on the cover, these silhouettes portray no

Figure 1. (left) Cover of *Feminary*, vol. 11, no. 1 & 2 (Sneddon, 1980).

features beyond their outlines, and a reader could easily miss their inclusion at all. They might signal blackness through the suggestions of afros and braids, or, much more crudely, through the shadowing of their entire bodies. Yet, it is this knowability of blackness—this iconicity—that these silhouettes productively trouble. The blacked-out images simultaneously signal absence and presence and imply ontologies that occur somewhere else than within recognizable symbolics and geographies. Returning to the front cover, I am inclined to revisit the transparent character as one of privilege. The images calls into question who has the freedom to be transparent about their disobedience, and who does not, and asks us to consider whose disobedience is knowable within movements of resistance. If we read the opacity of the silhouettes as an unknowability, then any signals of whiteness and blackness likewise cannot be read under a stable, essential ontology. Additionally, the layering of ink-on-photo suggests we cannot read the connections between past and present as fluidly linear, but instead as layered and piecemeal. The cover wrap, with its photograph of the slave cabin, its suggestion of displaced and privileged subjectivities, and its representation of body blended with space and environment, calls

Figure 2. (right) Back cover of *Feminary*, vol. 11, no. 1 & 2 (Sneddon, 1980).

attention to both feminist and southern reliance on black iconicity to articulate white resistance, while also destabilizing the certainty with which a reader can interpret such representations of disobedience. Rather than reading blackness, whiteness, southernness, lesbianism, etc. as knowable facets of self-hood, we can read them as transformational technologies of *being* that orient our bodies across time and space. In this instance and many others, the Feminary Collective demonstrates a commitment to confronting the complexities of an optics of resistance.

Afterward, and then

I have demonstrated that the journal *Feminary* ingeniously performs a praxis of *backward-onward* reflexivity that frames southern lesbianism as social movement rooted in historical awareness. However, it proves difficult to capture within the scope of an article how the Feminary Collective as a group of women created something special and intangible through their relationships to each other and their work. During our interview, Deborah Jamieson touched upon this impossibility:

If I say anything about this incarnation, about Feminary, is I'm very, very sorry for the readers who could not have the experience of Feminary. They could read the articles, and they can get a lot out of that, but they could not have the experience of our collective that I would have wished for them more so than the stuff they read. (p. 34)

Jamieson offers an important reminder that archival work, like all acts of remembrance, can only catch a small glimpse of the past, and what is more important in the case of Feminary and other histories of social movement is figuring out how to mobilize these pieces of our past toward collective visions. In lesbian studies, this means building upon the work from our predecessors to continue to effect necessary change, such as addressing classism in academic studies of identity, confronting histories of transphobia in the lesbian archives, and challenging the whiteness of much queer history that gets written and remembered. In the context of lesbian identity, I suggest that like the Feminary Collective did, we must resist dreams of a clean break from tradition, language, or community, but instead pursue creative practices that face these sites of belonging and meaning-making head-on to embrace what is usable and to articulate what is not. Backward-onward lesbian identities have no clear endpoints, but are instead complex, interlocking, and ever-expanding processes—like the ripples in a pond.

Disclosure of interest statement

The authors report no conflicts of interest. The authors alone are responsible for the content and writing of the paper.

Notes

1. Jamieson now has a step-son as well, but during her time with the Feminary Collective she had just the two daughters. This interview took place in Jamieson's home in Greensboro, NC, on November 29, 2019. We were joined by her wife Ann Clegg and her daughter Lalenja Harrington.
2. *Sinister Wisdom* has since returned to the South, and currently edited by Julie Enszer out of Dover, FL.
3. From *Feminary*, vol. 15, no. 1 (1985). This is the journal's final issue.
4. Vol. 1, no. 9 (1970) announces a "new look for the issue" (n.p.) and requests submissions of poetry, ads, song lyrics, and other non-news related items (though it is quite some time before the journal begins publishing these types of submissions); vol. 7, no. 21 (1974) includes an editorial note about the desire to find a focus and develop an editorial policy.
5. While prior to this issue, *Feminary* catered to a local, Durham-Chapel Hill audience of

"feminists," much of their content was geared particularly toward lesbian feminists, prompting readers like "Elizabeth" to encourage *Feminary* to "come all the way out" (vol. 6, no. 15, 1975).

6. In her reading of Marlene Nourbese Philip's work, Katherine McKittrick (2006) defines S/place as a "space between" that "subverts inner/outer and active/passive dichotomies by speaking through time/place/histories; it reproduces New World children; and, it signifies threat, reclamation and violation" (*Demonic Grounds*, 49).

7. While Deborah Jamieson frequently helped with the printing of issues, she indicated in her interview that Minnie Bruce Pratt, Mab Segrest, and Cris South were the core of the Collective, especially when it came to editorial decisions. According to Minnie Bruce Pratt's oral history on file at Smith College, they added "an African American and an Arab member about halfway through" the development of their final issue.

References

Beins, A. (2017). *Liberation in print: Feminist periodicals and social movement identity.* University of Georgia Press.

Cantrell, J. (2015). SUBSCRIBE to *Feminary*!: Producing community, region, and archive. In A. Stone & J. Cantrell (Eds.), *Out of the closet, into the archives: Researching sexual histories* (pp. 311–335). SUNY Press.

Cornwell, A. (1982). Backward journey. *Feminary*, *12*(1), 86–105.

Cloud, F. T. (1982). Adversity. *Feminary*, *12*(1), 106–109.

Elizabeth, (1975). Letters. *Feminary*, *6*(15), 2. Accessed via Duke University's Sallie Bingham Center for Women's History and Culture.

Enszer, J. R. (2015). Night Heron Press and lesbian print culture in North Carolina, 1976-1983. *Southern Cultures*, *21*(2), 43–56. https://doi.org/10.1353/scu.2015.0021

Female Liberation Newsletter of Durham-Chapel Hill. (1970). *1*(9). Accessed via Duke University's Sallie Bingham Center for Women's History and Culture.

Feminary Collective. (1979). Collective statement. *Feminary*, *10*(1), 4.

Feminary Collective. (1985). Table of contents. *Feminary*, *15*(1), 1. Accessed via Texas A&M's Don Kelly Collection.

Fleetwood, N. R. (2011). *Troubling vision: Performance, visuality, and blackness.* University of Chicago Press.

Gilbert, J. L. (1993). *"Feminary" of Durham-Chapel Hill: Building community through a feminist press* [Master's thesis]. Duke University.

Harker, J. (2018). *The lesbian South: Southern feminists, the Women in Print Movement, and the queer literary canon.* UNC Press.

Hogan, K. (2016). *The feminist bookstore movement: Lesbian antiracism and feminist accountability.* Duke University Press.

Jamieson, D. (2019, November 29). Interview by Sarah Heying. (Recording currently being processed by Duke University's Sallie Bingham Center for Women's History and Culture).

Lynn. (1976). Feminary process/progress report. *Feminary, 7*(21), 1. Accessed via Duke University's Sallie Bingham Center for Women's History and Culture.

McKittrick, K. (2006). *Demonic grounds: Black women and the cartographies of struggle.* University of Minnesota Press.

McPherson, T. (2003). *Reconstructing Dixie: Race, gender, and nostalgia in the imagined South.* Duke University Press.

Powell, T. M. (2000). Look what happened here: North Carolina's Feminary Collective. *North Carolina Literary Review, 9,* 91–102.

Pratt, M. B. (1980). Collective comments. *Feminary, 10*(3), 4–5.

Pratt, M. B. (1991a). Books in the closet, in the attic, boxes, secrets. In *Rebellion: Essays 1980-1991* (pp. 151–165). Firebrand.

Pratt, M. B. (1991b). Identity: Skin, blood, heart. In *Rebellion: Essays 1980-1991* (pp. 27–77). Firebrand.

Pratt, M. B. (2005). Oral history interview by Kelly Anderson, March 2005, transcript and recording, Voices of Feminism Oral History Project, Sophia Smith Collection, Smith College.

Ransom, J. C. (1941). *The new criticism.* New Directions.

Segrest, M. (1978). Collective statement. *Feminary, 9*(1), 2–3. Accessed via Duke University's Sallie Bingham Center for Women's History and Culture.

Segrest, M. (1985). "Lines I dare": Southern lesbian writing. In *My mama's dead squirrel* (pp. 100–185). Firebrand.

Sneddon, S. (1980). Cover illustration. *Feminary, 11,* 1–2.

Twelve Southerners. (1930). *I'll take my stand: The South and the agrarian tradition.* Harper.

Van Deurs, K. (1979). Excerpt from *The notebooks that Emma gave me. Feminary, 10*(1), 5–11.

Williams, K. V. (2020). "Saving the life that is your own": Southern women writers' great migrations. *Southern Cultures, 26*(3), 104–121. https://doi.org/10.1353/scu.2020.0042

Wynn, C. (2000). "Hearing me into speech": Lesbian feminist publishing in North Carolina. *North Carolina Literary Review, 9,* 82–90.

Between mother and daughter: Brown erotics and sacred notes

Sara Shroff

ABSTRACT

In this short essay, I offer an alternative ontology and episte-mology of the term "lesbian" vis-à-vis my relationship with my brown Pakistani mother. I bring into this reading a number of variables ranging from the geographic, historical, biopolitical, and economic to the embodied, affective, esthetic, and imma-terial. In recounting formative moments of my childhood – Quranic pedagogy alongside classical voice, singing and dance lessons – I re-read the spaces that produce homosociality and homoerotics as sites of brown maternal knowledges and fem-inist transgressions. This essay uses memory to examine the different ways that *lesbian*, both as a term and a mode of being, is not necessarily attached to sexual identity and prac-tices. Analyzing how desire and secrecy are mediated by global capital, postcolonial respectability, nation, and compulsory heterosexuality, *brown erotics and sacred notes* offers a close look into the nuanced relationality between a brown mother and brown daughter, and takes seriously questions of what constitutes living a feminist life, and being and becoming a lesbian.

There are times when I do not know whether my mother has always been a lesbian or is becoming one with me. I say this because my mother always makes sweeping statements, such as: "All women are lesbians" or "we are all lesbians" or "being a lesbian doesn't mean you leave your (hetero) marriage." She has made these statements to me when visiting me in Brooklyn (lesbian capital) where I lived during my doctoral studies after my divorce, to my cousin at the end of her decade-long marriage and scandalous coming out, to me again when she met one of my many lovers, to groups of my friends, to her own sisters and sisters-in law over chai and dirty conversations about sex. She made these statements noto-riously and unapologetically. This statement, and its varied iterations and movements over time and location and circumstance, clung to my psyche throughout my life, and now emerges as my feminist object, queer object lesson. To think about the question posed to us in this special issue: "Is

Lesbian Identity Obsolete?" I ruminate on my mother's words as a mode of maternal pedagogy that reveals the intimate workings across postcolonial, diasporic, and brown feminist lesbian worlds-in-the-making.

Moving through feminist studies as a student and now as a scholar, I came to understand that women like my mother – women who raised their daughters within the confines of strict heterosexual parenting, neoliberal Islamization, servitude (messy and irreverent) to patriarchy, and a deep deference to capital and postcolonial bourgeois class structure – were not part of hegemonic feminist archives. Indeed, as a maternal figure, my mother was an anathema to the very buzzwords worshiped in the feminist academy such as lesbian, radical, feminist, independent, working woman, single woman, career-oriented, secular, and queer. Conversely, my mother would be seen, if seen at all, as conservative and closeted. Women like my mother were either dismissed (as repressed) or loathed (as complacent), and thus seen as figures from whom daughters must depart (in both psychoanalytic and diasporic terms).[1] Thus, my mother's understanding and evocation of lesbian and her constant use of it (in jest and in seriousness) was initially unintelligible to my scholarly training.

It was decades until I understood that these utterances gestured toward a heterogeneous range of desires and survival strategies; that the erotic was far more capacious than the pornographic imagination (Lorde, 1984), the heterosexual matrix (Butler, 1990) and; that lesbianism can and does emerge out of contextual and colonial histories, class dynamics, and sacred formations (Alexander, 2005; Tinsley, 2018); and that my mother, like so many invisibilized brown women, lived and breathed her life on the lesbian continuum (Rich, 1980). Such a reading of my mother demands most obviously an engagement with Adrienne Rich's notion of compulsory heterosexuality, but it just as significantly demands a rethinking of how the frame of compulsory heterosexuality has not spoken to the nuances of state, nation, military, and imperial formations of heterosexuality and sexual deviance in the Global South. For example, Madhavi Menon (2018) shows how moving across and through coloniality to postcoloniality, sexual and gender deviance, including deviant femininities and lesbian sexuality, has been expunged and made straight in the service of presenting a coherent and pious history of brown desire and South Asian respectability. Thus, to speak about brown erotics and sacred notes alongside the dynamism that occurs between a brown mother and daughter necessitates a writing practice that takes seriously that we cannot tell in advance who or what is a feminist, who or what is a lesbian.

My mother was a toddler during the 1958 Pakistani coup d'état of General Ayub Khan, while I was born into the 1977 coup d'état of General Zia-ul-Haq. Both coups, twenty years apart, led to the installment of military regimes, and both military regimes trickled down into the domestic lives of Pakistani mothers, daughters, sisters, aunts, and wives. Women and girls came to carry the weight of coagulated nationalized masculinity, state-mandated Islam, and gendered postcolonial modernity. What this meant was a hyper emphasis on respectable womanhood, honor, insecurity, modesty, policing, repression, and perhaps most of all, fear. These were the early years of internalizing transnational circulations of middle-class womanhood, which implied that respectability came from relationality to men, marriage, and motherhood. The 1979 Hudood Ordinance concretized these biopolitical regimes of citizenship, gender, and religion into everyday social vernaculars. This law came to be popularly known as *chador aur chaar devari* (veil and the four walls of the home) precisely because it relegated women to the domestic space. Within these discourses, deviant women were the dancers, the artists, the feminists, the whores, and the sex workers. Along with the gendered and sexual violence this law enabled and produced, dance, theater, cinema, music, song, and the visual arts came to be considered "un-Islamic" and were subsequently banned (Gardezi, 2011; Rouse, 2004). But these 1980s censorship practices were cemented far earlier by both British Victorian morality and Indian urban reformers in the 19th century *anti-nautch* movement, a movement to abolish female entertainment (Dewan, 2019; Hinchy, 2019; Mitra, 2020). It was during this anti-dance movement that *tawaifs* (courtesans), *devadasis* (Hindu temple dancers), among others, came to be seen as deviant figures in the modern patriarchal imaginary.[2] It is within this matrix of law, governance, biopolitics, and postcolonial modernity that my mother taught me the costs, consequences, and crises of brown femininities.

My mother was twenty-one when she married the eldest of seven siblings, who had cashed in on a booming economy through their businesses in publishing and real estate, and within five years she had three children. Our class position within the Pakistani nouveau riche meant that I was enrolled in an all-girls British convent school, daily Shia Imami Ismaili Muslim night school, bi-weekly Quran training, and Gujrati lessons. I wore modest clothes and was carefully indoctrinated into my (gendered) lot in life. While my mother belonged to what is often classified as "progressive" Pakistani elite spaces shaped by domestication and patriarchal capital, the desires these formations cultivated and curtailed functioned in complicated ways in her life. On paper, my mother *owned* many properties and had a full domestic staff, but the men in the family had all the power of attorney. These properties were bought, sold, and developed, and wealth was accumulated but never controlled by my mother. Indeed, she was a pawn in men's decisions to accumulate wealth, property, and resources through the use of her name. Her ability to reproduce life and lineage gave her access to wealth but in ways that were unagentic, out of her control, highly incumbent on men's violence, men's desires, and men's supremacy over her and myself.

Regardless of these gendered, sexual, and class confines, my mother cultivated my mischief, my curiosity, my waywardness, my rebellion, my nascent feminism, and my desire to live, explore, and be in my body. She tells me that when I was a toddler, she would secretly watch me perform in front of the mirror, where I would choreograph *thumkas* and put together elaborate one-act plays where I was the villain, the hero, the heroine, the vamp, the martyr, the dancer, the devotee, and the backup singer. She eventually enrolled me in classical Indian dance *bharatanatyam* and voice training at the age of five, in a dance school founded by Sheema Kirmani, one of Pakistan's most celebrated and controversial Indian classical dancers, for both her commitment to the arts and feminist activism. At seven, I started training under Nighat Chaudhary, a leading *Sufi* and *Kathak* classical dancer who also trained in contemporary dance and ballet. The two dance forms in which I was training emerged from the devotional, sexual, and storytelling cultures of *devadasis* and *tawaifs*. It was in these afternoons that I learnt to love women's bodies, breasts, hands, hips, lips, eyes, and feet. I observed how my mother's mannerisms moved from restraint to flirtation, from formal speech to mischievous banter, from stillness to movement. Watching my mother interact with these two women was one of my first lessons in lesbian education (Gopinath, 2005). The way their hands organically landed on each other's hands, thighs, or backs during conversation, the way their gazes locked at a particular comment or joke, how they gave each other complete, enamored attention, or when they collectively taught me to move my hips, their hand on each other's bodies, close, and unafraid of mischievous, flirtatious proximity. I was learning the careful and playful ways feminine energies and femininity moves, and in this movement, crafts and unsettles space and sociality.

Learning to dance was complemented by voice training. My teacher was Ustad Baba Chahat Hussain, a maestro of Indian classical music. He also taught me the Quran. Babaji was one of the few musicians in Pakistan who had worked in Bollywood before the Partition of 1947. Once Babaji migrated to Pakistan, he was often secretly called upon to train *Imams* (mosque leaders) to make the *azaan* (the Muslim call for prayer) more melodious. I spent most of my childhood afternoons with Babaji, a seventy year old man who was relegated to the working-class due to pious narratives in and of Pakistan, where art and artists were marginalized figures. These art forms are usually passed down through patrilineage or apprenticeship, through the social structure of the *gharanas*, a term that indicates one's musical home and kinship. Our afternoons moved between Quran recitation, devotional music, Bollywood histories, erotic poetry, and vocal practice, as Babaji and I were making our own musical *gharana*. But just as I was being immersed in this new kinship network, I observed my mother's distinct shift in her embodiment with my Ustad. Mischief was replaced with deference, feminine energy with discipline, and seduction with respectability.

I recall my singing induction ceremony, known as a *bismillah*, in the name of Allah. I had just celebrated my first Bismillah, a few months ago, marking the first time I completed the Quran in Arabic script at the age of seven. The word marks a spiritual beginning. With closed eyes, I was guided to gently touch the accompanying instruments, *harmonium, tanpura,* and *tabla* and say the words *Sarasvati Devi mere galay mein aja* (Goddess Sarasvati, come into my throat). This beckoning of the Goddess into my throat, into my voice box, literalized for me how song, dance, poetry, rhythm, and melody were forms of divine feminine knowledges, forms of lesbian erotics, and modes of becoming a woman. I was being inducted into the erotic and sacred worlds of desires inherited from feminine deities and their powers to perform, invoke, transform and come inside my body. By literally suffusing my voice/box through the opening of my mouth with the energy of a Goddess, I was in that moment reminded of how desperately, how religiously, how hungrily, how devotionally my mother prayed for money, stability, nonviolence, and a future for her daughter that was not puppeteered by men. There were erotics in her prayers just as there were erotics in my performance. The erotic overtures of my spiritual song were not available to me at that age. But what was available to me in that moment was the affective bond between sacred knowledge, and deviant femininity. My mother was equipping and enabling me with a different kind of power.

By the time I was ten, I was already deeply immersed in the complex registers of racial capital and its relation to maternal knowledges, and inculcated into heteropatriarchy and secret lesbianism. Regardless of the mandated religiosity and strict gendered training that shaped my exteriority, I was also being strategically introduced into a world of spiritual eroticism vis-a-vis song, dance, Islam, and the maternal. I later learned how my mother paid for these extracurricular activities. The family money paid for my British education, religious training, and expensive tuition teachers. My mother used her small monthly stipend to underwrite a different world for me. Our afternoons of temporary refuge and rooms full of traveling desires were my first training in the intimate workings of heterocapital and desire, how capital is used to jolt, slap, train, punch, and seduce women into heterosexual submission. As an upper-class Pakistani Muslim girl, I learnt to challenge the dialectic between power

and powerlessness as well as masculinized capital and femininized accu-
mulation. This led me to center maternal strategizing and secretivity. I
did not know then that this, too, was a brown archive of deviant femininities (Gopinath, 2005; Lorde, 1984; Mitra, 2020).

Audre Lorde once wrote, "My mother has two faces and a frying pot/
Where she cooked up her daughters into girls/Before she cooked our
dinner" (Lorde, 1978, p. 6). Indeed, her words echo, as I now think
through the way my mother taught me how to become marriage material
– a becoming which mandated a certain kind of ascetic practice toward
my sexual self. But just as she offered me the pedagogy of "two faces,"
my mother made sure the asceticism did not erase or invalidate the erotic.
The erotic was presented as a method, a mode of feminist living, or in
Audre Lorde's words, "a resource within each of us that lies in a deeply
female and spiritual plane, firmly rooted in the power of our unexpressed
or unrecognized feeling" (1984, p. 48). Thus, when my mother evokes the
term lesbian, she is not evoking a sexual category or a sexual identity
unhinged from class, gender, ethnicity, spirituality, or nation. Rather, lesbianism becomes a sacred erotic methodology, an ethics of care, a strategic
refusal and a speculative possibility – what Leela Fernandes (2003) and
Jacqui Alexander (2005) call feminist spiritual work, work that recenters
the otherwise erased sacred (of the self) and refuses the separation between
the spiritual and the political. I have come to see lesbianism as a expression of feminist spiritual work that activates the erotic as a different set
of relations, that may be enmeshed in heteropatriarchy and racial capital
(in that nothing operates outside of a field of power), even as it is not
entirely determined by these formations of power. Rather, lesbian for me
is a spiritual subjectivity (a sacred sense of self) and a fragmented space
(women/femme-only spaces)[3] made and unmade through and in-between
the insidious negotiations with capital, social reproduction, desire, and the
feminine erotic.

In the regulatory and rhythmic reverberations of my childhood afternoons, I was learning a divine mother tongue, a feminist tongue, a lesbian
tongue, and all the promiscuous ways women like my mother move in
and out of worlds not of their making or choosing. This is perhaps why
my mother lovingly calls me a *mithee choore* (sweet knife), a popular
descriptor in Urdu and Hindi, which refers to a person who is trained in
the art of sweet duplicity. Embedded in this phrase was her maternal
pedagogy of how one becomes a brown lesbian woman – likeable and
resourceful, charming and covert, respectful, and, to use Sara Ahmed's
(2010) phrase, a feminist killjoy. This was but one lesson in rewriting (for
me) how brown lesbianism could be imagined and may come to move
through the world. She trained me in this strategic and furtive mode of

being. It is these archives of the brown maternal, deviant and hidden lesbian modes of being that I am indebted to. These rooms and afternoons my mother created through secret capital and feminist deviance allowed both of us the ability to make and maneuver a range of desires and divinities, and move between postcolonial respectability, diasporic racializations, class inconsistencies within the economics of empire. Unbeknownst to her, she rendered porous the hard lines often drawn between the erotic and sacred; safety and precarity; desire and embodiment; devotion and dance. I share these stories because, for me, this reading exceeds the peculiarity of our mother-daughter dyad, and offers instead a maternal and playful worlding (Lugones, 1987) of what constitutes living a feminist lesbian life.

Notes

1. For a close reading of the erasure of the brown maternal and the abject brown maternal body in the South Asian diasporic context, see Moon Charania's (2019) and her forthcoming book, *Archive of Tongues*. Also, for brown maternal archives as feminist and queer methods, see Jordache Ellapen's (2020).
2. For a critical and queer feminist engagement on devdasis and tawaifs see Anjali Arondekar (2012) Vanita's (2018).
3. In a forthcoming project, I am looking at women-only spaces, such as the zenana, in the brown and South Asian context. For a glimpse into this work, see my public lecture, titled, Sara Shroff (2021).

Disclosure statement

The authors report no conflicts of interest. The authors alone are responsible for the content and writing of the paper.

References

Ahmed, S. (2010). Feminist Killjoys and Other Willful Subjects. *The Scholar and Feminist Online, 8*(3), 1–8.

Alexander, J. M. (2005). *Pedagogies of the sacred: Meditations on feminism, sexual politics, memory, and the sacred*. Duke University Press.

Arondekar, A. (2012). Subject to sex: A small history of the Gomantak Maratha Samaj. In A. Loomba, & R. A. Lukose (Eds.), *South Asian feminisms* (pp. 244–266). Duke University Press. https://doi.org/10.1215/9780822394990

Butler, J. (1990). *Gender trouble: Feminism and the subversion of identity.* Routledge.

Charania, M. (2019). Making way for ghosts and mothers: Storied socialities, sexual violence, and the figure of the furtive migrant. *Meridians, 18*(1), 206–226. https://doi.org/10.1215/15366936-7297213

Charania, M. *Archive of tongues.* Forthcoming. Duke University Press.

Dewan, S. (2019). *Tawaifnama.* Context/Westland Publications.

Ellapen, J. (2020). Brown photo album: An archive of feminist futurity. *Kronos, 46*(1), 94–111. https://doi.org/10.17159/2309-9585/2020/v46a5

Fernandes, L. (2003). *Transforming feminist practice: Non-violence, social justice and the possibilities of a spiritualized feminism.* Aunt Lute Books.

Gardezi, F. (2011). "From Social Reform to Neoliberalism: Islamization, State Formation and Gender Formation in Pakistan, 1850-1988". Retrieved from Carleton University. Theses and Dissertations. Sociology.

Gopinath, G. (2005). *Impossible sesires: Queer Diasporas and South Asian public cultures.* Duke University Press.

Hinchy, J. (2019). *Governing gender and sexuality in colonial India: The Hijra, C. 1850-1900.* Cambridge University Press.

Lorde, A. (1978). *The Black Unicorn: Poems.* Norton.

Lorde, A. (1984). Uses of the erotic: The erotic as power. In A. Lorde (Ed.), *Sister outsider: Essays and speeches.* (pp. 49–55). Crossing Press.

Lugones, M. (1987). Playfulness, "world"-travelling, and loving perception. *Hypatia, 2*(2), 3–19. https://doi.org/10.1111/j.1527-2001.1987.tb01062.x

Menon, M. (2018). *Infinite variety: A history of desire in India.* Speaking Tiger Books.

Mitra, D. (2020). *Indian sex life: Sexuality and the colonial origins of modern social thought.* Princeton University Press.

Rich, A. (1980). Compulsory heterosexuality and lesbian existence. *Signs: Journal of Women in Culture and Society, 5*(4), 631–660. https://doi.org/10.1086/493756

Rouse, S. (2004). *Shifting body politics: Gender, nation, state in Pakistan.* Women Unlimited.

Shroff, S. (2021). "Between Brown Femininities: Queer Notes on Language, Erotics, and Devotion." Hosted by Mark S. Bonham Centre for Sexual Diversity Studies at the University of Toronto. Retrieved from https://www.youtube.com/watch?v=YQ_6I1URetM

Tinsley, N. (2018). *Ezili's mirrors: Imagining black queer genders.* Duke University Press.

Vanita, R. (2018). *Dancing with the nation: Courtesans in Bombay Cinema.* Bloomsbury Academic.

The institutionalization of queer theory: Where has lesbian criticism gone?

Maite Escudero-Alías

ABSTRACT
This contribution brings to the fore the lesbian silences veiled by dominant theorizations of queer studies in academia, nowadays more concerned with analyzing social affections such as queer diasporas, terrorism, human rights and necropolitics and positing intersectionality as the key configuration of queer epistemology. Yet, I am interested in eliciting how such existing approaches can help chart queer horizons in more inclusive ways without ignoring lesbian voices. Concomitantly, I will posit such lesbian positions as critical epistemologies we cannot do without, since only by unfolding past accretive knowledge on gender and sexuality will queer discourses become inclusive and relational. Hence, this article traces the evolution and theoretical shifts that queer theory has undergone in the last decades and further explores why "the lesbian" continues being dismissed as a marginal site of knowledge and material production, enacting a closeted identity, muted by other legitimate discourses in academia. Such a move toward new queer and affective frameworks, while convincingly essential, should not overshadow lesbian criticism. By drawing on relational and affective modes of being, I suggest recasting "the lesbian" as both a textual and ontological possibility capable of embracing the variety of lesbian-identified persons traditionally silenced by queer theory's canonical institutionalization.

1. Introduction

In 1989, under the title of "Postmodernism and Feminism: Where Have All the Women Gone?" Patricia Waugh (1989) pointed out the ambivalent relationship of feminism and postmodernism. Indeed, postmodernism's ontological disruption of the subject was acknowledged as deleterious not only by most feminist women but also by those excluded from the dominant culture for reasons of class, gender, race, and sexuality. This was so because the advent of postmodernism deconstructed and jeopardized the

The sharing of joy, whether physical, emotional, psychic, or intellectual, forms a bridge between the sharers which can be the basis for understanding much of what is not shared between them, and lessens the threat of their difference (Lorde, 2007, p. 56).

very site of minority identity configurations, as well as other forms of academic feminism that challenged patriarchal configurations of politics and society. In "What Ails Feminist Criticism?," Susan Gubar (1998) offered a critical approach to these questions and lamented the course of feminism at the end of the 20th century, claiming "a number of prominent advocates of racialized identity politics and of poststructuralist theories have framed their arguments in such a way as to divide feminists" (1998, p. 880). Gubar's contention was endowed with a censorious tone about race-based and lesbian critical enquiries, and condemned poststructuralism for delivering a language crisis that refuted alliances among women. Accordingly, Gubar stated: "I can only respond with my view that critical election, abjection, and obscurantism perform a disservice to the libertarian politics and pedagogies endorsed by many of those whose astute ideas play a justly prominent part in feminist thinking" (1998, p. 900).

Amid this war of feminisms, the emergence of queer theory in the early 1990s in academia contributed to casting more theoretical doubt and uncertainty on a historically robust corpus of feminist and lesbian studies. Significantly, Suzanna Danuta Walters (1996) made an important contribution to these critical conversations and interrogated "queer" as the perfect postmodern trope that lost sight of collective experience and displaced "radical and lesbian feminism, often positing itself as the antidote to a retrograde feminist theorizing [...] foregrounding lesbianism as the unfortunate absence" (1996, pp. 832, 847). In her thorough critique on "queer" as the new reigning subjectivity that vindicates postmodern sexual pluralism, Walters is wary of what is left aside in the marginalization and demonization of feminism and lesbian feminism, as she understands that "queer evacuates the specificities of racialized identities without seriously developing a race-based critique on heteronormativity" (1996, p. 860).

Three decades after such debate, this article aims to trace a parallel line of thought between the academic overshadowing of feminism in favor of postmodernism, and the rise and institutionalization of queer theory in the 21st century to the detriment of lesbian sexuality as an epistemological category. As will be argued, much of queer theorizing, initially fascinated by the Butlerian mantra of "gender performativity" (Butler, 1990) and currently interwoven with key social and political concerns, problematically ignores the relevant role that women of color and lesbian feminists have played in its genesis and praxis. Accordingly, by rethinking "queer" as a form of intellectual activism, I also intend to highlight the primary role of lesbian thinkers in the past as well as their contribution to the political utility of queer nowadays. So, after praising the main interventions of these lesbian writers in queer scholarship, I delve into the queer affective turn as an example of queer inquiry that has forgotten about lesbians.

This is not a negative aspect in itself, but the attenuation of queer's reference to race and sexuality, I contend, pushes lesbian criticism aside and favors research on queer theory from other perspectives such as posthumanism, ecocriticism, and new materialism.

The present contribution, then, attempts to bring to the fore the lesbian silences that have been veiled by dominant theorizations of queer studies, nowadays more worried about social affections such as immigration, terrorism, human rights, and necropolitics, thus broadening its exclusive focus on sexuality. Moreover, I am interested in eliciting how such existing approaches can help chart queer horizons in more inclusive ways without ignoring lesbian voices. Concomitantly, I posit such lesbian positions as critical epistemological sites we cannot do without, since only by unfolding past accumulative knowledge on gender and sexuality will action and transformation become real. By lesbian positions I do not exclusively mean the well-known lesbian categorizations of butch and femme, but also other identifications and lesbian genders such as the stone butch, the dyke, and transgender persons who identify themselves as lesbians. I also claim to acknowledge those lesbian positions and experiences that are detached from imperialistic logics and pleasures; namely, the racialized Other, the migrant, and the self-exiled (Spanish) working-class lesbian from rural and impoverished areas like myself, who must find our own path, either by living a lonely lesbian life or by being always already elsewhere, thus accentuating the importance of understanding lesbian lives in different geographical and cultural environments. Much grateful and indebted as I am to US-based scholars for their pioneering, valuable and precious work on queer theory, my point here is to highlight that the field has resulted in showing little interest in work from the periphery.[1] If we aim to build up a more inclusive and intersectional paradigm of queer identities, attention should be paid to these sites of oblivion. To do so, my article draws attention to those lesbian voices that have been erased from the centrality of queer scholarship. Forgetfulness breeds violence and other forms of oppression and discrimination: unless past and present lesbian practices are fully known and assimilated in our queer discourses and actions, the legacy of inequality will persist, for the same mistakes are liable to be made again, drawing us to elitist academic comfort.

2. The silencing of lesbian voices in the queer canon

The emergence of queer theory cannot be isolated from the enormous impact that feminist and lesbian studies had on the category of gender from the late 1970s onward. Historically, the category of the lesbian has conjured dissident voices, which called for the inclusion of sexuality within the prevalent paradigm of identity politics. Most feminist scholarship has redefined "the lesbian" by emptying it from its sexual content, overlooking the importance and complexity of sexuality in the formation of gender identity. As Eve K. Sedgwick reminds us, the concept of sexuality can be associated with "the social/symbolic, the constructed, the variable, the representational" (Sedgwick, 1990, p. 29), thus forging a cultural cornerstone that unveils the constructed status of heterosexuality. During the last decades of the 20th century, the perception of homosexuality as a socially constructed product contributed to the writing of a distinctively lesbian history, aimed at narrativizing our lives from varied cultural and social backgrounds. The main challenge to heteronormativity was more eminently defended in the 1980s with the demands of women of color and lesbian feminists. Influential works on the intersections of gender, race, and sexuality, were best encapsulated by theorists like June Arnold (1976), Cherríe Moraga and Gloria Anzaldúa (1983), bell hooks (1984), Audre Lorde (2007), Barbara Smith (1985), and Kimberlé Crenshaw (1989), to name but the most relevant. For example, Moraga and Anzaldúa (1983) denounced the systemic oppression they suffered because of their race, sexuality and class and, more specifically, they claimed that being lesbians constituted the venue through which their oppression became more fiercely silenced, thus making them more prone to suffering poverty and social exclusion. These feminists' protests against heteropatriarchy and white feminism offered not only new models of kinship centered on race, lesbianism and structural inequalities, but also a way for female agency that queer theory was to dismiss in favor of "antinormativity as the signature value of a newly emergent activist and academic movement" (Jagose, 2015, p. 32). Queer's anti-identitarianism paradoxically displaced the very gender norms that enabled these lesbian feminists to achieve political transformation.

Such feminist and lesbian critiques have forged not only arduous theoretical and methodological strategies, but have also cultivated affective habits of interpretation and prediction. The founders of non-heterosexual feminisms deeply mistrusted a white Western feminism that was aligned with an increasingly neoliberal and imperialist world, especially those critics narrating feminist criticism within the safe space of academia. By contrast, for black women embracing lesbianism as the fundamental site of freedom from coerced heterosexuality attested to their liminal identity position as both victims and rebels. And yet, they concurrently shared with lesbian critics an urgent impulse toward "resisting dogma, expanding the canon, creating a non-racist and non-classist critical vision, transforming our readings of traditional texts, and exploring new methodologies" (Zimmerman, 1981, p. 471). Ultimately, this antiracist and anti-imperialist stance has also been a prevailing defining trait of queer theory, which from its activist genesis, has aimed at rendering visibility to people of color, working-class, HIV positive, and trans persons as an inclusive pattern of political comportment and aesthetic theorization. For Anzaldúa (1987), queerness was both inherently linked to race and threatened by the nonspecificity of whiteness itself, thus defining it beyond sexuality: "we are the queer groups, the people that don't belong anywhere, not in the dominant world nor completely within our own respective cultures. Combined we cover so many oppressions" (1987, p. 208).

As Garber points out, queer theory should recognize the work of "insurgent, activist feminisms, including lesbian feminism and the poetry that constitutes some of its key early political theory" (2001, p. 177), whose voices confronted the heterosexism of women's studies and the sexism of the gay liberation movement. Yet, writers such as Judy Grahn (1971) and Pat Parker (1978, 1983) have been excluded from the lists of queer theory's compulsory readings, despite their blunt disruption of heteronormativity and racism. Furthermore, Lorde and Anzaldúa have been oft quoted among some queer theorists who are more interested in claiming a postmodern *mestizaje* that disrupts gender norms than in "exploring how queer theory is indebted to the work of black lesbian feminists" (Garber, 2001, p. 200). Yet, Anzaldúa's initial affinity with "queer" did not prevent her from accusing white academics of using it "to construct a false unifying umbrella which all queers of all races, ethnicities and classes are shoved under" (Walters, 1996, p. 843). Similarly, Moraga embraced the phrase "queer lesbian" for its difference from middle-class lesbians. Initially, then, queer was adopted by those who sought to acknowledge the "differences of class, or ethnic culture, generational, geographical, and socio-political location" (de Lauretis, 1991, p. iii).

On the other hand, Amber Jamilla Musser wonders if "claiming Lorde as queer has somehow erased her identity as a black lesbian feminist" (2016, p. 347). While Lorde defined herself as a woman, a black lesbian feminist mother lover poet, her legacy offers a way for us to re-think about queer female sexuality. In her 1978 essay "Uses of the Erotic" Lorde (2007) developed a powerful model of lesbian community through difference in which it was possible to think "about possibilities for coalition, solidarity and affect [...] marking the erotic as a binding force that supersedes differences of race and gender" (Musser, 2016, p. 349). This understanding of the erotic aimed to launch a critique upon heterosexist, racist and capitalist structures of oppression that objectified women, as well as to develop solidarity through difference. Thus, Lorde defined the erotic as a set of communal affective bonds that sought to forge feminist alliances based on coalition and joy: "the sharing of joy, whether physical, emotional, psychic, or intellectual, forms a bridge between the sharers which can be the basis for understanding much of what is not shared between them, and lessens the threat of their difference" (Lorde, 2007, p. 56).

I find Lorde's concept of the erotic a compelling site of resistance for black queer women and lesbians, as it allows us to cultivate affective relations outside a heteropatriarchal space that inevitably objectifies female bodies differently, depending on our material conditions. Interestingly, Musser (2016) also elaborates on Lorde's discussion of the maternal as an erotic site of black lesbian feminism: "Lorde's invocation of the maternal works to produce a particular mode of community formation across difference" (2016, p. 354), an idea that has not been much explored by queer theory as another positionality and experience for many lesbians. For Lorde, the maternal is a mode of care, of teaching, filled with optimism and eccentricity in as much as it posits a queer kinship filled with eroticism. Queering the lesbian mother would entail an active sexuality. Musser (2016) cites Lorde's poetry as the juncture where the terrain of the black lesbian and the black mother overlap, evoking "hands and tongues and textures and tastes, calling forth a sexuality that is embodied, active, and sensual" (2016, p. 358).

The need to decolonize heteronormative structures of power is a premise that women of color and black lesbians have traditionally claimed, for this dynamic involves the structural superiority of one race and gender over the others. To this positionality, I would also add the specificities of local and geographical sites. For example, María Lugones (2007) carried out substantial research in this direction, not only emphasizing the intersections of race, class, gender, and sexuality in feminist analyses, but most remarkably, in thinking that "transnational intellectual and practical work that ignores the imbrication of the coloniality of power and the colonial/modern gender system also affirms this global system of power" (2007, p. 188). Central to this task has been the defence by black feminists of intersectionality as the premise which will free feminism from its exclusionary practices, producing transformative counter-hegemonic politics of social justice.

According to Jennifer Nash (2019), the prevailing narrative of intersectionality among women of color has pigeonholed it as a rooted practice in black feminist thought, as "the system of value that aligns 'intersectional' with 'good feminist work', that presumes that intersectional scholarship is politically virtuous" (2019, p. 45). Drawing herself to the term "intersectionality wars" (p. 36), Nash explores the recent battles "rooted in intersectionality's citational ubiquity" (37), in its "whitening, commodification, and colonization" (p. 38). She further pinpoints intersectionality's critical limits when the nonblack critic—i.e. Jasbir Puar—is perceived as a race-traitor, as an outsider that makes intersectionality problematic. As a queer of color theorist, Puar (2008) "embraces black feminism, but only black feminist work from an earlier historical era than intersectionality" (Nash, 2019, p. 55).[2] Such a retrospective approach to black lesbian scholarship, particularly to Lorde, entails interpreting "the critic as engaged in a loving practice rather than a malicious one, a generative act rather than a destructive one" (Nash, 2019, p. 58). What it reveals is that women of color and queer of color critique can be complementary modes of examining the intimate relation between race and sexuality, thus foregrounding an affective engagement through a retrospective gaze to the past, a positionality that is essential for my arguments here.

Despite these women's conviction of paying critical attention to race and sexuality, the canonized texts which have achieved recognition and authority among queer theorists, were the ones written by Teresa de Lauretis (1991) and Judith Butler (1993). Both publications shifted the history of gay and lesbian studies, placing "queer" at the center of debates around gender and sexuality, and incorporating differences such as race and lesbian queer genders. Annamarie Jagose (2015) has insightfully acknowledged de Lauretis' insistence that "queer theory, unlike lesbian and gay studies, is a critical enterprise foundationally interested in race and, through the master term of *race*, in all the taxonomic classes by which social subjectivity is differentiated" (p. 29). Likewise, Butler (1990) includes "cultural practices of drag, cross-dressing, and the sexual stylization of butch/femme identities" (p. 174) as part of her model of gender performativity, thus featuring an archive of practices identified as antinormative. And yet, the decentering of the lesbians of color whose work was central to queer theory's origination in favor of white theorists continues to be a dilemma that needs reconciliation.

In the realm of theoretical criticism, queer's much claimed mobility, flexibility and adaptability allows for a postmodern theorizing of identity that, in Sedgwick's words, refers to "the open mesh of possibilities, gaps, overlaps, dissonances, and resonances, lapses and excesses of meaning when the constituent elements of anyone's gender, of anyone's sexuality aren't made (or can't be made) to signify monolithically" (1993, p. 8). The issue of queer antinormativity via a feminist perspective was revitalized by Butler and Sedgwick who routinely emphasized "its fundamental indefinability in the present and the unknowability of its future forms" (Jagose, 2015, p. 33), thus attesting to both its semantic malleability and the possibility of political transformation. Queer theory, then, is a theory always in the making, gesturing toward its own future emergence. Even though queer theory has sought to foster the study of cultural and literary modes of political alliances among minority groups, most of it strikes a chord that continues to overlook women of color and lesbian writers. Linda Garber (2001) suggests that the lesbian feminism/queer theory polarization is unproductive because "many queer theorists in the 1990s dismissed lesbian feminism wholesale as an unsophisticated, essentialist politics" (p.

11). The Manichean feature attached to the essentialism versus constructivism debate throughout more than three decades by both lesbian and queer studies has indeed prevented the field from recasting other issues permanently silenced not only by heteronormativity but also by a new homonormativity that excludes white lesbians, lesbians of color and transgender lesbians systematically.

Similarly, queer theory has been criticized by some queer of color scholars such as Puar (2008), whose work attempts to denounce queer theory for reproducing a historical amnesia that tends to erase non-Anglo-Saxon and regional, gendered, racial, and sexual differences. Puar challenges a regulatory queerness that not only excludes queer of color and queer immigrant communities but "conversely it also holds queer of color organizing and theorizing to impossible standards and expectations, always beholden to spaces and actions of resistance, transgression, subversion" (2008, p. 41). This is an important claim that should help us to critically interrogate both the de-racialization of queer and the simultaneous structural subversion that is allegedly defined as intrinsic to such queer of color identities. It is my belief that the commodification and gentrification of queer has stripped it of its radical and transformative meaning. Likewise, it has also enabled the institutionalization of an all-inclusive category that refashions queer scholarship and activism into a trendy and insipid practice that yields to a global dominance of US-based scholars in the field and erases geographical differences. This is also the case in academia where "queer" has become a prevailing trend in a publishing market that has manifested its own exclusions.

In being disassociated from sexuality, the "heterosexualization" of queer has contributed to effacing part of its political engagement. As Walters remarks (1996), we must acknowledge from where we speak, and the politics of experience should be part of this dynamics, for knowing about queer theory is not the same as being queer: "the concept of positionality tends toward a voluntarism that ignores the multiple, felt, structural determinations on people's everyday existence" (1996, p. 841). The same applies to questions of race, gender, disability, and so on. What values are lost or gained in the critic's passing as a lesbian? I believe that the heterosexual intellectual should explicitly address their positionality and experience in the classroom and their research; otherwise, it is a way of accentuating the invisibility of lesbians. Ironically, to quote Garber again, "the field that gave us *Gender Trouble* has gender trouble of its own" (Garber, 2001, p. 29).

While "queer" appeared as one solution to the allegedly reductive and problematic nature of identity categories such as "lesbian," it has failed to incorporate successfully the latter as part of its feminist theory and practice. Far from being essentialist and making a reductive and atomized proposal, my claim is to vindicate a more inclusive framework within queer studies in which lesbians can have a room of their own, if only to contest the well-known assumption of "out of sight, out of mind" (Castle, 1993). Undoubtedly, the question of where have all the lesbians gone in academia and the publishing market deserves more attention than ever.

3. Queer's reparative turn and lesbian oblivion

I now wish to explore some theoretical moves that may have triggered the obsolescence of the lesbian within queer studies.[3] The definitional turn of queer theorists to "the political utility of queer" was sensibly pondered by David Eng, J. Jack Halberstam, and José Esteban Muñoz in 2005. They insisted that "the political promise of the term resided specifically in its broad critique of multiple social antagonisms, including race, gender, class, nationality, and religion, in addition to sexuality" (2005, p. 1). Their work paved the way for emergent assumptions of queerness, challenging reductive forms of queer critique and moving away from an exclusive focus on sexuality. Since then, we have witnessed a progressive evolution in its praxis, one that seeks to analyze not only converging axes of identity categories but also the condition of present-day global emergencies such as "debt, crisis, precarity, bare life, biopolitics, neoliberalism, and empire" (Wiegman, 2014, p. 5). This insight enacts a robust commitment to academic interest in questions of immediate political urgency, currently prompted by the COVID pandemic, environmental alarm, refugee crises, the Black Lives Matter movement, etc. Such a shift toward more affective frameworks, I argue, is also the result of the current dominance of postcritical and posthermeneutic forms of analysis in academia, best illustrated by the turn to new materialism and postanthropocentric theory.

For several decades up to the threshold of the 21st century, queer discourse has been traditionally linked to the articulation of "critique," understood as the enactment of a paranoid reading against canonical heteronormative discourses. Robyn Wiegman (2014) has noted how Sedgwick famously called "paranoid reading" to the "rhetorical genre referenced as *critique*, which gives the critic sovereignty in knowing, when others do not, the hidden contingencies of what things really mean" (p. 7, italics in the original). To counteract the wielding agency of the critic over the text, Sedgwick elaborated on a "reparative reading" that could prompt more affective and intimate responses in the reader, such as hopefulness and creativity, inaugurating what is now known as "postcritique" (Sedgwick, 2003). Although Sedgwick called for reparative readings in the mid-1990s, queer theory has widely embraced them a decade after its first citation (Wiegman, 2014, p. 12). In her work, Wiegman discusses a body of work which she labels as *"queer feminist criticism*, which attends to the condition of the present through the converging analytics of affect and time" (2014, p. 5). While noticing the absence of lesbians in Sedgwick's work, Wiegman's list of essential scholarship founded on reparation calls on a variety of tactical strategies that may fuel queer feminist readers today: from Ann Cvetkovich's use of the productive possibilities of depression "as an entry point into a different kind of cultural studies" (2012, p. 13), to Heather Love's focus on negative affect in order to ask questions "about how 'feeling backward' can offer affective resources for queer survival in the political present where forgetting has become the keynote of a progressivist historical consciousness" (2007, p. 23). Such frameworks reinforce my belief in the need of tracing an affective genealogy of queer lesbianism if we are to cultivate a turn to reparative reading "as a practice of critical community formation" (Wiegman, 2014, p. 16).

This relational theory is fully aligned with the positing of lesbian affects as a platform of knowledge and experience from which to enact our desires and identity positions. In this respect, Kadji Amin (2016) offers "an *attachment genealogy* as a method of exposing, fragmenting, and reworking *queer*'s historical inheritances to enable *queer* to do different's work in new contexts" (p. 174). In Amin's view, it is urgent to ground queer in its affective histories that define it as well as to allow it "to do new kinds of work with different objects and archives in a range of historical, cultural, and geographic contexts. This may mean allowing *queer* to come not only to *mean* but also to *feel* differently than it does now" (2016, p. 185). Her *attachment genealogy*, then, has a double purpose: that of excavating queer's multiple pasts and that of thinking about "more historically distant times, racialized populations, and non-US contexts in general" (p. 186). Similarly, according to Mel Chen (2012), we need a queer politics of recognition, that is, a politics that seeks to undo normative patterns of affective kinship through the foregrounding of queer possibilities of intimacy: "queering is immanent to animate transgressions, violating proper intimacies, including between human and non-human things" (p. 11). There is strong evidence to suggest that although the very questioning of "critique" began in the mid-1990s, the growing popularity of the term "postcritique" is opening new paths for queer studies, among which a posthuman ethics of subjectivity is included, but overlooking the presence of lesbians at once.[4] And yet, these relational affective modes are not something new, for lesbians of color such as Anzaldúa, Moraga, and Lorde suggestively avowed an archive of affects, among which rage, shame, touch, solidarity, and generosity were included. Asserting these affective histories of queer through an excavation of multiple pasts would "re-animate it in new formations—thanks particularly to queer of color, transnational, disability, and trans scholarship" (Chen, 2012, p. 83).

Queer theory's amnesia toward this past legacy may alert us against its colonizing and neoliberal stance, albeit unconsciously enacted. One way of incorporating lesbian voices within its scope could be to forge an intersectional epistemology wherein the explicit presence of lesbian agency is not foreclosed. For example, Angela Willey (2018) has suggestively developed a "dyke ethics of antimonogamy" grounded in "notions of friendship, community and social justice [...] that renders its significance as a feature of humanness" (p. 237). In claiming diverse forms of affective ties and networks of social support outside the primacy of the lesbian couple, she draws on materiality and affect as new doors for thinking the lesbian body, as this quest is both erotic and epistemological. Interestingly, Karen Barad's notion of "ethical response-ability" (2012) also attests to our most sensible and sensitive ontological positions as lesbians, capable of weaving a relational net of knowledge, trust, and empathy that criss-crosses past and present accounts of queer sexuality.

If the lesbian is at risk of becoming an obsolete and void identity category, semantically deprived of her own sexual desire and aesthetics, then we should be alert not to create antagonistic spaces, and think, instead, of contingent and attracting possibilities in which the main aim is "to do collaborative research, to be in touch, in ways that enable response-ability" (Barad, 2012, p. 208). According to Barad (2012), "theorizing, a form of experimenting, is about being in touch. What keeps theories alive and lively is being responsible and responsive to the world's patterning and murmurings" (p. 207). By entangling the intimacy of different lesbian and queer epistemologies, and theorizing the sensual metaphor of "touch," a more communitarian ethics and productive aesthetic spaces could be drawn since, as Barad points out, "is touching not by its very nature always already an involution, invitation, invisitation, wanted or unwanted, of the stranger within?" (2012, p. 207).

On the other hand, the trope of "touch" was insistently vindicated by Lorde and Moraga not only as a source of pleasure and vulnerability among women, but also as a call for a return to the mother, as "a polit-ical gesture of making reparations" (Musser, 2019 p. 129). Moreover, Sedgwick developed the sense of touch as an attempt to move away from dualistic thought and raise new questions about phenomenology and affect. The association between touch and affect is obvious, and Sedgwick's approach to touching emphasizes a relational narrative reinforced by the title of her work, *Touching Feeling*, which metonymically suggests a wide range of desires, emotions, and attractions. In her own words: "to touch is always already to reach out, to fondle, to heft, to tap, or to enfold, and always also to understand other people" (2003, p. 14). As I see it, such generous and empathic formulations should stimulate the inclusion of (transgender and stone-butch) lesbians within the academic discussions of feminist queer pedagogies. In rethinking the evolution of queer's definitional openness and theorizing it as a form of action, we must pay attention to the recognition of lesbian sexuality as a key analytic category.

4. Conclusion

The renewal and political utility of "queer" cannot efface the word "lesbian" from its scope. By this assertion I do not imply an unequivocal essentialism, but rather that, just when lesbian voices started to be heard, they were surpassed by a new canonicity of queer studies. In this way, "queer" continues deploying a race while erasing others. Sara Ahmed (2006) argues that queer theory has been interestingly propelled by its own semantic disruption to describe unofficial paths of behavior, desire, and feeling, other than strictly queer. Such a shift reinforces the stereotype of the tragic lesbian, pointing to "the loneliness of the lesbian life, where the lesbian is 'on her own,' cut off from the family, and where her body is lived as an injury to others, which is conscious of feeling all wrong" (Ahmed, 2006, p. 104). In an analogous way, the lesbian may feel at odds with the imperialistic move of queer theory, consistently veiling lesbian subjectivity for the sake of liberal policies of knowledge control and production. My proposal here is cumulative; that is, the queer reparative turn must not isolate those lesbian voices that have laid the foundations of queer thought, but rather integrate them. So, the invocation of an imagined lesbian community defended by thinkers like Anzaldúa and Lorde should produce an alternative mode of all-female extended family that may counteract the current suture of queer (male) individualism. Similarly, Willey (2018) builds on versions of dyke resistance to normative kinship based on long-term intergenerational friendships, solidarity, multiple nonhierarchical romances, and investments in polyamory that are "simultaneously epistemological and corporeal" (p. 250).

If queer theory has engulfed the epistemological—and the material—conditions of lesbian studies, a new sociocultural, academic context emerges whereby the fascination for the former annihilates the visibility of the latter. Against the flattering promises of queer theory, the lesbian critic stands alone, tragically driving herself to academic neglect and semantic erasure. To put it in Terry Castle's well-known words: "The lesbian remains a kind of 'ghost effect', elusive, vaporous, difficult to spot. The lesbian is never with us, it seems, but always somewhere else; in the shadows, in the margins, hidden from history, out of sight, out of mind, a wanderer in the dusk, a lost soul, a tragic mistake, a pale denizen of the night" (1993, p. 2). To rephrase Wiegman's reflection on an anti-disciplinary "world of authorship-without-the-author, culture-without-literature, and the humanities-without-a-human-subject" (2014, p. 18), a queer theory-without-lesbians might leave the critic at war with the very discipline that has undone her. In weaving between the visibility of past lesbian voices and dominant theorizations of queerness as a trendy and convenient discourse, we must find our own place, one that interrogates silence so that a different genealogy of queer studies can emerge, enabling transformative connections among lesbians.

Significantly, the history of queer identities has been one of alliances, dialogues, and silences among different oppressed identity communities that have sought to open new ways to conceptualize the relations between gender, sex, sexuality, class, and race. While the commodification of "queer" entails a cultural visibility for affirming ontological and epistemological diversity, the "lesbian," however, has been dismissed as a marginal site of knowledge and material production. This, in turn, signals a lesbian identity no longer represented as a desirable locus of ontological certainty. The coalescence of "lesbian" and "queer," though simultaneously identity-enforcing, should be invoked as a way of vindicating nonheteronormative desire beyond its usual modes of representations, including racial and transgender ones. I am interested in how to embrace this openness, so as to welcome a queer theory capable of accommodating the very category—i.e. lesbian of color, lesbians, and transgender feminists—on which it was initially wrought. We need to examine the demise of lesbianism and assert it not only as an academic discourse aimed at a constant revision of the history of sexuality, but also as a relational locus from which to interrogate racist, transphobic, and colonialist assemblages of systemic violence and discrimination. To do this type of critique on queer theory is to keep it open and in constant dialogue with its own limitations. We, as lesbians, should unapologetically try to find a voice of our own, one that is inclusive and relational, rather than solipsistic, and one that combines reparative possibilities and imaginative dimensions of lesbian existence.

Declaration of interest statement

I wish to confirm that I do not have any conflicts of interest to declare.

Notes

1. As I have argued elsewhere (Escudero-Alías, 2008), the political force of "queer" is lost when used in other countries, mainly because it is not translated, and the centrality of the English language through which queer identities are defined erases the cul-

tural, social, and historical connotations of other words for naming queer lesbians like the Spanish *bollera* or *tortillera.*

2. In discussing the origins of intersectionality, Nash mentions several thinkers and innovators such as Combahee River Collective, Toni Cade Bambara, Deborah King, Frances Beal, Anna Julia Cooper, Patricia Hill Collins and Kimberle Crenshaw, and she notes that "it is crucial to note that Crenshaw's work has remained a touchstone to intersectional histories" (2019, p. 41).

3. Drawing on Nash's critique of intersectionality as an allegation invested with generosity, love and admiration (2019), my critique of queer theory's neglect of lesbians is also carried out as an intellectual practice of affection and, as such, I hope it is met with interest and fondness by the reader.

4. The field of critical posthumanism is also relying on queer affect theory in its appraisal of complex assemblages between human and nonhuman forces (Barad, 2003; Bennett, 2010: Braidotti, 2013).

Acknowledgments

I would like to express my gratitude to Lorraine Turner, and to the three anonymous readers for their generative and thorough feedback on this article.

Funding

My thanks are also due to the financial support of the Spanish Ministry of Economy and Competitiveness (METI), and the European Regional Development Fund (DGI/ERDF) (code FFI2017-84258-P); the University of Zaragoza and Ibercaja (code JIUZ-2019-HUM-02); and the Government of Aragón and the European Social Fund (ESF) (code H03_20R).

ORCID

Maite Escudero-Alías ⒾⒹ http://orcid.org/0000-0002-3116-3641

References

Ahmed, S. (2006). *Queer phenomenology. Orientations, objects, others.* Duke University Press.
Amin, K. (2016). Haunted by the 1990s: Queer theory's affective histories. *WSQ: Women's Studies Quarterly, 44*(3–4), 173–189. https://doi.org/10.1353/wsq.2016.0041

Anzaldúa, G. (1987). *Borderlands/La Frontera: The New Mestiza*. Aunt Lute Books.

Arnold, J. (1976). Lesbian fiction. *Lesbian Writing and Publishing. Sinister Wisdom*, *1*(2), 42–52.

Barad, K. (2003). Posthumanist performativity: Toward an understanding of how matter comes to matter. *Signs: Journal of Women in Culture and Society*, *28*(3), 801–831. https://doi.org/10.1086/345321

Barad, K. (2012). On touching—The inhuman that therefore I am. *differences*, *23*(3), 206–223. https://doi.org/10.1215/10407391-1892943

Bennett, J. (2010). *Vibrant matter: a political ecology of things*. Duke University Press.

Braidotti, R. (2013). *The posthuman*. Polity Press.

Butler, J. (1990). *Gender trouble. Feminism and the subversion of identity*. Routledge.

Butler, J. (1993). Critically queer. *GLQ: A Journal of Lesbian and Gay Studies*, *1*(1), 17–31. https://doi.org/10.1215/10642684-1-1-17

Castle, T. (1993). *The apparitional lesbian: Female homosexuality and modern culture*. Columbia University Press.

Chen, M. Y. (2012). *Animacies: Biopolitics. Racial mattering, and queer affect*. Duke University Press.

Crenshaw, K. (1989). Demarginalizing the intersection of race and sex: A Black feminist critique of antidiscrimination doctrine, feminist theory and antiracist politics. *University of Chicago Legal Forum*, *140*, 139–167.

Cvetkovich, A. (2012). *Depression. A public feeling*. Duke University Press.

de Lauretis, T. (1991). Queer theory: Lesbian and gay sexualities. *differences*, *3*, iii–xviii.

Eng, D., Halberstam, J., & Muñoz, J. E. (2005). What's queer about queer studies now? *Social Text* (Special issue), *23*(3-4).

Escudero-Alías, M. (2008). When (non) Anglo-Saxon queers speak in a queer language: Homogeneous identities or disenfranchised bodies?. In C. Caldas-Coulthard and R. Iedema (Ed.), *Identity trouble. Critical discourse and contested identities* (pp. 77–94). Palgrave Macmillan.

Garber, L. (2001). *Identity poetics: Race, class, and the lesbian-feminist roots of queer theory*. Columbia University Press.

Grahn, J. (1971). *Edward the Dyke and other poems*. Women's Press Collective.

Gubar, S. (1998). What ails feminist criticism? *Critical Inquiry*, *24*(4), 878–902. https://doi.org/10.1086/448900

hooks, b. (1984). *Feminist theory: From margin to center*. South End Press.

Jagose, A. (2015). The trouble with antinormativity. *differences*, *26*(1), 26–47. https://doi.org/10.1215/10407391-2880591

Love, H. (2007). *Feeling backward: Loss and the politics of queer history*. Harvard University Press.

Lorde, A. (2007). *Sister outsider: Essays and speeches*. Crossing Press.

Lugones, M. (2007). Heterosexualism and the colonial/Modern gender system. *Hypatia*, *22*(1), 186–209.

Moraga, Cherrie, and Gloria Anzaldúa. Eds. (1983). *This Bridge called my back: Writings by radical women of color*. Women of Color Press.

Musser, A. J. (2016). Re-membering Audre Lorde. Adding lesbian feminist mother poet to Black. In E. Patrick Johnson (Ed.), *No tea, no shade. New writings in Black queer studies* (pp. 346–361). Duke University Press.

Musser, A. J. (2019). All about our mothers. Race, gender, and the reparative. In *After queer studies. Literature, theory and sexuality in the 21st century* (pp. 122–136). Cambridge University Press.

Nash, J. (2019). A love letter from a critic, or notes on the intersectionality wars. In *Black feminism reimagined. After intersectionality* (pp. 33–58). Duke University Press.

Parker, P. (1978). *Womanslaughter*. Diana.

Parker, P. (1983). *Movement in Black: The collected poetry of Pat Parker, 1961–1978*. Crossing.

Puar, J. K. (2008). Homonationalism and biopolitics. In A. Kuntsman and E. Miyake, *Out of place: Interrogating silences in queerness/raciality* (pp. 12–69). Raw Nerve Books.

Sedgwick, E. K. (1990). *Epistemology of the closet*. Penguin.

Sedgwick, E. K. (1993). *Tendencies*. Duke University Press.

Sedgwick, E. K. (2003). *Touching feeling: Affect, pedagogy, performativity*. Duke University Press.

Smith, B. (1985). Toward a Black feminist criticism. In E. Showalter (Ed.), *The new feminist criticism: Essays on women, literature, and theory* (pp. 168–185). Virago.

Walters, S. D. (1996). From here to queer: Radical feminism, postmodernism, and the lesbian menace (or, why can't a woman be more like a fag?). *Signs: Journal of Women in Culture and Society, 21*(4), 830–869. https://doi.org/10.1086/495123

Waugh, P. (1989). Postmodernism and feminism: Where have all the women gone? In *Feminine fictions. Revising the postmodern* (pp. 1–33). Routledge.

Wiegman, R. (2014). The times we're in: Queer feminist criticism and the reparative 'turn'. *Feminist Theory, 15*(1), 4–25. https://doi.org/10.1177/1464700113513081a

Willey, A. (2018). Rethinking monogamy's nature: From the truth of non/monogamy to a dyke ethics of "antimonogamy". *Journal of Lesbian Studies, 22*(2), 235–253. https://doi.org/10.1080/10894160.2017.1340006

Zimmerman, B. (1981). What has never been: An overview of lesbian feminist literary criticism. *Feminist Studies, 7*(3), 451–475. https://doi.org/10.2307/3177760

"*Somos contra la 'queer-ificacíon'*"/"We reject the queer-ification of lesbianism": lesbian political identity and anti-queer politics among Mexican lesbians and queer Chicanas-Latinas

Stacy I. Macias

ABSTRACT

This essay provides a critical personal reflection contemplating a 2006 Mexico City-based cross- border dialogue in which sharp divisions emerged between a set of Mexicana lesbianas—declaring their pro-lesbian feminist and anti-queer politics—and a set of queer Chicanas- Latinas—pronouncing their queer women of color politics. The vexing exchange occurred on the eve of the 3rd annual Marcha Lésbica, an explicitly radical lesbian feminist political gathering and at the time the largest public action of its kind to be held in Latin America. I draw new insights about key historical and contemporary lesbian political identity issues by reviewing how Mexican lesbian politics informed by feminism and critiques of neoliberalism produced challenges to the U.S. based participants. I reframe the value of the lesbian Mexicanas' "anti- queer" proclamation, an affective statement especially unpopular in that period given the provincializing glance at lesbian politics and identity in the U.S. Finally, I revisit this difficult moment to historicize how lesbian remains a freighted category of political identity for Chicanas-Latinas who abide by women of color and trans coalitional politics, while it also opens up affinities for meaningful though precarious cross-border identifications. This multilayered reflection argues for a situated understanding of the meanings that can be ascribed to lesbian identity and politics, which are highly contingent upon spatio-temporalities. Thus, the category "lesbian" is replete with instructive energies whether as an affective critique of queer epistemologies that move along a Global North to Global South axis, or as a reminder of the limits of coalitional politics built across nation-state borders.

In the Spring of 2006, I traveled alongside several self-identifying Chicanas-Latinas and queer women of color to Mexico City to participate in the 3rd annual *Marcha Lésbica* [Lesbian March].[1] After several months of planning, fundraising, and media blitzing, Mexicana lesbians of the "*COMAL*" [*El Comité Organizador de la Marcha Lésbica de México*/The

Organizing Committee of the Mexico Lesbian March], with the support and participation of a few U.S.- based collectives, including Tongues of which I am a co-founding member, were about to stage this public march and demonstration.[2] Occurring the day before the *Marcha*, the *Reunión Internaciónal* ["International Meeting"] was intended for each country's participants to explore organizational strategies, review the history of the *Marcha*, preview the next day's events, and meet core participating members.[3] What began as an attempt to dialogue about each group's sexual and gender politics, however, quickly shifted into a verbally clashing, emotionally charged, and ultimately irreconcilable conversation about class, race, sexuality, lesbian feminism, and the limits of "queer" discursive travels.

In what follows, I retrace what led to the conversation breakdown to explore the Mexican organizer's claims of *lesbofeminismo*—an activist discourse and practice of lesbian feminists throughout Latin America that addresses the cultural, political, and social precarity of female lesbian existence due to the neo-liberal co-optations of feminism, gay identity, and human rights agendas. Pronounced by a *COMAL* member through an affectively punctuated "*contra*-queer" [anti-queer] stance, I consider the productive challenges of *lesbofeminismo* to the U.S. collectives' queer claims. As a participating organization in the *Reunión* and *Marcha* with deep investments in coalition-building projects between and among lesbian, queer, and trans women of color in the U.S. and Mexico, I explore how lesbian political identity espoused by Mexico City-based organizers of the *Marcha Lésbica* in the mid-2000s could both ignite and extinguish the coalitional desires of Tongues and some of the other U.S. queer women of color, Latina- Chicana participants. In this way, I situate this article as an historical, critical personal reflection within a very specific time and place to show how a series of un-translatable, vexing, and haunting moments exposed the problem of invoking lesbian political identity and lesbian feminism for those in the U.S. who abide by a queer women of color and trans coalitional politics. I also revisit this moment to meditate on the provisional breakthroughs that transpired in the event's aftermath. Thus, I argue that *lesbofeminismo* opened affinities for meaningful—even if fleeting—cross-border coalitional-building work.

At stake in reexamining this moment is a nuanced optic for understanding lesbian identity, *lesbofeminismo*, and queer concepts that circulated in Mexico City among Mexican lesbians in the early to mid-2000s. In effect, I reflect back on my and other Chicana-Latina organizers' unidimensional cultural feminist framework for understanding lesbian identity and lesbian feminism, which is symptomatic of white, U.S.-Eurocentric, global North to global South spatio-temporal logics and epistemic travels.

I also raise how these logics function not only to obscure *lesbofeminismo* for the Chicana-Latina participants as residents of the global North, but how queer women of color identity and knowledge claims are similarly muddled for Mexican lesbians as global South residents. The value of attending to the unique, thorny, and sometimes narrow conceptualizations of both lesbian identity and queer women of color politics in a U.S.-Mexico cross-border context propels these reflections.[4] Ultimately, I contend that an affectively infused *contra*-queer politics could hold instructive energies for queer Chicanas-Latinas if only underpinned by the *lesbofeminismo* circulating in that moment. This requires divesting from lesbian identity and lesbian feminist politics that signal archaic prescriptions of female-separatism at the exclusion of trans community members, and which have become predominant in the U.S., toward opening up *lesbofeminismo* into what queer diasporic and lesbian of color thinkers like Sara Ahmed (2015) proceed from: "lesbian feminism is a resource of the present."[5]

Un-translatable encounters at the 2006 *La reuníon internacional*

On the eve of the 3rd annual *Marcha Lésbica*, two distinct groups—one set of queer Chicana-Latina activists from California with whom I traveled, and a set of Mexican lesbian organizers—participated in a Mexico City-based cross-border meeting. This international meeting formed part of the activities of the 2006 *Marcha Lésbica*, which at the time of its occurrence was the largest public action of its kind to be held in Latin America. As a member of the U.S.-based collective, Tongues, I eagerly anticipated this more intimate engagement for the opportunity to dialogue about gender and sexual politics in Mexico and the U.S. and to gather insight from the *COMAL* on their successful large-scale lesbian political actions. After all, I could not imagine staging any parallel to the *Marcha Lésbica* due to the national dominance of lesbian, gay, bisexual, and transgender (LGBT) visibility politics and the state-wide mainstreaming of same-sex marriage campaigns.[6]

After settling into a big circle at a Quaker center, in a mixture of Spanish, English, and Spanglish, introductions began. Participating Mexican lesbians referenced the organizations of which they were a part, the neighborhood, city, or state from which they traveled, and their sexual and gender identities: "*Soy mujer lesbiana feminista de Tepos*" [I'm a lesbian feminist woman from *Tepotzlán*]. U.S. contingent members categorically highlighted sexual and gender identities that intersected with race, ethnicity, and class according to established U.S. variables, as in "working-class queer Chicana" or "first-generation bisexual *mujer*." Before the meeting could proceed, however, I noticed that murmurs, side-conversations, and questions from the scattered members throughout all points of the circle arose, eventually redirecting the energy and the objectives of the group gathering.

For the Mexican lesbians, U.S. identity claims rang as unfamiliar and inauthentic; for the U.S. Chicanas-Latinas, I thought that translating terms from English to Spanish was the main source of the problem.[7] In search of handy linguistic compatibles to aid in translation, I sensed the frustrations intensifying. Translating started to grow into a laborious task, extending the introduction period well into the second hour of the meeting. The main challenge, though, became one of clashing geopolitical realities which ushered in the politics of (mis)translation. It became clear that even with the most judicious word choices, there were incomprehensible contexts that could not be distilled into simple terminology. In essence, the sociocultural complexity of history, place, and politics of neither the queer women of color in the U.S. or the Mexican lesbians present could be captured. The inadequate translation of the U.S. designation "women of color" to "*mujeres de color*" is one telling example.

When Chicanas-Latinas identified as "women of color" and this was translated to "*mujeres de color,*" the *Mexicanas* corrected us. We were actually "*gringas*" because, in a Mexican context, we were citizens of the United States and not Afro-Mexican women.[8] I recall that the use of the term "*gringa*" felt like a punch to the gut because *gringa* in the U.S. is a pejorative term to hurl at a white, feminine presenting, non-Latina girl/woman. While naming the Chicanas-Latinas from the U.S. "*gringas*" was explained as simply the nomenclature for privileged U.S. passport holders, many of us experienced it as racialized insult to remind us that we could never make authentic claims to Mexican culture and belonging. We then attempted to explain that "women of color" is an umbrella term for African American-Black, Latina-Chicana, Asian American, and Native American feminists in the U.S. What we could not explore, however, was how in the post-Civil Rights era "women of color" was coined in feminist of color writing to denote shared sociocultural, political contexts of nonwhite racialized gender subjectivity formed in response to overlapping structural subjugation and state-based oppressions. Moreover, the Chicana-Latina collectives involved in the *Marcha* activities use "women of color" less as a referent to an essentialized notion of identity and rather to signal a nonwhite, anti-racist, feminist *practice* of social justice activism and knowledge production.

Grace Hong (2006), for example, explains the uses of "women of color" (xvi)

Furthermore, unlike single-axis forms of organizing, such as the mainstream white feminist movement, traditional labor organizing, or race-based movements, women of color feminism's insistence on difference, coalitional politics, and a careful examination of the intersecting processes of race, gender, sexuality, and class, which make singular identification impossible, displaces a U.S. nationalist subject formation based on homogeneity, equivalence, and identification.

In this way, translating "women of color" to capture its genealogical links to U.S. feminist, ethnic-nationalist, and anti-capitalist movements of the 1970s and 1980s, as well as its discrete methodological interests, was strained, if not altogether impossible.

Likewise, many of the U.S. contingent participants did not fully comprehend that in Mexico *"mujeres de color"* refers solely to African-descent or *Afro Mexicana* women who are racially marked as Black. Much like in other Latin American countries, the Atlantic slave trade and the Spanish colonizer's *sistema de castas* [caste system] introduced to Mexico a race-based hierarchical classification system. The term *"mujer de color"* captures both the racist codification of the early caste system in which blackness was highly marked as "subordinate other," and the occlusion of the African-descent presence in the idealized production of Mexican national identity.[9] It became obvious that although "women of color" and *"mujeres de color"* were both race-based terms of identification, they were fundamentally un-exchangeable. The freighted histories of race, immigration, and nation-state making efforts in the U.S. and Mexico are fundamentally different, and these perplexing differences were unable to be explained with precision and attentiveness amidst the heated moment.

Following the shortcomings of accurate translations, several more flare-ups prompted our collective descent into what I would call an affective zone of debate and confrontation. Affect, as Juana María Rodríguez (2014) offers, involves the process through which feelings operate in the social sphere. In her work, Rodríguez identifies affects that are undesirable, confrontational, or inappropriate as they emerge in discourse, gesture, and performance to reassess their outwardly political and embodied meanings. I identify key affective moments at the *Reunión* that set off a series of unsettled and unsettling discursive exchanges among the participants. There was an assumption that none of the Chicanas-Latinas maintained familial or cultural connections to Mexico, and this especially offended those who identified as Mexican, whose parents were non- documented in the U.S., or who spoke only Spanish at home to oppose cultural assimilation imperatives. Some of the U.S. members hastily believed that Mexicana lesbians were unable to reciprocate support because Mexican lesbians must be more oppressed as residents of a Global South country. The next climatic moment occurred when a *COMAL* organizer took to the microphone and began the following inspired manifesto: *"Somos contra la queer- ificaccion. somos contra la bisexual-ificaccion...somos contra la gay-ificaccion...y somos contra la corportizacion de nuestro movimiento de lesbianas feministas aqui y en el mundo total"* ["We are against the queerification/queer coopting... we are against the bisexualizing/bisexual coopting...we are against the gayifying/gay coopting...and we are against the corporatization of our lesbian feminist movement here in Mexico and in the entire world"].[10] In the following sections, I unpack this bold, staunchly delivered manifesto, or what I call an affective *contra-* queer politics, which I suggest can only be apprehended through a fuller rendering of how lesbian Mexicans of the *COMAL* articulated their *lesbofeminismo*.[11]

Situating *lesbofeminismo* in Mexico City, 2006

The *COMAL* member renouncing the transnational travels of queer indicated that she was doing so in the name of preserving *lesbofeminismo*.[12] In her research, Cristina Serna (2017, p. 51) constructs a definition of *lesbofeminismo* combining her insights with those of Mexican scholar of Communications, María Isabel Barranco Laguna:

> a Latin American political discourse and practice developed during the seventies, eighties, and nineties 'whose enunciative charge was centered mainly on the denunciation of repressive acts against homosexuals and lesbians by the authorities and their respective ideological apparatuses (State, church, family), and the mass media' (qutd in Barranco Laguna, 2001, p. 53).

The rise and formation of *lesbofeminismo* in Mexico was catalyzed by the contempt and exclusion lesbian women experienced in progressive moments of the 1970s and 1980s (2017, p. 54). Furthermore, *lesbofeminsimo* in practice espouses an expansive agenda, advocating for changing the curriculum taught to middle and high school students in order to reflect the multiplicities of sexuality; placing more women and out lesbians in political office; addressing the globalization of female sex work; reforming health initiatives that demonize female sexuality; and the general affirmation that in order for any society to achieve a successful revolution and supplant the existing social order, the issue of lesbian sexuality must be elevated by characterizing heterosexism as a systematic, structural issue.

The contemporary manifestation (early 2000s onward) of *lesbofeminismo* emerged in response to the conditions of neoliberalism, where the necropolitical realities of *femicidio* (the killing of women usually accompanied by sexual violence and torture due to their gender), transnational corporate capitalism, and global gay visibility converge. Mexican scholar Norma Mogrovejo (2000) delineates how *lesbofeminismo* marked important differences among gay men, bisexuals, and lesbians, but moreover exposed the fault-lines between national organizing models supported by global gay identity allure and grassroots organizing models supported by a politics of transformation. Mexican lesbian feminists were critical of the dominance of pride and visibility efforts in the gay liberation movement that relegated fights against imperialism, capitalism, heterosexism, and other systemic problems to the feminists or other social movement activists. While lesbians invoked an agenda inclusive of human rights, the most radical gay liberation rights agenda was, in the words of one organizer of Mexico's first *Marcha*, "more about pride and less about politics." Identifying these conditions as the necessary starting points from which to develop a politics grounded in something other than pride, *lesbofeminismo* became ideologically consolidated among some Mexico City-based activists and organizations in particular. These activists organized the *Marcha Lésbica* as a direct critical response to the pernicious effects of misogyny, religious fundamentalism, heterosexism, and neoliberalism while serving as a testament to feminist collective work amidst the corporatization of lesbian and gay identity and the NGO-ification of human rights agendas.[13]

Given these historical specificities, the value of *lesbofeminismo* in the context of Mexico is undeniable. For the Mexico City *Marcha* organizers and *COMAL* members, persistently resisting "queer" via an affirmative *lesbofeminismo* is rooted in the feminist practice of resisting localized forms of gendered state-violence inaugurated by neo-liberal processes of globalization. *LeSVOZ*, a primary organizing body of the *Marcha Lésbica*, has detailed in their organizational mission and eponymous magazine that a *lesbofeminista* agenda seeks a radical restructuring of sociocultural institutions throughout Mexico such that lesbian desire, lesbian sexuality, and lesbian community are supported and sustained across all areas of social life.[14] Emphasizing resistance to dominant regimes of the nation-state and its transnational dealings that produce Mexican women as commercialized objects, *lesbofeminismo* in this way cannot be severed from the gendered and sexualized trappings of the neo-liberal nation-state. Unlike *lesbofeminismo*, "queer" does not hold the same political force or ideological power. *Lesbofeminismo* is also conceivably at odds with an all-encompassing notion of queer that has indiscriminately jumped borders with little regard for local analyses or ongoing struggles. Such a fulmination against queer— however keenly contextualized within Mexican socioeconomic politics and local gay history—can nevertheless be read as a problematic that similarly conjures lesbian feminists in the U.S. and *lesbofeministas* in Mexico: those who refute queer vocabularies are inflexible separatists or tran sexclusionary radical feminists (TERFs).

In the U.S., lesbian feminism historically has been understood as a political philosophy that exposes and resists the institutionalization of heterosexuality. Lesbian theorists like Adrienne Rich (1993) infamously argued for a version of lesbian feminism that is less about erotic desire and same-sex sexuality but rather a "woman-identified-woman" subjectivity constructed out of rejecting heteropatriarchal demands. Some versions of lesbian feminism in the U.S. remain out of scholarly and activist favor due in large part to the fabled split between women's studies and queer studies, which is narrativized as an issue of competing approaches to the same objects of study (Cohen, 1997; Jagose, 1996; Muñoz, 1999). Furthermore, in contemporary contexts, lesbian feminism is overly correlated with the transphobia and cissexism of TERFs and lesbian feminist separatists, a narrative that some scholars of trans* theory and trans feminisms (Stryker and Bettcher, 2016) have unraveled. While gender and feminist scholars have written about the height of the tensions occurring in the mid-1990s, my collision with this related-issue happened in a context outside of the U.S.—Mexico City, specifically— and in an historical moment in which "trans" as in "transnational" and "transgender" were becoming, if they had not already become, robust methodological frameworks and fundamental considerations in women's, gender, sexuality, and feminist circles and fields of thought. In other words, I want to resist evaluating that *contra-queer* moment of *lesbofeminismo* as in temporal step with 1980s -1990s lesbian feminist moments and movement in the U.S, or as teleologically bound to eventually align with the radical gender possibilities and trans feminist queer timescape that we are in. Comparing the 2006 tenets of *lesbofeminismo* in Mexico City to U.S. lesbian feminist separatist discourses of an earlier era decontextualizes what transnational feminists like Maylei Blackwell (2014, p. 300) argue are "unaligned geographies of difference." This term emphasizes "the fact that the political construction and social meaning of differences surrounding racial formation, class stratification, and gender and sexual identities [are] highly differentiated in local contexts" (Blackwell: 300). While Blackwell addresses incompatible spatialities across nation-states and within political cultures of a single nation, I extend Blackwell's insight here to emphasize spatialities as they relate to epistemic contact within temporal frames, specifically a *lesbofeminismo* political identity discourse among *Marcha* organizers in Mexico City, 2006.

I also acknowledge that broaching *lesbofeminismo* runs the risk of validating the reductive, harmful ideologies about bisexuality, non-lesbian sexualities, transgender identity, and trans* frameworks that some practitioners of *lesbofeminsmo* historically have defended and contemporaneously have championed. Rather than continue to moor lesbian feminist and lesbofeminismo claims of relevance to these debates, it may be as valuable to document transnational feminist lessons, archive critical queer takeaways, and co-construct activist fundamentals around spatial-temporal contexts rather than "new" or "old" claims. This is why I insist that in order to value that *contra*-queer affective moment, *lesbofeminismo* must be situated in the spatio-temporality of the *Marcha* in Mexico City, 2006. Thus, while *lesbofeminismo*, and its English-language cousin, lesbian feminism, may share in some overarching epistemological objectives, notably the deconstruction of heterosexuality, the two are not thoroughly aligned due to the political exigencies surrounding their discrete emergences. The idea of *lesbofeminismo* as a critique of how transnational corporate power and neo-liberal capitalism had flattened out the radical dynamics of non-heterosexual politics reframed the cliched narratives of U.S. lesbian feminism and lesbian identity to which some of the U.S. queer women of color ascribed it. To put it plainly, *lesbofeminismo* cannot be seamlessly equated with lesbian feminism despite the commonsense move to do so.

Meditating on South to North & North to South movements of knowledge

Although the *contra-queer* politics expressed in manifesto form opened affective registers replete with anger, bewilderment, and denouncement without a quick way to close them down, I caution against writing off this moment as merely caught in a series of un-translatables. The temptation to read this moment as having fallen into incommensurability or even worse, tempestuousness, diminishes the productive tensions of what I am borrowing from the *lesbofeminismo* promulgated in that moment of the *Marcha*'s preevent meeting—a "*contra- queer*" or anti-queer politics. What can a *contra-queer* politics that is articulated through *lesbofeminismo* in Mexico signify and accomplish outside of the U.S? One insight is that a *lesbofeminista* analytic can illuminate early turn of the 21st century uneven cross-border movements of queer women of color knowledges and lesbian feminisms.

The proclamation, "*Somos contra la queer-ificacion...*" is a bold statement established in the negative form that leads with "being against" rather than the affirmative form of "being with." This prescriptive seemed to counter the coalition-building objectives of the meeting; however, to understand this move as merely indicting U.S. queer-ing processes and politics in order to elevate *lesbofeminismo* is a misreading that necessarily places these two projects in opposition to one another. To reach another kind of understanding requires adjusting the dominant epistemic frame that overdetermines these conclusions. To do so entails not only acknowledging the specific geographically inflected meanings of 'queer' between the U.S. and Mexico, but reevaluating transnational movements of knowledge and feminist resistant practice so that emergent "misreadings" in a global South country like Mexico might productively reconstruct that which some U.S. scholars and activists might overgeneralize or write off, like lesbian feminism.

Reacting defensively to the resentment uttered in taking a stand against queer-ing processes highlights how the project of queer cannot conceal its very U.S.-Western-centric epistemic starting point. By "the project of queer," I am referring to the various theoretical discussions, activist efforts, and field formations informally and formally implicated in constructing an ironically stable notion of queer that has facilitated its nimble movements globally. It was apparent that the dominant conceptualization of queer—narrowly white, often gay male-centered, and always U.S.-Euro-centered—that some U.S scholars in the early-mid 2000s began to deconstruct also dominated in its North to South epistemic travels. Thus, I was not surprised by the *COMAL* member's un-mistakeable critical distancing from our self-declared queer women of color politics and identification. As U.S. queer of color writers and thinkers like Cathy Cohen (1997) and Martin Manalansan (2003) theorize, although "queer" stores within its five-letter word a complex of identities, practices, and politics, its history and relevance are shaped by the particular queer genealogy that any one narrator excavates and prioritizes.

For the U.S. queer women of color participating in the *Marcha Lésbica*, queer is inextricably linked to critiques of heteronormativity that early lesbian of color feminists, like Gloria Anzaldúa and Cherríe Moraga (2015) and many of the contributors of *This Bridge Called My Back*, advanced.[15] These lesbians of color exited feminist movements and ethno-nationalist organizations to initiate their own critical projects because their lesbian sexuality was ferreted out from—rather than vitally incorporated into—radical visions of social justice. With demands to repudiate heterosexism and include sexuality as a constitutive site of power that is always active and already present within race, gender, and class formations, lesbians of color ignited a new era of U.S. anti-racist, feminist politics while theoretically grooming the next generation of scholars and activists. Their under-acknowledged contributions to the intellectual and cultural projects of queer sit at the heart of a genealogy aligned with what Cathy Cohen (1997, p. 453) reminds readers: "LGBT people of color have increasingly taken on the responsibility for at the very least complicating and most often challenging reductive notions of heteronormativity articulated by queer activists and scholars." While the staunch claims of the *lesbiana Mexicana* stand in contrast to how queer women of color contextualize and deploy queer, this difference must be attributed in part to the ways in which the contributions of U.S. radical lesbian of color history—rather than radical or cultural lesbians—are occluded from and warped within the dominant queer epistemological record on both sides of the border.

In addition to contextualizing *lesbofeminismo* within its specific time-space emergence, another way to avoid mapping *lesbofeminismo* onto U.S. temporal-spatial grids is to identify feminist of color, queer of color, and feminist diasporic queer frameworks that offer intersecting, complimentary, and relational alternatives. For example, queer diasporic thinker Gayatri Gopinath (2005) qualifies a notion of queer in relation to how female bodied women interact in Indian home spaces "as pertaining not simply to sexual identity or even sexual practices" but "[r]ather to a mode of resistant feminist cultural practice." Gopinath cleverly roots queer in *feminist* diasporic cultural practice rather than in U.S. sexual identity or expressions. This notion of "feminist cultural practice" can be read as closely resonant with *lesbofeminismo*'s sociopolitical cultural objectives that are unabashedly "resistant." I also imagine the capacious potential of *lesbofeminismo*'s resistant politics not only to patriarchy, heterosexuality, and neo-liberal policies but to the range of punishing normativities that feminists can resist including those that nation-states and cultures impose on queer and trans subjects. Accordingly, I find Gopinath's formulation of "queer" as another astute reminder of the feminist, even cultural lesbian, roots of queer. With this recognition, the desire to create idealized shared grammars through which to collaborate can be brought into sharp relief.

Such was the case when after the affective, incontrovertible rejection of queer, one of the Mexico-based organizers posed a challenge: could the Chicanas-Latinas organize the 4th annual *Marcha Lésbica* in their own backyard and in accordance with their own queer women of color politics? At first blush, the question seemed confrontational given the sudden turn to the future of the *Marcha* while the present palpable tensions had not been resolved. After a few minutes of pondering it, the U.S-based participants began to imagine and idealize organizing a large-scale political demonstration of queer women and trans of color communities.

After afterthoughts on *lesbofeminismo*

Upon the *Reunión* meeting ending, the Mexican lesbians shared that they were exhausted, and while remaining politically committed to sustaining the *Marcha Lésbica*, they desperately needed a break from the year-round, emotionally and physically debilitating planning on an under-resourced budget. After some initial apprehension, I remember Tongues' collective enthusiasm about sponsoring a similar type of action to be held in the U.S., noting that much of the public, social justice work of queer communities of color had been overrun by pro-gay marriage advocacy efforts. In fact, by 2008, the same-sex marriage campaigns had displaced the Tongues office, leaving us and several other queer of color organizations' offices that West Hollywood's Gay and Lesbian Village was mandated to provide at the time of its construction in the early 2000s as phantom presences.

This idea was also attractive politically because the public demonstration component of the *Marcha Lésbica* happened to have coincided on the same day as an historic call for a National Day of Protest in the U.S. on March 26, 2006. This action was touted as a public outcry against the vast and increasing anti-immigrant policies of the U.S. government, and large demonstrations were planned throughout Los Angeles. As part of our participation in the *Marcha* planning, Tongues was tasked with taking the stage at the end of the marching route to deliver comments (Figure 1). We gathered in one of our hotel rooms to compose a much more thoughtful set of remarks than we had initially planned. The short Spanish-language speech highlighted the overlapping connections among citizenship status, immigrant rights, sexuality politics, and racialized identity to stress how we understood our presence at the *Marcha Lésbica* in light of the concurrent protests in the U.S.

These comments cobbled together after the *Reunión* would later become the thematic focus of our U.S.-based event. We all agreed that whatever form the event took, we would delve deeper into the interlocking social issues that position immigrant, trans, bisexual, queer, lesbian, and other non-heteronormative women and people of color in vulnerable states of injurious existence. This three-day event, and the nearly year-and-a-half period of intense community organizing preceding it, would not have transpired if not for that particular charged contra-*queer* affective moment in defense of *lesbofeminismo*. In effect, the anti queer-ification exhortation on behalf of one vocal organizer may have ruptured the transnational coalitional-building momentum between queer women of color Mexicans

Figure 1. Los Angeles-based Tongues members on stage at the Lésbica Marcha, Monumento a la Revolución Plaza, Mexico City, March 25, 2006. Photograph by Judy Ornelas Sisneros.

lesbians, but it productively led to the community conference, "Tongue-to-Tongue: Provoking Critical Dialogues Among Queer and Women of Color" held September 7th-9th 2007 in Los Angeles.

After Tongue-to-Tongue in 2007 in the midst of a pointedly queer cultural and scholarly turn, a provincializing glance back at LGBT identity politics, and a desire for meaningful change outside of state-based offerings, I again contemplated how lesbian identity or *lesbofeminismo* maintained any currency; how could it travel from South to North? With more urgency and to a different effect, I now raise a related query: how can lesbian identity and *lesbofeminismo* be reimagined contemporaneously, and reinvented if necessary? This reflection presents one narrativization of a critical moment in the annals of lesbian identity and *lesbofeminismo* that pivoted on an affective counterstance to the neo-liberal byproducts of queer ideologies disavowed by Mexico City-based lesbians in March 2006. While I irrefutably oppose the anti- trans discourse of the *Marcha Lésbica*'s online blog[16] with endorsements of British author, J.K Rowling and Australian lesbian feminist theorist, Sheila Jeffreys, due to their shared beliefs in dismissing trans studies and undermining transgender lives, these blatant trans and queerphobic statements do not nullify the critical takeaways of *lesbofemimismo* in Mexico City 2006. Then and there, Mexican lesbians of the COMAL provided a supple model of doing resistant feminist practice in which *lesbofeminismo* was the means through which to push to secure safe social and cultural spaces for lesbians and cisgender women against the forces of transnational capitalism. The *contra*-queer politics of *lesbofeminismo*, in particular, remind queer women of color in the U.S like me that it remains imperative to understand the interlocking structures of domination that create neo-liberal policies, threaten cross-border organizing, increase racializations, and breed new forms of sexuality and gender-based phobias. This is one way to epitomize the value of lesbian identity of the past while constructing its upgrade into the present.

Notes

1. The Tongues collective sponsored or traveled with self-identifying Black, Asian-American, Puerto-Rican, Indigenous, Mexican, and White women among those identifying as Chicanas-Latinas. I use "Chicana-Latina" to reference those U.S.-based non-Black women of color participants from Tongues and *Las Mujeres de la Costa Central de California* [Women of the Central California Coast] who variously identify as "Latina" and/or "Chicana," thus the hyphen represents the interconnected relationship of these two gendered, racialized, ethnic identity terms.

2. I use "Mexican lesbians" to refer to the female identified lesbian feminists who were representative members of several organizations and collectives throughout Mexico and participated in the international meeting of the *Marcha Lésbica* in Mexico City on March 25, 2006. Most Mexican lesbian participants at the meeting were also

members of the *COMAL*.

3. The international meeting idea was purportedly posed by a U.S. participating member in order to secure funding and meet an institutional mandate. However, the meeting grew into a central component of the *Marcha* 2006 with bi-national bodies involved in its planning.

4. It's important to note that due to the bordered geographies and geo-political entanglements of Mexico and the U.S., trans border linguistic politics between Mexicanas and Chicanas-Latinas pose distinct conundrums than other feminist of color coalitions that work among non-dominant ethno-racial communities. For example, see T. Carrillo, "U.S. Cross-Border Talk: Transnational Perspectives on Labor, Race and Sexuality" (1998).

5. As this special issue's provocation suggests, lesbian identity matters merit our collective and individual critical contemplation partly due to the preponderance of lesbian identity's oft taken-for-granted white, cisgender, and female-centered ontological construction historically and contemporarily. It is this notion of lesbian identity that is informed by the ideological formation, lesbian feminist separatism, that I characterize as predominant and worthy of interrogation.

6. The political battle staged against passing Proposition 8 which would bar legal same-sex marriages in California garnered much financial support, leading various marriage equality efforts to crop up.

7. While there was advance preparation in anticipation of practical translation challenges, dialogue was conducted in Spanish and thus challenging for those who did not fully comprehend or speak Spanish.

8. I acknowledge that the use of "gringa" was not meant to include the African American-Black women present, just as Afro Latinas-Chicanas who are visually marked as Black are likely never to be named "gringa" in the U.S. or Mexico.

9. Dependent on the Enlightenment era's scientific racist discourse, ethnocentric religious ideology, and anatamo- politics captured in the concept *limpieza de sangre* (purity of blood), race was structured into a social hierarchy in which the purest embodiments of whiteness were positioned at the highest and thus most desirable point, endowing sociocultural power and belonging. Moving away from whiteness and its positive ascriptions were the various mestizo (mixed-race) designations and an attenuated social standing, while ultimately blackness was substantially distanced from any social power and sense of belonging. By the early 20th century, the concept of mestizaje (mixture of Spanish and Indigenous) as an affirmative racial ideology came to challenge and replace the original colonial racial logic. For more on the Mexican colonial race and gender system, including mestizaje, see María Elena Martínez 2008.

10. These are my interpretative translations based on the novel uses of "ificación" to modify queer, bisexual, gay, and corporate, which works like the gerund "ing."

11. While beyond the purview of this essay, one might consider how Mexican lesbian's reliance on an affective register suggests a way to orient "queer" towards "cuir." For further engagements with "quir" in Latin America, see the Special Issue of *GLQ* Queer/Cuir Américas: Translation, Decoloniality, and the Incommensurable.

12. It should be noted that the Mexicana lesbian reading this manifesto had not been actively involved in the conversations with the Latinas/Chicanas in the U.S. during the earlier organizing period; however, she was a member of the *COMAL*, and the views she expressed were not interrogated by the *COMAL* members. I have intentionally kept her name out of this out of a concern for anonymity.

13. It is notable that *lesbofeminismo* is particularly on display in Mexico since the

February the Associated Press 2020 (See https://www.latimes.com/world-nation/story/2020-02-18/killing-of-7-year-old-stokes-anger-in-mexico-over-femicides) news of the brutal femicides of a 7-year-old girl and a 25-year-old woman have been met with the current government's nonchalance and inaction, attributing the killings only to neoliberal economic policies while the opposing conservative party (with an anti-abortion platform) decries the killings as sexist and injust.

14. The Mexico City based *lesbofeminista* organization and publication, *LeSVOZ*, is a prominent organizing body of the *Marcha Lésbica*, which held its 7th annual *Marcha* in March 2019.

15. For additional examples, see the contributions of Barbara Cameron, Chrystos, Audre Lorde, and Merle Woo.

16. See both the *Marcha Lésbica COMAL* webpage: https://www.marchalesbica.com/comal/ and the LeSVOZ blog entry posted December 4, 2020: https://www.lesvoz.org

Acknowledgments

I wholeheartedly thank and acknowledge all of the organizing members of Tongues who coordinated the *Reunión*, raised funds to travel to Mexico City, planned Tongue-to-Tongue, and who remain active in Tongues, especially Aurora Garciacruz, Marissa Medina, Judy Ornelas Sisneros, and Cristina Serna. I am grateful to the anonymous reviewers for their astute comments to improve this essay.

Disclosure statement

No potential conflict of interest was reported by the authors.

References

Ahmed, S. (2015, February 26). Living a lesbian life. *Feminist Killjoys (blog)*. https://feministkilljoys.com/2015/02/26/living-a-lesbian-life/

Anzaldúa, Gloria and Cherríe Moraga (Eds.) (2015). This Bridge Called My Back: Writings by Radical Women of Color. 4th Edition. New York, NY: SUNY Press.

Associated Press. (2020, February 18). Killing of 7-year-old adds to anger in Mexico over femicides. *Los Angeles Times*. https://www.latimes.com/world-nation/story/2020-02-18/killing-of-7-year-old-stokes-anger-in-mexico-over-femicides.

Barranco Laguna, María Isabel. (2001). "La construcción social de la mujer a través de la toma de decisión sobre su propia determinación sexual." In María Elena Olivera Córdova (Ed.), Mujeres Diversas, Miradas Feministas (pp. 20–89). México City: Editorial Grupo Destiempos.

Blackwell, M. (2014). Translenguas: Mapping the possibilities and challenges of transnational women's organizing across geographies of difference. In S. E. Alvarez, C. L. Costa, V. Feliu, R. Hester, N. Klahn, & M. Thayer (Eds.), *Translocalities/Translocalidades:*

Feminist Politics of Translation in the Latin/a Americas (pp. 299–320). Duke University Press.

Cohen, C. J. (1997). Punks, bulldaggers, and welfare queens: The radical potential of queer politics?*GLQ: A Journal of Lesbian and Gay Studies, 3*(4), 437–465. https://doi.org/10.1215/10642684-3-4-437

Combahee River Collective. (2015). A Black feminist statement. In C. Moraga & G. Anzaldúa (Eds.), *This bridge called my back: Writings by radical women of color* (4th ed., pp. 210–218). SUNY Press.

Gopinath, G. (2005). *Impossible desires: Queer Diasporas and South Asian public cultures.* Duke University Press.

Hong, G. (2006). *The ruptures of American capital: Women of color feminism and the culture of immigrant labor.* University of Minnesota Press.

Jagose, A. (1996). *Queer theory: An introduction.* New York University Press.

Manalansan, M. (2003). *Global divas: Filipino gay men in the diaspora.* Duke University Press.

Martínez, M. E. (2008). *Genealogical fictions: Limpieza de sangre, religion, and gender in colonial Mexico.* Stanford University Press.

Mogrovejo, N. (2000). *Un amor que se atrevió a decir su nombre: La lucha de las lesbianas y sus relaciones con los movimientos homosexuales y feminista en América Latina [A love that dared to say its name: Lesbian riots and their relationships with homosexual and feminist movements in Latin America].* Centro de Documentación y Archivo Histórico Lésbico.

Muñoz, J. E. (1999). *Disidentifications: Queers of color and the performance of politics.* University of Minnesota Press.

Rich, A. (1993). Compulsory heterosexuality and lesbian existence. In H. Abelove, M. A. Barale, & D. M. Halperin (Eds.), *The lesbian and gay studies reader.* (pp. 227–254) Routledge.

Rodríguez, J. M. (2014). *Sexual futures, queer gestures, and other Latina longings.* NYU Press.

Serna, C. (2017). Locating a Transborder Archive of Queer Chicana Feminist and Mexican Lesbian Feminist Art. *Feminist Formations, 29*(3), 49–79. https://doi.org/10.1353/ff.2017.0030

Stryker, S., & Bettcher, T. M. (2016, May). Introduction: Trans/feminsims. *TSQ: Transgender Studies Quarterly, 3*(1–2), 5–14. https://doi.org/10.1215/23289252-3334127

Women who prefer "lesbian" to "queer": generational continuity and discontinuity

Jessica Megarry (iD), Catherine Orian Weiss (iD), Meagan Tyler (iD) and
Kate Farhall[c] (iD)

ABSTRACT
The legitimacy of the term and identity "lesbian" has long been
contested, but has come under renewed scrutiny, with some
suggesting it is exclusionary and dated. Along with these suggestions is the implication of a generational divide. Supposedly,
older women—unaware of contemporary queer discourses—are
more likely use the term "lesbian," whereas younger women
are more likely to choose queer affiliated identities. In this
paper we draw on survey data investigating why some women
might seek to retain the identity "lesbian." These narratives
complicate simplistic accounts of a generational divide. We
discuss themes of cross-generational continuity in participants'
sense of historical connection; connection to politics; lesbian
visibility; and specificity and boundaries. The theme of lesbian
community demonstrated discontinuity: participants of all ages
agreed on the importance of lesbian community, but there
was generational discontinuity in the access that participants
had to it. Our respondents were aware of, and reflective about,
current debates situating the category "lesbian" as problematic
or obsolete, and nonetheless found utility and meaning in the
term. Through their analysis we hope to destabilize discussions
about a generational divide defining the use of the term "lesbian" with corresponding questions around ongoing
relevance.

Introduction

The currency and value of the term and identity "lesbian" have been
contested for decades, but have come under renewed scrutiny with recent
suggestions that "lesbian" is too exclusionary (Ellis, 2015) and too dated
(Morris, 2016) to still be of use. Along with these suggestions is the
implication of a generational divide, where older women—unaware of
contemporary alternative discourses—are more likely to opt for the

terminology of "lesbian," whereas younger women are more likely to choose queer-affiliated identities. In order to explore some of these (re)emerging debates, this paper provides a qualitative thematic analysis of data collected for a wider project investigating how and why some women seek to consciously retain the identity of "lesbian."

In this paper we explore the ways in which an analysis of this data complicates simplistic or straightforward accounts of a generational divide in valuing a specifically lesbian identity. Instead, we suggest that there are more fundamental political and conceptual continuities in valuing "lesbian" that cut across generations. Although a range of motivations were detailed by participants, we identify significant consistencies in themes across diverse age groups. Respondents were often aware of, and reflective about, current debates situating the category "lesbian" as problematic or obsolete—particularly in contrast to queer discourses—and nonetheless found utility and meaning in continuing to use the term in their everyday lives, for both personal and political reasons. Our paper makes space for the voices of such women and our analysis maps a number of themes, across age ranges, regarding conscious decisions to retain a lesbian sense of self and community. We note a shared sense of historical and political connection as well as the importance of visibility, specificity, and sexual boundaries. In addition, we note some discontinuity around the experience of lesbian community.

Background

Reflecting the central concern of this special issue, contemporary media and scholarly narratives have suggested the term "lesbian" is outdated, disappearing, or not reflective of progressive, youth politics (e.g. Bendix, 2019; Cauterucci, 2016). Within such discussions, there are assumptions of a generational split, between "'lesbian feminist longtimers' and 'postidentity-politics newcomers'" (Forstie, 2020, p. 1769) mirroring findings by social movement scholars who have charted the move away from more "fixed" sexual identities (e.g. "lesbian," "gay") among US college students (Miller et al., 2016).

At the same time as queries around obsolescence have been raised, however, there has also been interest in the reassertion of lesbian identity (e.g. Jones, 2018; Obinwanne, 2018; Waterhouse, 2015), particularly in contrast to the increasing popularity of "queer" as a label, identity and ethos. Within the broad context of these seemingly contradictory portrayals of the lesbian/queer landscape, there has been little contemporary research that addresses "lesbian" in terms of its political and personal value to lesbian identified women (for notable exceptions that touch on these themes see: Ellis & Peel, 2011; Harris, 2010; Morris, 2016). Our paper seeks to address this gap through an analysis of data exploring women's desire to retain the term "lesbian," which fleshes out the lived reality of some of these shifts and tensions.

Friction between "lesbian" and "queer" is not new. In the 1990s, the tension between "queer" as an umbrella term and the political aims of lesbian feminism, in particular, were noted by several authors—often drawing on personal testimony (e.g. Stein, 1992, 1997; Walters, 1996). Others highlighted concerns within the academy as queer theory took precedence over a feminist analysis of marginalized sexualities (Jeffreys, 1994; Wilkinson & Kitzinger, 1997). Others again have noted tensions between lesbian and trans identities and politics, in particular localities – especially the US (Earles, 2019; Weiss, 2007) and the UK (Hines, 2019; Jeffreys 2008) – as well as potential synergies (Beemyn & Eliason, 2016; Green, 2006). The more specific tension between maintaining "lesbian" within a broader context of mainstreaming "queer," however, has been noted again in more recent literature (e.g. Harris, 2010), including a special issue for *Feminism and Psychology*, where Ellis and Peel (2011, p. 202) note:

> [D]espite being seen in some circles as rather passé, lesbian feminism still has a profound relevance currently. While the "lesbian feminism" that was prevalent 25 years or so ago has all but vanished, it has left a legacy that still influences the lives, values, and work of those who both identify as "lesbian" and "feminist".

Although not all respondents discussed below identified themselves as feminists, Ellis and Peel's observation echoes what we found: that the term "lesbian" still holds a "profound relevance" for many.

Of particular interest in this paper is that the enduring relevance of the term and identity "lesbian" appealed to women across different age brackets in the data. This was a noteworthy finding in comparison to existing work addressing a sense of generational *difference*. For instance, in understanding how historical trends in gay and lesbian rights movements, in particular geographical locations, have shaped identity formation for lesbian women (Parks, 1999). As well as work on generational differences in interpreting the need for lesbian-specific public space and visibility (Fobear, 2012) and barriers to cross-generational friendships with older lesbian women (Stanley, 2002). In some ways a generational lens to understand an attachment to "lesbian" can be seen to mirror particular narratives about feminist generational splits that (mis)cast or reduce political differences as being largely or solely age-based (Hogeland, 2001; Mackay, 2015). As Hogeland (2001) and Mackay (2015) both, separately, contend, such a framing can slip into a suggestion that newer or "younger" political positions are inherently superior to "older" or more established political positions without real engagement with the ideas underpinning different perspectives. It is therefore particularly interesting to consider where there are points of continuity as well as difference across age groups.

Data collection

Our initial research project was designed to explore some of the contemporary tensions between "lesbian" and "queer," as well as the potential value that some women ascribe to the concept and identity of "lesbian." We set up an online survey that was open for two weeks in 2018 and contained a set of open-ended questions (without word limit, per Smyth et al., 2009), mostly encouraging narrative-style responses. The screening question was simply: "Are you a woman who prefers the term "lesbian" to "queer" to describe yourself?" Our focus in this research was intentionally on women who prefer the label lesbian: while our data may include women who identify as both lesbian and queer (but prefer lesbian), it excludes women who engage in homosexual relationality but prefer queer, or a different label. Further survey questions included elaboration on understandings of queer and lesbian, why it was important to them to use the term "lesbian," whether or not respondents found the LGBTQIA+ framework useful, their experiences of lesbian community and their understandings of the relationship (if any) between feminism and lesbianism. We provide a full list of our survey questions in the Appendix.

Participants

We were aiming for around 40 participants, but the survey received more than 200 responses in less than two weeks, indicating this research provokes strong interest in particular communities. In order to capture responses of our intended population of women who prefer the word "lesbian" to "queer" to describe themselves, we used purposive sampling. Purposive sampling is a common approach to accessing hidden populations, which "relies on the researchers' situated knowledge of the field and rapport with members of targeted networks" (Barratt et al., 2015, p. 5). Our purposive sampling approach tapped four key avenues for participants: activist networks, online groups, academics and authors in the field and social networks. We sent our survey advertisement and link to 1) activists we knew personally or through contacts, who were active in lesbian politics; 2) online lesbian and/or feminist groups on social media platforms; 3) academics who had written recently about lesbian politics, as well as authors of media articles detailing the tensions between "lesbian" and "queer"; and 4) our social networks of lesbian women. From this sampling approach, we had an overwhelming response.

Our respondents were split across seven age brackets, ranging from 18 to 85 years old. Discounting the oldest age bracket of 76–85 years (five responses), the spread across older and younger age groups was fairly even (approximately 35–40 responses in each age category), with a markedly lower level of responses in middling age brackets for 36–45 years (13 responses) and 46–55 years (28 responses). Participants were from 16 different countries, although roughly two thirds lived in Australia or the United States. As demonstrated in the following analysis, the themes cut across age groups and localities. However, we have chosen to make more visible those living outside the United States, in line with the direction of this Special Issue. The high proportion of Australian respondents reflects the authors' embeddedness in the Australian-based research context. The study is further shaped by the fact that we are all feminist researchers who consider sexuality within our work. As such, we were conscious of the growing media commentary regarding tensions between "lesbian" and "queer," a tension which was also reflected in our extended networks. Overall, our research team comprises three lesbians and one heterosexual woman. The three lesbians attach particular value to asserting ourselves as lesbian women. We would like to take this opportunity to acknowledge the generosity of our participants in donating their time and sharing their experiences in order to make this research possible.

Our participants do not constitute a representative sample. As such, we do not make claims regarding the prevalence of these views among all same-sex attracted women, or the broader LGBTQIA + community. Our point here is to demonstrate these views exist, and that make an important contribution to discussions regarding lesbian identity and terminology. Furthermore, in terms of limitations with the data, it should be noted that we did not ask participants to disclose their race/ethnicity or whether they lived in a rural or urban location. These areas would, however, provide fruitful avenues for future research.

Method

The survey data were initially analyzed using theoretical thematic analysis (Braun & Clarke, 2006). All four members of the research team participated in the process of determining codes and coding the data, which was done by hand rather than with an analytic program. From this work, we began to discuss a sense of similarity in responses across different age groups. The analysis in this paper arose from the following steps; we began with a more inductive approach to determining themes from the questions: "Why is it important to call yourself a lesbian?" (Q.1) and "What is your understanding of the term lesbian?" (Q.2). Again, all four members of the research team participated in this process and a number of responses were shared for analysis during the coding process to ensure consistency. From this, coding was expanded to include a search of the whole data set for the following terms: old(er); young(er); visible; visibility; history; politics; political; boundary and boundaries. All responses found with these searches were read in their entirety to ensure a full under-standing of context. In keeping with the kind of qualitative analysis put forward by Braun and Clarke (2006), we simply emphasize the existence of broad themes, rather than focussing on the specific number of times particular terms appeared.

Analysis and discussion

Through our process of thematic analysis, the major themes where we identified continuity across age groups were: historical connections, con-nections to politics, visibility, and a sense of importance around boundaries and specificity. These are discussed, in turn, before a section on experiences of lesbian community as discontinuity. Overall, this shows considerable ideological continuity regarding the concept and identity of "lesbian" across the age groups in our data set, but a level of material discontinuity in terms of the lived experiences of lesbian community. In these sections we provide a couple of overarching, contextual quotes from different age groups before providing context and sub-themes. Please note that all quotes in these sections are reproduced as provided, inclusive of spelling and grammatical errors.

Historical connection

The word has a specific meaning and has a history. (26–35, UK).

It is the word we chose to call ourselves when we began coming out publicly in the 1970s. It is what I have called myself for my entire adult life (45 years now). It is what I choose to call myself. It is my identity. It is the identity I share with other lesbians. (66–75, Australia).

Respondents' sense of connection with a long history of lesbianism was a noteworthy theme identified in our data. For example, a number of participants mentioned the origin of the term with Sappho, the Ancient Greek poet, and one participant also mentioned the Amazons: "To choose not to call myself Lesbian would be to deny my identity and disrespect all the fierce Amazons who came before me" (46–55, USA).

Connections were also made with the more recent past. A few of the older participants linked their identification with the term "lesbian" to activist movements of the 1970s, for instance:

As the term lesbian was hard won by activists during the 1970s in particular and there's no other term that is comparable I am proud to be a lesbian will continue to call myself and act out my life as a lesbian. (66–75, Australia).

Some younger women also situated themselves and their choice of a lesbian identity within a long and apparently continuous tradition: "[The term lesbian] connects me with a long and rich, albeit not very well known, history and culture of women who were also lesbians" (18–25, Australia). This continuous lesbian tradition was often framed in terms of a history of resistance and struggle. In this vein, one participant explains: "[t]he term lesbian has a Herstory of strength, female energy, subverting the patriarchy" (46–55, Australia).

Others gave a sense of inscribing a personal journey within a larger historical movement, making links between past struggles of women and their own continuation of these struggles into the future:

Calling myself a lesbian... allows me to access a history of other proud, defiant women who have lived, succeeded and been happy before me. It gives me hope that I will do the same. (26–35, New Zealand).

Many reasons which include the significance of personal identity, the long fight to claim the title by those before me, and quite simply it best describes who I am, how I live, my underlying philosophical belief system, and how I walk in the world. It took me until my mid 30ies to stand strong in my lesbian shoes, and standing strong I remain. (66–75, Australia).

This strong sense of a connection to historical women and lesbian's struggles was echoed in our participants' thoughts on the connections between lesbianism and feminism more generally.

Connection to politics

Lesbian is a personal and political identity. (26–35, Australia).

It is my identity, the Basis for my political/feminist work. (76–85, Germany).

Participants across age brackets stressed the value of the term "lesbian" on the basis of its connection to politics and, often, to feminism. Respondents frequently understood "lesbian" to signify more than a sexual orientation, and many emphasized they preferred the term because it also conveys a political commitment or identity. For many, this related to their drive to center women, rather than men, in their lives:

I put women first i[n] all things. I see that as feminist but I also see that as inherently lesbian, and that [i]s not necessarily about sex/sexuality. I am oriented towards women in all things, including my sexuality. (46–55, Canada).

[A lesbian is a] woman born woman who is romantically and philosophically drawn to other women, she may or may not have sex with women but her partners are women. (46–55, Australia).

This political commitment to centering women was also highlighted by younger women: "[c]alling myself a lesbian means refusing to sugar coat what I am, which is a woman who chooses to center my life around women and make my love for them my number one priority" (18–25, Scotland). A number of older women pointed to how lesbian, understood as a political commitment, represents a rejection of, and thereby a sense of freedom from, heterosexual norms: "for me 'lesbian' describes a politcal Standing and denies understanding a woman as part of a man. To be a lesbian describes freedom from heterosexual norms" (76–85, Germany).

Some said that using the term "lesbian" is political because it carves out a space for discussing issues specific to women who love women, which they suggested can be disappeared in both heteronormative and queer settings. The latter claim was based on sense that queer (when used as an umbrella term) can obfuscate differences between lesbian, gay, bisexual and transgender individuals, as well as competing political interests: "terms like queer makes [...] it seem as gay men and lesbians have the same position and issues" (18–25, Sweden). Other women said they consciously called themselves lesbians because the term is connected to their political analysis of women's oppression and their explicit commitment to the feminist, or lesbian feminist, movement: "'lesbian' is a denomination that implies, or contains a commitment to women's liberation and feminism. 'Queer' is about sexuality alone" (56–65, Australia). Respondents often pointed to the impact of male dominance upon their lives—"I am a lesbian who has been born and raised as a female and treated as a female/girl/woman/old woman in this patriarchal society" (66–75, Australia)—and they highlighted how the term "queer" is unable to capture the specific experience of being a homosexual *woman* under patriarchy:

T]he vast majority of lesbophobia is rooted in misogyny rather than in homophobia and the "queer" movement largely ignores that, and has many misogynistic ideologies in itself. (18–25, Scotland).

Some participants saw lesbianism and the term "lesbian" as a direct challenge to a patriarchal ideology that insists women exist for men and male pleasure: "[l]esbianism is rooted in rejection of men and patriarchy" (18–25, Scotland). Many preferred the term "lesbian" because it signals "a certain form of feminist resistance to women's oppression by men" (18–25 UK) and to "patriarchal roles such as marriage, and the sexualization of women for mens benefit" (56–65, Australia).

Visibility

The term [lesbian] makes us visible. (46–55, USA).

[L]esbians are being made invisible and rendered meaningless within "queerdom" (26–35, New Zealand).

The importance of lesbian visibility—both broad public visibility and visibility within queer and LGBTQIA + spaces—is another theme that cut across age groups in our data set. This was particularly evident in response to the question "why is it important to call yourself a lesbian?." Taking pride in the term "lesbian" was sometimes declared in these responses. Both older and younger participants mentioned, for example, the need to claim or reclaim pride in the term "lesbian" in the face of stigma. One woman, in an older age bracket, noted that using the term "lesbian" is important to her "because 'lesbian' was the word that was used to condemn me until I chose to own it and be proud of it" (66–75, Canada), while another woman, in our youngest age category, shares similar sentiments:

> [Using the term lesbian] is important to me because I spent my adolescence ashamed of my sexuality because of the heterosexist society we live in but also the stigma attached to the term lesbian. I now find it important to use the term 'lesbian' to refer to myself to reclaim it and be proud. (18–25, Australia).

This can be seen as tied to a sense that using the term "lesbian" was not only a personal choice but an act of making oneself visible to other lesbian women. As one respondent noted: "It's important for me to call myself a lesbian because I want to set a positive example for young people" (26–35, USA). Others categorized this as a consciously political act (echoing the previous section) linked to visibility—"it meant for me a political choice for being visible as a lesbian woman" (66–75, Australia)—or fighting invisibility:

> [It is important to call myself a lesbian] to honour all those lesbians who fought against the oppression on all levels to bring us into the light and gain visibility, legality and…not be diminished and our story made invisible once again. to stand up and say we are and have always been here. (56–65, Australia).

Another woman in our final "Do you have anything else you would like to add?" section offered: "We need to fight this invisibility curse." (36–45 Australia).

For others there was a sense, more specifically, of lesbian visibility asserted against the labels of "queer" frameworks. For example:

> [Q]ueer is not inclusive of lesbians, it in fact attempts to eradicate them or make lesbians invisible. (36–45 Australia).

Its important for me to call myself a lesbian because we lesbians; at least lesbian feminists; have a woman focussed, woman loving culture that is not visible in the term queer. (56–65, Australia).

These themes overlap with the next section, showing the specificity of the term "lesbian" is seen as valuable in maintaining boundaries, especially within the context of the rising prominence of "queer".

Specificity and boundaries

Queer is ambiguous as to whether or not I'm attracted to men. The word lesbian simply and definitively states that I am only attracted to women. (18–25, New Zealand).

[B]ecause it's who i am [lesbian]. it describes me as a part of a community of women who exclusively love women. (46–55, Ireland).

Connected to a desire for visibility as lesbian women, and the political and historical resonance of lesbianism for our participants, a key cross-generational theme in the data was the importance of retaining the term "lesbian" due to its specificity and the associated invocation of sexual boundaries. Younger participants explained that lesbian "accurately describes my experience in this world" (18–25, Australia), "doesn't obfuscate what I am" (18–25, USA), and that "It's not ambiguous and it's straight to the point" (18–25, Scotland). Women in older categories echoed these sentiments, noting that "The word queer is obfuscating and diluting" (56–65, Australia) and "Queer is fluid. Lesbian is firm and nonnegotiable" (56–65, USA). A young respondent from Canada clearly illustrated the drive for specificity, in terms of her understanding of herself and the way she wanted to be interpreted in the world:

Lesbian (at least for the most part) has an immediately identifiable meaning: a woman who is exclusively into women. I also feel that people invariably assume "bisexual" when I say queer. I feel as though recently ths term has become synonymous with bisexual...Sometimes when I say "queer" people assume I am not a woman, which I find insulting, especially as a butch lesbian facing constant scrutiny of my gender even in non-lgbt spaces. (Canada, 18–25).

We can see here that her previous use of the term queer to self-describe led to misinterpretations regarding her sexuality or assumptions about her gender identity. She describes already feeling surveilled as a non-gender conforming woman; "queer," for her, further complicates this picture and erases her experience as a butch lesbian.

Closely tied to valuing specificity was participants' desire to clearly and firmly state and enforce their sexual boundaries. This sentiment was particularly prevalent in younger age brackets. For example, one young woman reflected that the word lesbian is important to her because it is "explicitly clear to those around me (including other lesbians) that I am same-sex attracted and am not available to men" (18–25, Australia). Another young respondent drew connections between the specificity of the word "lesbian" and the exclusion of men from her sexuality: "Lesbian delineates a specific set of desires and boundaries... With terms [such as] queer there is ambiguity, the possibility that a woman might well be open to sex or relationships with men – it's not really equipped to describe lesbian reality" (18–25, Scotland).

A need to refute the "possibility" of relationships with men came up frequently within the data. Young respondents noted that lesbian "denotes the exclusion of males from my sexuality/lifestyle" (18–25, Australia), and that it involves "no ambiguity, 'fluidity' or chance of that changing. It's a firm assertion of a boundary" (26–35, Ireland). For some women, demarcating sexual boundaries was a political decision, reflecting the discussion of connections to politics earlier in this paper:

> Lesbian is a word that denotes a woman with sexual boundaries that exclude men, and I believe using the word communicates a specific pride in being a homosexual woman and a bit of a fuck you to a society that makes lesbians a porn category, insult or punchline. (26–35, Ireland).

While the importance of delineating sexual boundaries was less pronounced in the data from older women, it was still apparent. One woman explained the term lesbian clearly demonstrates that "Who I choose to have sex with, who I want to have sex with is women, and that is about our bodies and minds and loved experience in the world" (46–55, Canada). This grounding in lived/loved experience resonated throughout the data and across age groups. Participants asserted that their personal, political and sexual experiences, as well as their personhood or connection to lesbian legacy, required the specific delineation provided by "lesbian."

A theme of discontinuity in lesbian community

> [I]t means being free. (66–75, New Zealand).

> [I]t means what community always means: not being alone. (18–25, UK).

Only one theme showed significant discontinuity between younger and older age groups: lesbian community. While there was near universal consensus, regardless of age, of the *importance* of lesbian community, there was significant discontinuity in the *access* that women of different ages had had to that sense of community.

Women of all ages spoke of specifically lesbian community (as opposed to community including gay men, queer-identified individuals or heterosexual women, all alternative options discussed by participants) in highly positive, even rapturous terms:

> I experienced lesbian community at a [feminist camp] that was mostly attended by lesbians, and it was honestly the most amazing week of my life... I never thought that I would be able to feel like that at the age of 22, but there I was with the weight of the world off my shoulders just singing and dancing and talking and running and swimming with lesbians. I didn't stop smiling the whole time. (18–25, UK).

> It meant being in spaces which were explicitly women's spaces, that put us first, where men were our secondary concerns or not at all. It was a source of power, a source of gathering strength as individuals and as groups of women. A place to plot, heal, laugh, flirt, be safe, find a way towards wellness, beyond trauma. It was about love and relationship and hope and relief. Being seen, being our truest selves without fear. Never being alone. Sisterhood meant putting women first and showing up for each other. (46–55, Canada).

Over and over, women emphasized the importance of a community of shared lesbian experience, with a number even expressing ideas along the lines that "[i]t has saves my life and my sanity" (66–75, Australia). They identified the solidarity and support found in lesbian community as crucial to their wellbeing.

Older participants were able to list a dizzying variety of groups and activities that made up the lesbian community in the past. A selection of these: camping, potlucks, music, softball teams, radio programs, communes, bathhouses, mothers' groups, art workshops, and a wide range of political activities. However, while many older respondents were still active in their lesbian communities, a number of them commented with sadness, indignation and anger that this rich and varied community life was a thing of the past.

> [I]t's everything, especially in these hostile times, to be with other lesbians. it feels like a huge weight is lifted when im in the company of women like me. i used to be able to be with my community in bars, bookstores, cafes, festivals, and political groups. now, i can only experience our community in private dinner parties. it's depressing... im so sad that young butches no longer have this. (46–55, Ireland).

Meanwhile, younger women reported that access to lesbian community was much more limited. As one respondent explained:

> I have noticed most women my age and younger feel absolutely starved of this sense of community, and very few will have it in real life-I am lucky to have a few lesbian friends. Most people are forced to find this community online, as numerically we are so few, and lesbian spaces are becoming vanishingly rare. (26–35, Ireland).

Other younger women expressed their feelings of sadness, loneliness and isolation, some even defining community around these experiences:

I am in a couple of facebook groups but apart from that I am not. Mostly because I fear that their take on Lesbian is not my take on it. I wish I had a group of friends or a community to turn to. (18–25, Sweden).

Lesbian community for me is the shared sense of being excluded. (18–25, Canada).

Some young women did define themselves as experiencing lesbian community, and were able to list activities and groups they participated in. However, these activities did not show the same variety and institutionalization as those mentioned by older respondents. Instead, they often revolved around individual friendships or friendship groups, and some of these were international and/or online.

Unable to find lesbian community among their peers, some younger women discussed creating community with older lesbians. These respondents valued such intergenerational connections, though some also mentioned the importance of lesbian friends their own age:

My positive experiences of lesbian community come from spending time with middle-aged and older lesbians. I do not have any lesbian community my age… and i have looked for them. Older lesbians remember the fights and struggles that they still face today and do not take it for granted the way younger people do. (26–35, Australia).

Thus, while there was strong consensus across age groups that lesbian community was important and positive, there was also strong material discontinuity in terms of access to this community: while older respondents had been able to access it in the past, and to some extent in the present, younger participants' access was much more limited, and many respondents were conscious of, and saddened by, this situation.

A note on participants as reflexive subjects

I think the term lesbian is viewed as outdated and unsophisticated by queers [...] I was looking at the Facebook profile of a queer identifying woman I vaguely knew. Within a thread she was having a discussion with another person about the usefulness of label 'lesbian'. In her reply to another person she said "lesbian? What is this 1970?". (26–35, Australia).

The above quotation is indicative of the narrative that lesbian is a label used by older, less fashionable, and less politically progressive homosexual women, while younger women are more likely to prefer and use the term queer to describe themselves. Our study does not support this narrative, but it does point to its dominance, and our participants' awareness of it. The analysis presented in this paper troubles the popular conflation of youth and political progressiveness with the presumed rejection of lesbian as an identity or self-descriptor. Participants' responses highlight how, rather than being obsolete, women of various ages and from various localities still find utility and value in the term and identity "lesbian." Nonetheless, some older participants did assume that younger women prefer the label queer, and some younger women did express feeling little support among their peer group for preferring "lesbian." This finding may relate to our discussion above, in that access to intergenerational lesbian centric spaces, where women can bond with other lesbians, formulate shared understandings, and generate collective political analyses, is lacking in many localities today.

The participant responses in our research demonstrate politically engaged reasoning around the choice to use the term lesbian (a choice which was not necessarily static). They also demonstrate that some women make the decision to describe themselves as lesbian on the basis of a reflexive process linked to significant thought and activism over time. For instance:

> For me it shows myself that I'm able to hide less than I did when I was younger. Being able to say something so true instead of the excuses or misdirections I'd say when the topic came up makes up for those times I lied to everyone (including myself). (18–25 Scotland).

The decision to retain the term "lesbian" also shows women identifying, critiquing, and pushing back against particular shifts. This suggests women who prefer and use the term "lesbian" are active political subjects engaged in debates, not unaware of alternative perspectives. Some women even pointed to the inadequacy of academic frameworks such as postmodernism and queer theory for trying to understand their life circumstances: "[q]ueer is a postmodern term that colludes with theories that remove all meaning from all of language" (36–45, UK).

A number of respondents—across age groups—were engaged in conscious pushback against a perceived dominance of queer perspectives in LGBTQIA + spaces. They understood such dominance to be disadvantageous to their understandings of themselves, and contra to their political identification as feminists or lesbian feminists. In this sense, the decision to retain the term "lesbian" is ideological, rather than generational. This mirrors Mackay's (2015, p.157) work debunking fixed generational differences in feminist positions: it has "nothing to do with their age, and everything to do with their politics." Perhaps also reflecting the time lag produced by slow moving academic publishing norms, and the disconnect that can occur between academic and activist-centred narratives and discourses (Bevington & Dixon, 2005), this pushback against a perceived increase in the dominance of "queer" by lesbian women has not yet been discussed in recent academic literature.

Critical theories have a long history of privileging counternarratives and acknowledging lived experience (e.g. Möschel, 2011). While maintaining a commitment to anti-essentialism and social constructionism, critical movements such as critical race theory and many strands of feminist thought also seek to elevate the authority of lived experience (Delgado & Stefancic, 2017; Rowland & Klein, 1996). While our results are not generalizable, they do provide details of a wealth of lived experience and a strong counternarrative to the notion that the term "lesbian" is obsolete, and that women who continue to use it are unaware of alternatives.

Conclusion

This paper points to the need for greater nuance in discussions around lesbian identity beyond broad-brush characterizations of a generational divide—a divide that even a number of our participants believed existed. Contrary to assumptions of concrete distinctions based on age, our work suggests some level of ideological continuity across age groups, especially with regard to the value and importance of "lesbian," and in spite of an element of material discontinuity in terms of access/deprivation of access to lived experience of lesbian community. Participants were also aware that their decisions are not made in a cultural vacuum, and many shared views on tensions between "lesbian" and "queer." Taken together, these insights suggest that claims regarding the obsolescence of lesbian identity are overstated and also fail to account for those who consciously, reflexively resist them.

Our analysis in this article is inevitably limited by the sample size, the feasibility of managing large quantities of qualitative data and the particular idiosyncrasies of the respondents. While this does not render the research invalid, we would like to note that respondents came from 16 countries, roughly two thirds lived in Australia or the United States and as the survey was in English, responses were limited to those comfortable responding in English. Additionally, we did not ask participants about their race or ethnicity, or whether they lived in a rural or urban location. Consequently, this study cannot give information about the prevalence of these views among all same-sex attracted women. Further, since it focussed on women who consciously embrace the term "lesbian" over "queer," it does not give any indication of the existence (or not) of these views within the broader LGBTQIA + community.

Nonetheless, this article makes important contributions to the understanding of lesbian identity through its insight into an under-studied group:

women who seek to consciously retain the identity of "lesbian" in the face of the continually growing influence and popularity of the term "queer." Further, it adds to the limited literature on generational similarities and differences among lesbian-identified women and on the political and personal value of the term "lesbian" to lesbian-identified women today. Consequently, this article provides evidence of the existence of views that are generally overlooked and under-valued, and suggests that these views may be more widespread than is often imagined. It demonstrates, too, in opposition to widespread assumptions, that such views are not limited to an older generation of lesbians whose views are outdated and in the process of disappearing, but are held by women across all age groups. Across generations, the participants' arguments in favor of lesbian identity are passionate, intelligent and considered and deserve to be taken seriously by academic and activist communities.

Disclosure of interest statement

The authors report no conflicts of interest. The authors alone are responsible for the content and writing of the paper.

ORCID

Jessica Megarry ⓘD http://orcid.org/0000-0002-9522-2823
Catherine Orian Weiss ⓘD http://orcid.org/0000-0001-9549-6675
Meagan Tyler ⓘD http://orcid.org/0000-0001-8779-0663
Kate Farhall ⓘD http://orcid.org/0000-0003-3737-1860

References

Barratt, M., Ferris, J., & Lenton, S. (2015). Hidden populations, online purposive sampling, and external validity: Taking off the blindfold. *Field Methods*, *27*(1), 3–21. https://doi.org/10.1177/1525822X14526838

Beemyn, G., & Eliason, M. (2016). "The intersections of trans women and lesbian identities, communities, and movements": An introduction. *Journal of Lesbian Studies*, *20*(1), 1–7. https://doi.org/10.1080/10894160.2015.1076232

Bendix, T. (2019, April 27). How to make lesbians cool (and inclusive) again. *NBC News: Think*. Retrieved December 14, 2020, from https://www.nbcnews.com/think/opinion/how-make-lesbians-cool-inclusive-again-ncna999066

Bevington, D., & Dixon, C. (2005). Movement-relevant theory: Rethinking social movement scholarship and activism. *Social Movement Studies*, *4*(3), 185–208. https://doi.org/10.1080/14742830500329838

Braun, V., & Clarke, V. (2006). Using thematic analysis in psychology. *Qualitative Research in Psychology*, *3*(2), 77–101. https://doi.org/10.1191/1478088706qp063oa

Cauterucci, C. (2016, December 20). For many young queer women, *lesbian* offers a fraught inheritance. *Slate*. Retrieved May 1, 2021, from https://slate.com/human-interest/2016/12/young-queer-women-dont-like-lesbian-as-a-name-heres-why.html

Delgado, R., & Stefancic, J. (2017). *Critical race theory: An introduction* (3rd ed.). New York University Press.

Earles, J. (2019). The "penis police": Lesbian and feminist spaces, trans women, and the maintenance of the sex/gender/sexuality system. *Journal of Lesbian Studies*, *23*(2), 243–256. https://doi.org/10.1080/10894160.2018.1517574

Ellis, S. (2015). Lesbian psychology. In C. Richards & M. J. Barker (Eds.), *The Palgrave handbook of the psychology of sexuality and gender* (pp. 109–128). Palgrave Macmillan.

Ellis, S. J., & Peel, E. (2011). Lesbian feminisms: Historical and present possibilities. *Feminism & Psychology*, *21*(2), 198–204. https://doi.org/10.1177/0959353510370178

Fobear, K. (2012). Beyond a lesbian space? An investigation on the intergenerational discourse surrounding lesbian public social places in Amsterdam. *Journal of Homosexuality*, *59*(5), 721–747. https://doi.org/10.1080/00918369.2012.673942

Forstie, C. (2020). Disappearing dykes? Post-lesbian discourse and shifting identities and communities. *Journal of Homosexuality*, *67*(12), 1760–1778. https://doi.org/10.1080/00918369.2019.1613857

Green, E. (2006). Debating trans inclusion in the feminist movement: A trans-positive analysis. *Journal of Lesbian Studies*, *10*(1–2), 231–248. https://doi.org/10.1300/J155v10n01_12

Harris, A. (2010). Back seat girls: Where do dykes sit with queer theory? *Inter Alia: A Journal of Queer Studies*, *5*, 1–16.

Hines, S. (2019). The feminist frontier: On trans and feminism. *Journal of Gender Studies*, *28*(2), 145–157. https://doi.org/10.1080/09589236.2017.1411791

Hogeland, L. (2001). Against generational thinking, or, some things that "third wave" feminism isn't. *Women's Studies in Communication*, *24*(1), 107–121. https://doi.org/10.1080/07491409.2001.10162429

Jeffreys, S. (1994). The queer disappearance of lesbians: Sexuality in the academy. *Women's Studies International Forum*, *17*(5), 459–472. https://doi.org/10.1016/0277-5395(94)00051-4

Jeffreys, S. (2008). They know it when they see it: The UK Gender Recognition Act. *The British Journal of Politics and International Relations*, *10*(2), 328–345. https://doi.org/10.1111/j.1467-856x.2007.00293.x

Jones, J. (2018, June 13). Queer women say they feel uncomfortable at pride events. *Star Observer*. Retrieved December 14, 2020, from https://www.starobserver.com.au/news/international-news-news/queer-women-uncomfortable-pride-events/169534

Mackay, F. (2015). Political not generational: Getting real about the second wave. In M. Kiraly & M. Tyler (Eds.), *Freedom fallacy: The limits of liberal feminism* (pp. 155–165). Connor Court Publishing.

Miller, S., Taylor, V., & Rupp, L. (2016). Social movements and the construction of queer identity. In J. E. Stets & R. T. Serpe (Eds.), *New Directions in identity theory and research* (pp. 1–25). Oxford Scholarship Online.

Morris, B. (2016). *The disappearing L: Erasure of lesbian spaces and culture*. State University of New York.

Möschel, M. (2011). Race in mainland European legal analysis: Towards a European critical race theory. *Ethnic and Racial Studies*, *34*(10), 1648–1664. https://doi.org/10.1080/01419870.2011.566623

Obinwanne, A. (2018, April 26). Why I'm lesbian (not queer). *After Ellen*. Retrieved February 8, 2020, from https://web.archive.org/web/20201111213950/https://afterellen.com/columns/545781-im-lesbian-not-queer

Parks, C. A. (1999). Lesbian identity development: An examination of differences across generations. *The American Journal of Orthopsychiatry*, *69*(3), 347–361. https://doi.org/10.1037/h0080409

Rowland, R., & Klein, R. (1996). Radical feminism: History, politics, action. In D. Bell & R. Klein (Eds.), *Radically speaking: Feminism reclaimed* (pp. 9–36). Spinifex Press.

Smyth, J., Dillman, D., Christian, L., & Mcbride, M. (2009). Open-ended questions in web surveys: Can increasing the size of answer boxes and providing extra instructions improve response quality? *Public Opinion Quarterly*, *73*(2), 325–337. https://doi.org/10.1093/poq/nfp029

Stanley, J. L. (2002). Young sexual minority women's perceptions of cross-generational friendships with older lesbians. *Journal of Lesbian Studies*, *6*(1), 139–148. https://doi.org/10.1300/J155v06n01_13

Stein, A. (1992). Sisters and queers: The decentring of lesbian feminism. *Socialist Review*, *22*(1), 33–55.

Stein, A. (1997). *Sex and sensibility: Stories of a lesbian generation*. University of California Press.

Walters, S. (1996). From here to queer: Radical feminism, postmodernism, and the lesbian menace. *Signs: Journal of Women in Culture and Society*, *21*(4), 830–869. https://doi.org/10.1086/495123

Waterhouse, L. (2015, February 24). Is the 'L' in LGBTI silent? *Star Observer.* Retrieved December 14, 2020, from https://www.starobserver.com.au/opinion/is-the-l-in-lgbti-si-lent/133104

Weiss, J. (2007). The Lesbian Community and FTMs: Détente in the Butch/FTM Borderlands. *Journal of Lesbian Studies, 11*(3–4), 203–211. https://doi.org/10.1300/J155v11n03_03

Wilkinson, S., & Kitzinger, C. (1997). The queer backlash. In D. Bell & R. Klein (Eds.), *Radically speaking: Feminism reclaimed* (pp. 375–381). Spinifex Press.

Appendix

Queer inclusion or lesbian exclusion? Survey questions

This survey is designed to try and capture the experiences of lesbian women who use the term "lesbian" to describe themselves. The researchers are based in Australia, but we welcome international responses.

Screening question

Are you a woman who prefers the term "lesbian" to "queer" to describe yourself?

Demographic questions

1. Age:
2. Country of residence:
3. Content questions
4. Why is it important for you to call yourself a lesbian?
5. What is your understanding of the term "lesbian"?
6. What is your understanding of the term "queer"?
7. Do you find the term 'queer' to be inclusive of lesbians?
8. Do you find the LGBTIQA + framework useful for lesbians? If so, why? If not, why not?
9. Have you ever experienced hostility or negativity in queer designated events or spaces (online and/or offline)? If so, please provide a description of these experiences.
10. Have you ever experienced hostility or negativity for expressing that you prefer the term "lesbian"? If so, could you explain circumstances in which this has happened (online and/or offline)? If you have experienced hostility or negativity, is this a recent issue, and, if so, when did you first notice this occuring? (approximately)
11. In your opinion/experience, what is the relationship between lesbianism and feminism? Please describe relevant examples or experiences.
12. Do you have any experience of lesbian community? If so, could you describe this?
13. Do you have anything you would like to add?

Comparing conceptions of gender, sexuality and lesbian identity between baby boomers and millennials

Ella Ben Hagai, Rachelle Annechino and Tamar Antin

ABSTRACT

To answer this special issue provocation, *Is Lesbian Identity Obsolete?* we analyzed interviews with people who had identified at some point in their lives as lesbians, or as women/femmes who were attracted to women – some of them part of the Baby Boomer generation and some part of the Millennial generation. Participants from both generations rejected the gender binary. Nevertheless, we found a shift away from understanding gender as an oppressive category to an understanding of gender as a proliferating identity in which one may play with gender in an intentional and creative manner. It appears that participants across generations articulated their sexual identities strategically to express not only a sexual orientation but more importantly political and community alliances. For Baby Boomer lesbians, lesbian identity connoted an alliance with feminism, and for Millennials their sexual identity indicated a political alliance with queer and trans* movements. In order to sustain solidarity between lesbians of different generations, we suggest that narratives about gender should include both intrinsic and extrinsic components. We further suggest that the political project of ending the oppression of all lesbians/women who love women is fraught, but essential in a world that hates women.

This special issue begins with the provocation "Is lesbian identity obsolete?" As conceptions of gender and sexuality have shifted in recent decades, tensions over the constitution of Lesbian, Gay, Bisexual, Trans, and Queer (LGBTQ+) identity have surfaced. As articulations of gender and sexual identity categories have shifted, some writers have framed lesbian identity as "disappearing" or "going extinct," (Morris, 2016). Media accounts that conflate transmasculinity with "lesbians in denial" (Herzog, 2020, Kiss, 2018; Serano, 2021) have positioned "lesbian" as an identity category in flux.

In this research, we examine the provocation "Is lesbian identity obsolete?" using qualitative interviews with LGBTQ+participants living in the San Francisco Bay Area. For our purposes, we compared interviews with study participants from two generations: "Baby Boomers" (born between 1946 and 1965) who came of age in the 1960s and 1970s, and "Millennials" (born between 1981 and 1996) who came of age in the first two decades of the millennium, with dramatic gains in the social and legal inclusion of LGBT people in the US. An example of some of the legal and social inclusion can be found in the 2003 US Supreme Court invalidation of anti-sodomy laws (Lawrence et al. v. Texas, 2003). National polls indicate that in 2013, for the first time most people in the U.S. supported the rights of same-sex couples to get married (Silver, 2013), and in 2015 the US Supreme Court approved same-sex marriage (c.f., Ben Hagai & Crosby, 2016, for a review). Given the shift in social and legal inclusion, we are interested in how people of different generations understand gender and sexual identity. Specifically, how do conceptions of lesbian identity differ for people who came of age before and after these social shifts?

Our interview sample focused on participants who either (1) identified as lesbians or women/femmes who are attracted to women at the time of the interview (In response to a multiselect question about their gender, these participants selected the option "woman"; two selected an additional category, ex. "genderqueer"), or (2) had identified as lesbians in the past (ex., a transman who described an earlier period of lesbian identification). We used the resulting set of 24 interviews to explore how these participants understand their gender and sexual identities.

Our investigation does not aim to represent the attitudes of all Baby Boomers and Millennials who have identified as lesbians at some point in their lives. Instead, we offer an empirically-grounded account of how these Baby Boomer and Millennial study participants – all with direct personal experience of the narrativization of lesbian identity– articulated their own narratives of gender and sexual identification. Rooted in a constructive paradigm that understands identities as historically constituted, socially contested, and always in flux (Balzer Carr et al., 2017; Foucault, 1978; Seidman, 1996), we foreground the role of feminist, queer, and transgender political movements in the construction of participants' narratives. We juxtapose articulations made by these movements with psychological frameworks on gender and our interviewees' voices. Our aim, in this brief article, is to offer an empirically grounded account of how participants of different generations narrativized lesbian identity in their own lives and understood their gender and sexual identities. By illuminating different approaches to gender and sexuality among people of different generations, we hope to increase understanding and reduce friction and alienation in LGBTQ + communities.

The framing of sex/gender in the 1970s feminist and lesbian movements

At the root of lesbian movements of the 1970s was an understanding of gender as an oppressive category that disenfranchizes women (De Beauvoir, 1949/2010; Firestone,1970/2003; Wittig, 1980). Radical lesbian feminists argued against compulsory heterosexuality and for the political importance of lesbian identity and intimate relationships between women in the battle against oppressive gender norms. In a famous manifesto the Radicalesbians group writes,

> What is a lesbian? A lesbian is the rage of all women condensed to the point of explosion. She is the woman who, often beginning at an extremely early age, acts in accordance with her inner compulsion to be a more complete and freer human being than her society - perhaps then, but certainly later - cares to allow her... She may not be fully conscious of the political implications of what for her began as personal necessity, but on some level she has not been able to accept the limitations and oppression laid on her by the most basic role of her society–the female role. (Radicalesbians, 1970/2020 p.41).

Following the Radicalesbians manifesto, lesbians are understood as women who reject social imperatives to conform to feminine gender roles. Motivated by an "inner compulsion to be a more complete and freer human being than her society... cares to allow her," lesbian rejection of traditional feminine roles is a political act. Although lesbians are othered and policed through homophobia, their marginalized position affords them more awareness of women's oppression (Rich, 1980). Both radical lesbians and gay liberation activists argued that the categories of homosexuality and heterosexuality are only possible in societies with rigid sex roles that foreclose desire between people of the same sex (Wittman, 1970). Liberation for women is grounded in rejecting the compulsory heterosexuality that separates women from one another and turns them into objects of desire for the male gaze (Rich, 1980). In this formulation, the creation of strong bonds of intimacy and love between women can liberate women from their subordinate roles in a society dominated by men.

A foundational assumption of these lesbian and feminist movements was a conceptual separation between sex and gender (Bem, 1993). The gender category "women" was regarded as cultural, whereas the sex category "female" was understood to be based in biology and common to women universally (De Beauvoir, 1949/2010). Biological sex (understood as natural, intrinsic and relatively unchanging) is the background from which arises gender (understood as cultural, extrinsic and relatively dynamic). Patriarchal domination is reproduced through the gender roles and stereotypes that construct women as passive, domestic and weak, compared to the construction of men as agentic, public and strong (Bem, 1993). Feminist psychologists focused on understanding how these gender roles become internalized by children as they develop (Bem, 1981; Maccoby, 1999; Markus et al., 1982).

Psychological research on women's sexuality, and in particular lesbian sexuality, has suggested that within patriarchal society the objectification and sexualization of women, propelled by billion dollar cosmetic, clothing, and porn industries, constrain women's sexual agency (Kitzinger, 1987; Kitzinger & Wilkinson, 1995; Rothblum, 1994; 1999). For many women, sexual identity is not necessarily in congruence with their sexual desire and or romantic attraction (Diamond, 2008). For instance, Carla Golden demonstrated that some lesbians understood their sexual identity as determined by biological and innate factors whereas other lesbians saw their erotic attraction as a conscious choice. While some lesbians experienced their orientation toward women at a young age and felt that this orientation was immutable, others experienced their erotic attraction as fluid and variant across contexts and people. These women identified as lesbian yet experienced their romantic attraction as bisexual (Golden & The Boston Lesbian Psychologies Collective, 1987). Because research on lesbian identity suggests enormous fluidity and diversity in lesbian sexuality, in this study we included participants who described their sexual orientation as shifting between lesbian and bisexual and/or between lesbian and queer. (We did not, however, include participants who did not identify themselves as lesbians at some point in their lifetimes.)

Queer thought and the transgender revolution

In the late 1980s and 1990s queer movements arose in the wake of governmental neglect of the AIDS pandemic ravaging gay communities across the US (Schulman, 2021). Queer scholars who were part of ACT UP and other radical queer activist groups (e.g., Queer Nation) critiqued the scientific, literary, and popular discourses constructed around the logic of the heterosexual matrix (Seidman, 1996). They argued against the assumption, prevalent among feminists of previous decades, of the biological origins of sex differences. Specifically, Butler (1990/2011) argued that sex differences are seen through the lens of culture. The historical and social processes that cast men and women into binary and hierarchical positions shape how scientists understand gender differences. As such biological sex is not separated from but intertwined with cultural genders. To explode the sex/gender binary, queer scholars called for a proliferation of gender identities that they believed would render the male/female gender binary nonsensical (Butler, 1990/2011).

Transgender scholars who were part of the first wave of transstudies, such as Lesley Feinberg (1992/2013), Kate Bornstein (2016), Sandy Stone (1992), and Susan Stryker (1994), also argued for the propagation of "gender outlaws" and their inclusion under the transgender umbrella, a joint political identity and political force including "transvestites, trans-sexual, drag queens and drag kings, cross-dressers, bull-daggers, stone butches, androgynes, diesel dykes or berdache—a European colonialist term" (Feinberg, 1992/2013, p. 5). In addition to creating a political force around gender deviances of different kinds, transgender thinkers have highlighted the manner in which an individual's sense of self and/or identity can be attached to a particular gender formation. As such gender is not only a force of oppression but also a productive force (Bornstein, 2016; Stryker, 1994).

Transgender writers have theorized about ways in which cisgender people may fail to recognize gender identification as an internalized awareness that can be incongruent with sex assigned at birth. For instance, Julia Serano describes the cognitive dissonance that can result when an individual experiences a subconscious sense of gender that is not affirmed by others (2016):

> By this time, I was already consciously aware of the fact that I was physically male and that others thought of me as a boy. During this time, I experienced numerous manifestations of my female subconscious sex: I had dreams in which adults would tell me I was a girl...I had an unexplained feeling that I was doing something wrong every time I walked into the boy's restroom at school." (p.78)

In this model, complex genetic, hormonal, neurological and environmental processes are associated with the emergence of subconscious sex, gender expression, and sexual orientation. Although hetero- and cis-normativity enforce dominant alignments between each of these components and dimorphic sex traits, they are independent of one another, and can be static or dynamic to different degrees for different people (Serano, 2016).

To further account for gender variance, current transgender inclusive psychological models deconstruct gender into several components, facets, or dimensions. For example, Charlotte Tate's (Tate et al., 2014) Gender Bundle Model suggests that there are five components of gender that come together into a gender identity bundle. Following empirical research on gender variant children and adults, these components include: (1) sex assignment at birth, (2) the gender a person feels they belong to or identify with, (3) the extent to which a person understands and follows gender role behavior, (4) gender presentation and (5) how people evaluate their gender ingroup compared to outgroups. In psychology, Sari Van Anders,(2015) Sexual Configuration Theory reiterates previous distinctions between sexual attraction, sexual behavior, and identity while further accounting for variability in the extent to which people may be attracted to a particular kind of gender/gender expression/sex (ex., masculine men, nonbinary people, butches or femmes), or have a more fluid disposition that is not specifically oriented toward a particular gender/sex.

Method

In this article, we conduct an Interpretive Phenomenological Analysis (Eatough & Smith, 2008) of nine interviews with Baby Boomers and 15 interviews with Millennials, which are taken from a larger dataset of interviews that were conducted in 2016 on sexual and gender identities as well as stigma and smoking. (Some of the interviews used in this study were also used in a study on LGBTQ identities more generally; see Ben Hagai et al., 2020.) Participants were recruited through announcements circulated via online media and in person through LGBTQ community centers and organizations. Trained qualitative researchers conducted semi-structured interviews (typically lasting for one hour) featuring questions about gender and sexual identities. Interviews began with the question "In your own words, please tell me a little bit about yourself. How would you describe yourself to/someone who doesn't know you?" and included questions such as "How do you identify your sexuality?" and "How do you identify your gender?"

Our sample of 24 interviews comprises participants from this larger dataset who:

1. met age criteria for either Baby Boomers (born between 1946-1965) or Millennials (born between 1981-1996), and
2. identified as lesbians and/or as women who were attracted to women at the time of the interview, or who described having identified as such in the past.

Notably, the resulting sample is not comprised solely of women or solely of lesbians. Because we were interested in lesbian identity across lifetime trajectories, the sample includes, for example, a transman and a bisexual woman who described a period of lesbian identification in their lifetimes. Individuals who did not indicate that they were lesbians at present and who did not describe this experience are not included. Given the fluidity of gender and sexual identity described by some participants – as well as the dynamic nature of "lesbian identity" posited by this issue's framing question – we believe that the narratives of people who have moved through a period of lesbian identification can be especially illuminating. However, most participants in our sample (22 out of 24) did select both "woman" in response to a survey question about gender, and "lesbian" or "queer" in response to a question about sexual orientation.

We note here that participants were asked a multiselect survey question that allowed them to select more than one gender descriptor or write in their own gender descriptor. Participants were also asked if they identified as transgender or had been assigned a different gender at birth. As our analysis illustrates, individual narratives do not always mesh neatly with answers to survey questions. For consistency, however, we will introduce participants' narratives using a standard combination of their responses to these questions. Thus, a participant who indicated that they are a woman, genderqueer, and not-transgender is introduced as a "genderqueer cis woman"; a participant who indicated that he is a man and transgender is a "transman"; and a participant who indicated that she is a woman and not-transgender is a "cis woman." In general, we use "women" (without "cis" or "trans" modifiers) to refer to a group of women, and we specify "cis women" or "transwomen" as a group where relevant.

The average age of Baby Boomer participants at the time of the interview was 56.33 (4.38) and ranged from 50 to 62. In response to a survey question about gender, of the eight Baby Boomer participants who identified as women, one indicated that she was a transwoman, and one indicated that she was a genderqueer woman. In addition, one Baby Boomer identified as a transman (who described his experience of having previously identified as a lesbian). In response to a survey question about sexual identity, one participant identified as queer, 7 as lesbian, and one woman identified as bisexual. In response to a survey question about race, five Baby Boomer participants identified as White, 3 as Black, and 1 as mixed race.

There were 15 Millennials in the sample. Their average age was 24 (3.03) and ranged from 19 to 30. In response t0o a survey question about gender, of the 14 Millennial participants who identified as women, one indicated that she was a transwoman and one indicated that she was a genderfluid woman. In addition, one Millennial identified as a genderqueer femme. In response to a survey question about sexual identity, eight identified as lesbian and 7 as queer. In response to a survey question about race, nine identified as White, one identified as Black, 1 as Latinx, 3 as mixed race, 1 as Asian (See Table 1).

Our analysis of the interviews followed the procedure of Interpretive Phenomenological Analysis (Eatough & 569860Smith, 2008). We first familiarized ourselves with the Baby Boomer interviews by reading and

Table 1. Demographic variable.

	Baby Boomer participants $n = 9$	Millennial participants $n = 15$
Average age	56.33	24.03
Gender: Women	8*	14*
Genderqueer or gender nonbinary, gender fluid	1	2
Trans men	1	0
Trans women	1	1
Sexuality: Lesbian/Gay	7	8
Bisexual	1	0
Queer	1	7
Ethnicity: African American or Black	3	1
Latinx	0	1
Asian	0	1
White	5	9
Mixed	1	3
Income** 0-30,000	4	10
30,000-74,999	2	1
75,000 and above	1	3
Employment status**: Full time	0	2
Part time	2	6
Disability	1	
Unemployed	3	6
Retired	2	

*Participants were able to identify as one or more genders.
**Some participants did not answer this question.

rereading. We wrote memos and conducted initial coding focused on groups of three interviews at a time. With each iteration, we compared codes across interviews and developed and refined a list of themes. We followed the same process moving from initial notes to codes. The first and second author met on a weekly basis to discuss codes and themes. Special attention was given to delineating reoccurring themes across generational groups. The first author created a document that was used as a theme table. The second author checked the themes based on their own coding and added additional notes. The third author checked the final list of reoccurring themes.

Findings

The reoccurring themes identified in our Baby Boomer sample were: 1. Understanding gender categories as constraining one's humanity; 2. Finding resistance within lesbian and feminist communities; and 3. Framing Lesbian identity as dynamic sexual orientation and as political category. Reoccurring themes that emerged from the Millennial sample included: 1. Understanding gender as potentially both intrinsic and extrinsic, multifaceted, fluid, and context dependent. 2. Adopting queer identity as part of an inclusive community identity, and 3. Using sexual identity terms strategically to avoid stigma. To protect confidentiality, the names used below are pseudonyms chosen by the participants.

Baby boomers' understanding of gender categories as constraining one's humanity

Baby Boomer participants often described their early sense of gender in the context of constrictive binary gender norms that foreclose women's agency and position them as socially derogated compared to men. This was especially true for Baby Boomers in our sample who discussed being "tomboys." For instance, Bebop (all names are pseudonyms), a 50-year-old Black, lesbian, cis woman, explained:

> I think I'm the one who should have been a boy, because I love – I was always getting in fights with boys and stuff... they called it a tomboy. I played football, basketball, everything.

Like many tomboys Bebop wished she were a boy and saw herself as breaking traditional gender norms in which women and girls are expected to support others rather than compete with them. Similarly, Gertrude – a 62-year-old White, lesbian, cis woman who saw herself as "a boy spirit" and tomboy in her youth –elaborated on an early aversion to traditional gender roles that position women as caregivers:

> ...My dad came home with a baby doll, and in my head, I actually said, "I'm not buying into the role. I'm not-- " I actually used the word, role. Even, I must have been eight or nine, and I just looked at this thing, it was like, I'm not doing that role... I think a lot of tomboys go through that.

Seeing oneself as different because of a rejection of traditional gender roles was also important to people in our sample whose gender identification shifted or who went through gender transition. For instance, Andrew, a 61-year-old White, queer, transman who identified as a member of the lesbian community for several years, also described himself as a youthful "tomboy" who had rejected the traditional gender roles assigned to him early in life:

> I was a tomboy and I did not conform to sex and gender norms. I didn't like dresses. When I was going to be baptized, my mom – and I don't remember this, but my mother told me, she said, I had you all dressed – I guess I was two or something and she said, you came out and you didn't have your dress on anymore and you had your cowboy boots on and you announced that nobody was going to "assitize" you. You know, for "baptize"...

Other Baby Boomer participants who did not describe themselves as former tomboys also experienced the traditional gender roles assigned to women as oppressive. Rachel, a 58-year-old White, lesbian, cis woman who described herself as more "feminine" observed:

I remember encountering sexism. I don't even remember what the incident was, but I remember being told I couldn't do something because I was a girl. And my immediate response, just boom, was, well then, I'm a boy! Now did I actually ever think I was a boy? Absolutely not. But really, the response was, no, you can't tell me I can't do that... So, I have actually never wanted to be a boy, but I sure as hell wanted the privilege as a little girl.

Baby Boomer participants like Rachel described their understanding of their gender in relationship to the oppression of women and privileging of boys and men in society.

Finding resistance within lesbian and feminist communities

Organic to the rejection of women's oppression and traditional notions of femininity in the narrative of several of these participants was their participation in women's and feminist movements of the 1970s. In these movements, participants found a safe haven and collective support for resisting gender role constraints. For instance, Rachel described her search for community growing up in Missouri:

[My mother and I] were close. So the fact that she clearly thought that the way I looked, my lifestyle issue, as she described it, was disgusting – it was painful.... When I came out in high school, I got actively involved in the women's community and the lesbian community in Kansas City. Kind of sneaking around so that my parents didn't know exactly what I was doing.

For Rachel, gender deviant attraction to women was embedded in feminist and lesbian communities, the praxis of consciousness raising, and the political agenda of women's liberation. Like Rachel, a teenaged Andrew also experienced feminist and lesbian communities as a refuge from certain gender constraints:

I was gonna transition – I told my mom I was going to transition when I was 17. Right about that time is when I discovered feminism. And I looked at that and I thought, maybe I don't need to be a man. Maybe what I want is to live my life the way that men are entitled and are allowed to live their lives, and take the power, as a woman, as a female. Stand up, take what I want from the world and be who I am and that's enough. I mean, feminism, yeah go! So I went off on this trajectory of being very involved in the women's movement, and oh my God, doing that in 1970-71, '72, is fabulous. I mean, feminism was just exploding, and I read books, and the consciousness raising groups, and I met some of the most fabulous women ever.

Although Rachel and Andrew's experiences of gender are categorically different, each found some support in feminist movements for the ability to live "the way that [similarly situated] men are entitled." At the same time, Andrew found that feminism was not enough; he needed to transition. Mainstream feminism may have been inadequate to addressing intersectional contexts of power and entitlement. For example, Corinne, a 50-year-old White, lesbian, transwoman, experienced feminine gender expression as "mortifying" – devalued and shameful, as Baby Boomer feminists have observed – but also as a privilege not afforded to her as a transwoman.

Framing Lesbian identity as dynamic sexual orientation and as political category

Some Baby Boomers discussed their sexuality as based in a sole attraction to women. For instance, Rachel explained "I have always been interested in women. Before I knew there was such a category as lesbians, I consistently had crushes on other girls and on women." Other Baby Boomers who identified as lesbians, such as Nome, Gertrude and Joey, discussed the fluidity of their attraction or bisexual attraction. For instance, Gertrude recalled her first attraction to a woman:

> I was convinced I was straight, on the outside. But I had this massive attraction to my friend's piano teacher, for some odd reason. I mean, I just couldn't wait for my friend to have her piano lessons. And you know, it was only in retrospect that I understood what was going on...And then, in high school, I had a mad crush on my friend, and I actually had a mad crush on her boyfriend too. So, I was equally attracted to both of them.

Destiny, a 58-year-old bisexual, Black, cis woman, described herself variously as "lesbian," "bisexual" and "gay" in her interview, centering the rejection of heterononormativity in her use of sexual identity terms.

Although Baby Boomer participants discussed the fluidity of their attraction or their experiences of attraction to men, early lesbian identification was often understood as a political act grounded in the rejection of racism, sexism and/or heteronormativity. Considerations of cisnormativity, however, were largely absent or secondary. For instance, Nome, a 54-year-old Black, lesbian, cis woman, framed her racial and sexual identity as political: "my Blackness is a political term just like ... I call myself a lesbian, is a political term." However, Nome also observed that some political terms were less available to her generation, commenting that "I see myself as transgendered as a kid, but I didn't have the language, I didn't know what that meant."

Like other Baby Boomers, Nome grew up with little access to language – or a collective political framework – for challenging cisnormativity. The relative lack of collective support for transidentities is further evidenced in Andrew's path as an older transman who believes his identification as a lesbian woman earlier in life was a mistake. Contrary to narratives that frame young transmen who love women as "really" lesbians, Baby Boomer participants such as Nome and Andrew highlight the complexity and variability of individual experiences of gender in relation to collective social support.

Millennials' understanding of gender as potentially both intrinsic and extrinsic

Compared to Baby Boomers, Millennial participants tended to invoke an understanding of gender identity situated in a sense of intrinsic or felt gender. Whereas Baby Boomers tended to focus descriptions of their gender on a rejection of traditional gender norms as manifestations of sexism and heteronormativity, Millennial participants had more access to collective support for their sense of internal gender identification. Along with centering their felt sense of gender, Millennial participants often used multiple categories to describe their gender and rejected the centrality of sex assigned at birth in describing gender identity. For instance, Ana, a 20-year-old White, queer, non-binary transfemme person, explained,

> In a way for me, a lot of my gender identity is a choice. Which also makes it sound strange, but I don't – I make decisions every single day about how I want to present and gender's performance, or, gender being performative. But I think for me specifically, I very much choose to present as femme.

Another participant, Kimmy, a 30-year-old Black, lesbian, cis woman, highlighted the intentionality that she felt toward her femininity, "I like being a woman, I'm really into femininity. I'm intentional about being feminine." S.B., a 24-year-old White, queer, cis woman, also framed her gender in intentional terms that highlighted an internalized sense of gender identification as distinct from gender "perform[ance].".

> I don't consider myself trans. I'm a little genderqueer. And how I square that is I don't need any trans resources. I don't experience dysphoria, which you don't need to be, to be transgender. When I see the word queer, I'm like, that's me. It resonates. And when I see trans, I don't get the same experience. So, although I don't consider myself transgender, I consider myself a little gender weird. I just don't perform – I'm gender nonconforming. So, I like to tell people I'm probably like 80 percent female, 20 percent filler.

For several cisgender Millennial participants, using the word "cis" before their gender marked their recognition of gender identification as distinct from sex assigned at birth. For instance, Violet, a 26-year-old Latina, lesbian, cis woman, explained what being a cis woman means to her. "I'm a cis woman. I'll explain what that means to someone who doesn't know, you know, being assigned at birth as a female, feeling like a female my whole life." In addition to the use of "cis," Millennials highlighted the fluidity of gender. Because gender was not framed in rigid biological or social categories, fluidity in expression was highlighted by several of the participants. For instance, Ruby, a 23-year-old White, queer, genderfluid woman, discussed gender fluidity in their life:

> Gender fluid... for me, it's kind of like, Today, I feel like kind of being more tomboyish, and other days, I'll put on more makeup and maybe wear a skirt or something... it's more really on just how I feel as a person for that specific time. And so for me, it's just not something that's set in stone based on your genitals or biological.

Along with deemphasizing biological sex and assigned dichotomous categories, Millennial participants emphasized a sense of felt gender as well as the fluidity of gender and the ways in which not only gender presentation, but also gender identification, may change across space and time. Some participants who rejected the stability of gender also expressed disidentification with gender itself as a concept.

Adopting queer identity as part of an inclusive community identity

Among Millennials, some participants who identified consistently as women (i.e., not genderqueer or genderfluid). such as Jane, Lisa, and Nikki, discussed their identification with lesbian identity. For instance, Jane, a 19-year-old White, lesbian, transwoman explained, "I'm a woman," or, "I'm a girl," or, "I'm a transgender girl," but "what I really identify as is a lesbian, but I feel hesitant to tell most people that, because people-- I have this fear that people will think it's a joke." Despite increased affirmation of transgender identities compared to prior generations, in Jane's experience the rejection of assigned gender roles was still perceived primarily as an indication of "outlaw" sexual identity rather than gender identity. As Jane explained:

> A big part of my identity in growing up has been questioning my sexuality, just since it's always been kind of questioned for me since I was in fifth grade... I couldn't find any answers until I got to college... I realized I was transgender... and realized I wasn't a gay man and really had no attraction for men.

Many Millennial participants discussed a strong identification with the queer community. For instance, Janet, a 25-year-old Latina, queer, cis woman who was organizing the San Francisco Dyke March explained,

> You're a part of the queer community... there's all of these things that fall under queer, and that's why I like it so much. That's why I identify with it, 'cause it's like, it doesn't have to be something specific really. Queer is queer... And you can

be gender queer *and* queer at the same time, or I can be queer and not gender queer, and that's fine too.

Janet, like other Millennials in our sample, preferred the word queer because she felt she was part of the queer community, and she embraced "queer" as an inclusive term that endorses both gender queerness and queer, i.e., not straight, sexual attraction. Some participants further identified with queer, as opposed to lesbian or bisexual, because it encompassed their attraction to people who did not identify exclusively as either women or men. Queerness allowed them to remain open to different gender configurations. For instance, Violet explained,

> I'm allowing the door to be open to many genders and not just women…Just calling myself a lesbian can't feel really true, because I wasn't just dating cis women… and I wasn't just dating trans women either. Like, it was very much like a range of genders that I started to date, at least in the last couple of years. So, it was, it just didn't feel real.

Violet added that the term lesbian "felt outdated, and the stigma was pretty intense too." In the Bay Area, she further explained, "it feels like queer is an identifier for people who are progressing, and any other term that you have, whether it's gay or lesbian or bisexual, those type of terms are starting to go obsolete because they're not all-encompassing of different genders." Millennial participants like Violet who embraced the social construction, performativity, and fluidity of gender also described themselves as "open to many genders", rather than attraction to "just women."

Using sexual identity terms strategically to avoid stigma

Stigma around lesbian identity further reinforced rejection of the term "lesbian." Kay, a 27-year-old White, queer, cis woman, echoed the endorsement of queer identity as more inclusive and less stigmatized. She said,

> I don't like the word, lesbian, 'cause it's been used negatively in my life around me, to me, about me. So, queer's more just like, open-minded, I guess, and it's the closest equivalent to like, not straight, that I have. And I dated this chick who was super closeted, but they were trans, and they were like, Oh, well, you said you were gay for a while. So, I was like, Oh, whatever… My mom sometimes still asks to say, lesbian, 'cause she's like, Well, you're only ever going to be with a woman, and I was like, Nah, not necessarily. I'm not ever going to be with a cis guy, yeah, but I could still be with a trans man. Like, I'm not going to write myself off before I've even started. And I've noticed, when someone in the community calls me a lesbian, if it's in a joking way, I'm actually okay with it.

The term queer allowed participants, particularly Millennials, to define their sexuality in a way that they felt did not exclude transmen and genderqueer people. Moreover, the term lesbian was associated with homosexual stigma, sexism, and othering not only from straight people but also within LGBTQ + communities.

Although many participants endorsed queer identity because of the political term's ability to include people of different gender and sexual identities, participants also used other gender and sexual identity terms. For instance, Kimmy explained:

> I use "queer" if I'm referring to myself in relation to the rest of the community, just like the umbrella. Just to be clear, I fall under the umbrella. If I'm talking to people who I know are gay and also queer, then a lot of the time I don't feel like being like, oh, I'm a lesbian, because we already know that someone is some shade of that. So just for the sake of the conversation or to not say like, LGBTQ or just queer people, queer this, queer that. That includes that. And then I don't call myself anything in front of my family or my parents. I don't say I'm lesbian or gay or bisexual. I would never say I was queer in front of them. I would not use that word. That is like, too much for them and then they also use that derogatorily too. So I don't want to identify with that in their heads.

For participants like Kimmy, sexual identity categories were used strategically. In certain contexts they identified as lesbian and in other contexts they used the term queer.

Discussion

In this research we aimed to trace the meaning of sexual and gender identity among individuals who have identified as lesbians/women who love women in their lifetimes, comparing Baby Boomers and Millennials. Baby Boomers in our sample tended to understand themselves as gender nonconforming and as clashing with oppressive gender categories rooted in patriarchy. For these participants, feminist and lesbian communities offered a space to resist repressive gender norms. Similar to discourses rooted in the lesbian and gay liberation movement and articulated by feminist psychologists, gender was understood as a cultural category that should be resisted and rejected in order for humans to be fully free (Bem, 1993). As has been found in previous research, some participants adopted the term lesbian because throughout their life they were attracted exclusively or primarily to women, while others who were attracted to both women and men adopted the term because they saw it as a political category associated with a community they were part of (Golden & The Boston Lesbian Psychologies Collective, 1987).

Millennials in our sample tended to understand their gender identity not only based on an oppressive social construction but also as a term related to intrinsic feelings. Gender as an internal experience was understood as detached from sex assigned at birth. Some Millennial participants who had identified as lesbians/women who love women in their lifetimes saw their gender as shifting across contexts, and as a performance. Many preferred sexual categories such as queer or pansexual because these labels conveyed attraction to people of many genders (i.e., not just men and women, but also agender, nonbinary, etc.). This evolving understanding of both gender and sexual categories is in line with the politics of queer and transgender movements that argued for the proliferation of gender and sexual categories for the purpose of exploding the gender and sexual binaries of man/women and straight/gay (Bornstein, 2016; Butler, 1990/2011; Feinberg, 1992/2013). The gender categories and queer politics articulated by participants, particularly among Millennials, necessitate a more complex gender framework that accounts for facets including felt gender, expressed gender, and gender assigned at birth (Tate et al., 2020, Serano, 2016). It also requires a more complex theoretical configuration to account for the fluidity and specificity of sexual attractions (Van Anders, 2015).

Our research suggests differences as well as commonalities in the ways that people who have identified as lesbian and queer women in their lifetimes understand their identities. Many of the older participants, like the younger ones, rejected gender roles and binary genders. Many of the older participants, like the younger ones, saw their sexual identities shaped by political goals and social movements. As such their sexual identity was less like sexual orientation and more like a community or political identity.

Our research findings further suggest that sexual identities are fluid, used strategically, and associated with communities and political projects. When psychologists focus on identities and infer from them a distinct experience, they may essentialize differences while ignoring the overlap among people of different identities. For instance, a person who grew up in the 1970s or 80s may see themselves as lesbian, but if the same person came of age in the early 2000s they may call themselves queer, bisexual, or pansexual. When psychologists conceptualize lesbian, bisexual, or queer as dichotomous, nonoverlapping categories of identity, they ignore some of the similarities across identities and the political and community based aspects of identity. Our findings imply that researchers should approach identity categories in more critical terms, focusing on the ways in which social forces may lead people with a similar understanding of their gender and sexualities to use different labels.

This study has several limitations. First, since we sought thick, nuanced, and rich, textured description of basic narratives around gender and sexuality our sample is small. The findings from this study should serve as conceptual tools to understand shifts in the understanding of gender and sexuality among people of different generations. Since we didn't use a representative sample, we cannot generalize the results to Baby Boomer or Millennials. Furthermore, while our sample was relatively diverse, we didn't have a large enough sample of participants of different racial groups to analyze how, for instance, Black lesbians of different generations may understand their identities. Finally, since the data were collected as part of a larger study on stigma and smoking, some directed questions related to the aims of this analysis were not included. However, the interviews themselves were conducted to elicit thick descriptions of identities therefore facilitating this sort of analysis. Nevertheless, we were not able to ask our participants directly about generational differences among lesbians. Future research should examine how participants reflected on these generational differences themselves.

In terms of advocacy, our findings suggest that lesbian communities of different generations form around different political projects. Baby Boomers lesbian communities have tended to focus on the feminist political project, whereas Millennial LGBTQ communities have focused on a queer political project of affording space for a wide range of identities as well as transgender inclusion. These differences may lead to clashes and misunderstandings across generations. Nevertheless, these political goals necessitate a large movement that brings together lesbian and queer women of different generations to work in solidarity.

To create solidarity, a narrative should draw from intergenerational conceptualizations of gender and sexuality. An inclusive narrative that supports coalition between lesbian of different generations will expand the understanding of gender not only as an oppressive category, but also a personal identification (which at times does not correspond with physical signifiers). Sexual identity should be articulated primarily as community making identity and as a political project (as opposed to a personal disposition). The political project of lesbian identity should reject compulsory heterosexuality, support cis and transwomen, and fight the oppression of women and people who do not fit within the gender binary.

Disclosure statement

No potential conflict of interest was reported by the authors.

Funding

This research and preparation of this manuscript were supported by grant #R01CA190238 (Antin, PI) from the National Cancer Institute (NCI) of the National Institutes of Health (NIH) and the Tobacco-Related Disease Research Program (TRDRP) of the University of California, grant number T30IR0890 (Antin, PI). The content is solely the responsibility of the authors and does not necessarily represent the official views of the NCI, NIH, or TRDRP. Also, sincere appreciation is due to the research participants who shared their insights and time with us. Without them, this research would not have been possible.

References

Balzer Carr, B., Ben Hagai, E., & Zurbriggen, E. L. (2017). Queering bem: theoretical intersections between Sandra Bem's scholarship and queer theory. *Sex Roles*, *76*(11–12), 655–668. https://doi.org/10.1007/s11199-015-0546-1

Bem, S. L. (1981). Gender schema theory: A cognitive account of sex typing. *Psychological Review*, *88*(4), 354–364. https://doi.org/10.1037/0033-295X.88.4.354

Bem, S. L. (1993). *The lenses of gender: Transforming the debate on sexual inequality*. Yale University Press.

Ben Hagai, E. B., Annechino, R., Young, N., & Antin, T. (2020). Intersecting sexual identities, oppressions, and social justice work: Comparing LGBTQ Baby Boomers to Millennials who came of age after the 1980s AIDS epidemic. *Journal of Social Issues*, *76*(4), 971–992. https://doi.org/10.1111/josi.12405

Ben Hagai, B. E., & Crosby, F. J. (2016). Between relative deprivation and entitlement: An historical analysis of the battle for same-sex marriage in the United States. In C. Sabbagh, & M. Schmitt (Eds.), *Handbook of social justice theory and research*. Springer. https://doi.org/10.1007/978-1-4939-3216-0_26

Bornstein, K. (2016). *Gender outlaw: On men, women, and the rest of us*. Vintage.

Butler, J. (1990/2011). *Gender trouble: Feminism and the subversion of identity*. Routledge.

De Beauvoir, S. (1949/2010). *The second sex*. Knopf.

Diamond, L. M. (2008). *Sexual fluidity*. Harvard University Press.

Eatough, V., & Smith, J. (2008). Interpretative phenomenological analysis. In C. Willig, & W. Stainton-Rogers (Eds.), *The SAGE handbook of qualitative research in psychology* (pp. 193–211). SAGE Publications.

Feinberg, L. (1992/2013). *Transgender liberation: A movement whose time has come*. Routledge.

Firestone, S. (1970/2003). *The dialectic of sex: The case for feminist revolution*. Farrar, Straus and Giroux.

Foucault, M. (1978). *The history of sexuality, Vol. 1: An introduction* (R. Hurley, Trans.). Pantheon.

Golden, C. (1987). Diversity and variability in women's sexual identities. In Boston Lesbian Psychologies Collective (Ed.), *Lesbian psychologies: Explorations and challenges* (pp. 19–34). Champaign, IL: University of Illinois Press.

Herzog, K. (2020). *Where have all the lesbians gone?*https://andrewsullivan.substack.com/p/where-have-all-the-lesbians-gone-0a7

Kiss, C. (2018). The idea that trans men are "lesbians in denial" is demeaning and wrong. The Economist. https://www.economist.com/open-future/2018/07/03/the-idea-that-trans-men-are-lesbians-in-denial-is-demeaning-and-wrong

Kitzinger, C. (1987). *The social construction of lesbianism*. Sage.

Kitzinger, C., & Wilkinson, S. (1995). Transitions from heterosexuality to lesbianism: The discursive production of lesbian identities. *Developmental Psychology*, *31*(1), 95–104. https://doi.org/10.1037/0012-1649.31.1.95

Lawrence, et al. (2003). v. Texas., 539 U.S. 558 https://supreme.justia.com/cases/federal/us/539/558/

Maccoby, E. E. (1999). *The two sexes: Growing up apart, coming together*. Harvard University Press.

Markus, H., Crane, M., Bernstein, S., & Siladi, M. (1982). Self-schemas and gender. *Journal of Personality and Social Psychology*, *42*(1), 38–50. https://doi.org/10.1037/0022-3514.42.1.38

Morris, B. J. (2016). Hey, young queer women, baby boomer lesbians are not the enemy. *Slate Magazine*. https://slate.com/human-interest/2016/12/disappearing-lesbians-and-the-need-to-preserve-dyke-culture.html

Radicalesbians. (1970/2020). The woman-identified woman. In B. Fahs (Ed.), *Burn it down!: Feminist manifestos for the revolution*. Verso.

Rich, A. (1980). Compulsory heterosexuality and lesbian existence. *Signs: Journal of Women in Culture and Society*, *5*(4), 631–660. https://doi.org/10.1086/493756

Rothblum, E. D. (1994). Transforming lesbian sexuality. *Psychology of Women Quarterly*, *18*(4), 627–641. https://doi.org/10.1111/j.1471-6402.1994.tb01051.x

Rothblum, E. P. (1999). Poly-friendships. *Journal of Lesbian Studies*, *3*(1-2), 68–83. https://doi.org/10.1300/J155v03n01_08

Schulman, S. (2021). Let the record show: A political history of ACT UP New York, 1987–1993. *Farrar, Straus and Giroux*.

Seidman, S. (1996). *Queer theory/sociology*. Blackwell.

Serano, J. (2016). *Whipping girl: A transsexual woman on sexism and the scapegoating of femininity*. Hachette UK.

Serano, J. (2021). Transgender people, "gay conversion," and "lesbian extinction": What the data show. *Medium*. https://juliaserano.medium.com/transgender-people-gay-conversion-and-lesbian-extinction-what-the-data-show-dea2a3e70174

Silver, N. (2013). How opinion on same-sex marriage is changing, and what it means. FiveThirtyEight. https://fivethirtyeight.com/features/how-opinion-on-same-sex-marriage-is-changing-and-what-it-means/

Stone, S. (1992). The empire strikes back: A posttranssexual manifesto. *Camera Obscura: Feminism, Culture, and Media Studies*, *10*(2), 150–176. https://doi.org/10.1215/02705346-10-2_29-150

Stryker, S. (1994). My words to Victor Frankenstein above the village of Chamounix: Performing transgender rage. *GLQ: A Journal of Lesbian and Gay Studies*, *1*(3), 237–254. https://doi.org/10.1215/10642684-1-3-237

Tate, C. C., Hagai, E. B., & Crosby, F. J. (2020). *Undoing the gender binary*. Cambridge University Press.

Tate, C. C., Youssef, C. P., & Bettergarcia, J. N. (2014). Integrating the study of transgender spectrum and cisgender experiences of self-categorization from a personality perspective. *Review of General Psychology*, *18*(4), 302–312. https://doi.org/10.1037/gpr0000019

Van Anders, S. M. (2015). Beyond sexual orientation: Integrating gender/sex and diverse sexualities via sexual configurations theory. *Archives of Sexual Behavior*, *44*(5), 1177–1213. https://doi.org/10.1007/s10508-015-0490-8

Wittig, M. (1980). The straight mind. *Feminist Issues*, *1*(1), 103–111. https://doi.org/10.1007/BF02685561

Wittman, C. (1970). *Refugees from Amerika: A gay manifesto*. Council on Religion and the Homosexual.

Lesbian, feminist, TERF: a queer attack on feminist studies

Carly Thomsen and Laurie Essig

ABSTRACT

While much has been said about the diversity industry and about transexclusionary radical feminists (TERFs), little has examined their relationship to one another or to academic feminist, queer, and trans studies. This article considers a "queer attack on feminist studies" at our small liberal arts college as a case study for thinking through these relations. A handful of students and diversity staff termed feminist studies faculty TERFs not because of any actual transphobic behavior, but because of our work to question gender systems and ideologies. By examining how some students and diversity office staff alike mobilized the TERF, as well as the ideologies that allow for slippages among the terms "lesbian," "feminist," and "TERF," we outline how the lesbian and the feminist are in danger of becoming permanently reactionary figures. In so doing, we reflect on the relationship between performing diversity work and policing academic studies of gender and sexuality, ultimately arguing that the mobilization of the TERF can function both to further extend the work of the diversity industry and also to call into question academic feminist, queer, and trans studies.

There is something about rural New England that evokes horror. Whether it is the 19th century Headless Horseman or 21st century film "Get Out," it is a place where oft-perfect facades are cracked open to reveal things not being as they seem. So it was that at a small liberal arts college tucked into the green mountains of Vermont, two lesbian professors teaching feminist, queer, and critical race theory were accused of being TERFs, or transexclusionary radical feminists. According to the college's Diversity, Equity, and Inclusion (DEI) staff and the few students making these accusations—none of whom had taken their courses, or any other feminist studies courses for that matter—their crime was in their construction of a survey question. Their punishment was to be branded with the scarlet letters of TERF.

In what follows, we examine this queer attack on feminist studies to consider the logics undergirding the mobilization of the figure of the contemporary TERF by DEI staff and students, as well as its potential for disciplining unruly subjects, including, in this case, both feminist scholars and feminist studies. Journalists and scholars alike have commented on the dangers of diversity work (Ahmed, 2007; Newkirk, 2019). As Sara Ahmed argues, such initiatives can function to make historically white institutions appear as if they are diverse by using the presence of nonwhite bodies as a "happy sign" to signal that racism has been overcome (Ahmed, 2007, p. 164). We suggest here that DEI staff used the figure of the TERF to signal that transphobia could also be overcome. Their approach suggested that the eradication of transphobia need not require a re-thinking of dominant ideas about femininities or masculinities—indeed, precisely the roots of transphobia—but did require, in a deeply ironic twist, the disciplining of lesbian feminists who teach about gender as ideology, analytic, and regime.

We suggest that, in this case, the TERF was phantasmatic. This is not to say that the TERF does not exist. Let us be clear: TERFs exist and transphobia is real. Violence against trans people occurs with depressing regularity. Some self-identified feminists are transphobic; a simple search for "gender skeptical" demonstrates how much transexclusionary feminism exists. The grossly disproportionate rate at which trans people, and especially transwomen of color, are murdered speaks to the cultural panic that transness incites. At the same time, it is the figure of the TERF who produces horror in the types of leftist queer feminist academic and activist spaces in which we tend to find ourselves. In the case we discuss here, we suggest that the TERF functioned as a bit of a folk devil. Like all folk devils, the TERF created a moral panic, producing concerns that its profanity would pollute our ostensibly diverse institution. We argue that TERFs as folk devils can function both to further extend the work of the diversity industry and also to call into question academic feminist, queer, and trans studies.

In his now-classic work on folk devils and moral panics, sociologist Stanley Cohen suggests that folk devils are created in three stages: (1) Simplification of the figure in question such that they are easily recognizable, (2) Exaggeration or fabrication of facts, and (3) Anticipation of future engagement in immoral actions (1972). These elements, each of which was present in the case we consider here, are crucial for the pursuit of folk devils to intensify into a broader movement that Cohen describes as a moral panic. Queer theory has long considered the place of such panics in the production of ongoing sexual hierarchies. Gayle Rubin, for instance, points out that "no tactic for stirring up erotic hysteria has been as reliable as the appeal to protect children" (2006, p. 271). Although not exactly a sex panic, the queer attack on feminist studies did center the student-as-vulnerable-child and positioned feminist lesbian scholars as the source of harm. As Cohen and Ruben make clear, moral panics occur because of real dangers, just not necessarily the danger at the heart of the panic.

In order to avoid creating folk devils ourselves, we want to emphasize that the students publicly shaming feminist studies faculty they considered TERFs did so because they earnestly believed they were making the institution less transphobic. Furthermore, even within the student organizations primarily responsible for critiquing feminist studies, some members resisted characterizations of the department as TERFy. By examining how some students and DEI staff alike mobilized the TERF, as well as the ideologies that allow for slippages among the terms "lesbian," "feminist," and "TERF," we outline how the lesbian and the feminist are in danger of becoming permanently reactionary figures. In so doing, we reflect on the relationship between performing diversity work and policing academic studies of gender and sexuality, ultimately considering how the larger cultural anxieties about lesbians, feminists, and sexism can be mobilized by the diversity industry to shrink possibilities for feminist, queer, and trans inquiry. In this way, a diversity office can incorporate not just institutional imperatives, but also those of student activists to increase institutional control over those deemed difficult or in need of disciplining. Such strange bedfellows are not unusual during moral panics, as Gregory Mitchell shows in his work on sex panics, sporting events, and the strange mix of state, feminist, and religious constituencies willing to come together in the name of the child (2016).

Always already TERFs: a case study

In the Spring of 2019, Carly Thomsen, a feminist and queer studies scholar and coauthor of this article, co-taught a course entitled "Beyond Intersectionality: Developing Anti-Racist and Anti-Capitalist Feminisms" with a colleague in Black studies. As part of the course, the instructors organized a symposium that brought well-known scholars of intersectionality to campus. Prior to the event, we sent out a campus-wide survey about intersectionality. Our primary goal was to gain information regarding how the term circulates in different campus environments so that we could better tailor our opening remarks to our specific context.

The survey began: "What gender do you consider yourself?" Options for answering included: "Man," "Woman," "Transgender," and an open-ended box titled "Self-Identify." Respondents could check as many boxes as they desired, write in any gender, or skip the question altogether. Students in the Queers & Allies student group sent the two professors who crafted the survey the following email:

> After viewing your survey on the circulation of academic theories, we were disappointed about the first question, dealing with gender identity. While we noted that the option to check multiple terms is present, the inclusion of transgender as an option without including cisgender contributes to the othering of transness while considering cis to be the default. Additionally, including common gender options such as nonbinary and agender as well as the option to write in an answer would be more inclusive.

The faculty responded by offering to have a conversation about the "thought processes and hours of conversation that went into our decisions regarding question design for a quantitative survey," which included consulting with colleagues who are experts in survey design. There were, we said in our email responses, good methodological and epistemological reasons for the construction of our questions. For instance, including additional (and uncommon) gender categories would have meant that respondents were more likely to be identifiable. In addition, we explained that there are trans studies critiques of the term "cis" (Enke, 2012) and, further, that having a fill-in-the-blank box—which our survey did include, despite students' claim to the contrary—actually offered greater potential for gender articulation than simply adding additional categories.

We were told that these responses, like our survey questions, were TERF-y. We were told that we "othered" trans students and made them feel un-seen by creating a box labeled "other." (We actually used the word "self-identify.") We were told that the wording of the question in which we asked what gender respondents "consider" themselves, rather than what gender they "are" was transphobic. Apparently, people don't consider themselves a gender; they are a gender. To be clear, this was mostly a whisper campaign. We were not directly called TERFs. We were rarely told these things by the people saying them—just by college staff "supporting" students or by our students who wanted us to know about conversations swirling around us.

From here, a mind-boggling and wildly time-consuming series of meetings unfolded. First, we met with a DEI staff member who handed us a packet that included student affairs' version of "best practices" for survey design. According to this person, we should have included every possible gender category. We pointed out that this belief approaches gender in a less capacious way than did our survey, in which people could self-identify as they please. We also outlined Finn Enke's transfeminist critique of "cis," a term that refers, of course, to "the condition of staying with birth-assigned sex, or congruence between birth-assigned sex and gender identity" (2012, p. 61). In tracing students' paradoxical deployment of the term "cis" in feminist studies classrooms, Enke troubles the idea that gender can possibly stay put, be static, or be something one is born with and then lives out simplistically. Feminist, queer, and trans studies rest on the position that gender is, in fact, not simple and, instead, that it is always becoming and unbecoming. Enke goes so far as to say that the ideas driving the circulation of "cis," "encourage[s] investments in a gender stability that undermines feminist, trans*, queer, and related movements (2012, p. 61). As bad, taking the categories of sex and gender as "natural" (for anyone) rather than as effects of power stabilizes the hierarchical relationship between "cis" and "trans." We also noted that the idea that one "is" a gender runs counter to the most commonsensical trans studies ideas about gender, including articulations of trans as a "redhot zone of ontological uncertainty" (Eng & Puar, quoting Steinbock, 2020, p. 15). Not so incidentally, it also goes against foundational assumptions of feminist studies, including Judith Butler's notion of "gender performativity" and her questioning the "metaphysics" of gender whereby one claims to be one (1990).

In short, throughout this meeting, we drew from feminist, queer, and trans studies to show that the survey was in line with commonly accepted approaches within our academic fields of expertise. In response, this white DEI staff suggested that the Black butch lesbian professor in question was "aggressive and defensive" and the white femme queer woman professor was "condescending and harmful," simultaneously furthering racist stereotypes of angry Black women and sexist stereotypes of uppity feminists. Having been told how to do our jobs by a DEI staff without academic training in critical feminist, queer, trans, or Black studies, we left the meeting disheartened.

The following fall—nearly six months after we sent out the survey—a new LGBTQ affairs staff person arrived on campus. Soon after, she organized a meeting with leaders of LGBTQ student groups, including Queers & Allies, Trans Affinity Group, Queer and Trans People of Color, and the Queer Studies House, for which Thomsen is the highly involved academic advisor. A student who had never met Thomsen commented at the public meeting that Queers & Allies would not partner with students associated with the Queer Studies House because Thomsen and the Gender, Sexuality, and Feminist Studies (GSFS) department to which the house is connected are TERFs. According to students in attendance, GSFS students responded in defense of Thomsen and the GSFS program. The new staff member insinuated that she would take care of this TERFy faculty member and chastised students (including trans students) who defended GSFS, suggesting that those students were being transphobic themselves.

GSFS students, many of whom are gender non-conforming or trans-identified, responded in various ways. Several students immediately emailed GSFS faculty to request meetings. Students attended individual meetings with this staff member, who had not yet met with GSFS faculty, to suggest that this reading of GSFS was inaccurate. In one of these meetings, this non-trans staff person told a transidentifying GSFS major that "cis people don't get to decide who is transphobic." GSFS students also met with the non-GSFS students perpetuating these claims. Queer Studies House residents met with members of other LGBTQ student organizations. GSFS students met with GSFS faculty. GSFS faculty met with one another.

These meetings exhausted everyone involved. GSFS faculty and students decided to host a community conversation and dinner to address the issue collectively. We invited members of all LGBTQ campus organizations. On a campus with 2500 students, approximately twenty-five students attended, as did all GSFS core faculty. Students who had never taken GSFS courses made claims about gender, sexuality, and GSFS, insisting that they knew about gender and sexuality through their lived experiences. They used discourses and ideas that GSFS students had learned to critique in their courses. In response, GSFS students offered feminist and queer ways to think about gender and sexuality, but their ideas were met with resistance rooted in the assumption that to question gender is to be transphobic. As it turned out, the non-GSFS students had no interest in conversing critically about gender or sexuality, a point one transidentified critic of GSFS made clear when they noted that their gender is always challenged and they don't need any more of that. For this student and others who had not taken GSFS courses, questioning gender systems and ideologies was synonymous with threatening their individual gender.

The following morning, Thomsen's Queer Critique class met. Some students who had attended the meeting were angry at their fellow students, and others who had heard about the meeting were confused. Students wanted to talk, in part because of Queer Critique's focus on the "translation" of ideas we discuss in class with those outside of it. Students' final course projects include, for example, creating board games that translate academic texts into playable formats. In short, a belief in the possibilities of moving queer theory beyond the classroom undergird the course. Was this meeting, and the related conversations swirling around it, evidence for the need for increased "translation" skills, students earnestly asked, or, actually, evidence that the entire pedagogical approach was futile?! As we addressed this question, we discussed the difficulty of "living a feminist life," to use Sara Ahmed's phrase, which so often includes talking across epistemological and political lines (2017). Having started the course with Cathy Cohen's classic "Punks, Bulldaggers, and Welfare Queens," students were primed to recognize in this situation the limits of the identitarian politics against which Cohen writes and that amplify the difficulties of talking across epistemological and political differences. Cohen argues that the radical potential of queer politics has not been realized because too often it "reinforce[s] simple dichotomies between heterosexual and 'everything queer'" (Cohen, 1997, p. 438). This approach, Cohen says, not only makes addressing racism, classism, and sexism within LGBTQ spaces more difficult but also makes it impossible to recognize the ways in which certain heterosexuals—i.e. the so-called "welfare queen"—do not benefit from heteronormativity and might actually occupy a "queer" social location. An ability to articulate such arguments clearly in moments when DEI staff and non-GSFS students were employing ideas that run counter to those of feminist, queer, and trans studies did not, however, result in more generative discussions. It simply made clear to our students and to us the depths of the epistemological clashes between feminist, queer, and trans studies and the diversity industry.

In the days that followed, the saga continued. Without telling anyone, a student from Queers & Allies took rough notes at the meeting and circulated what they incorrectly described as a "transcription" among students and staff. Students who recognized the gross inaccuracies riddling the document shared the document with GSFS faculty. Through this document, we gained additional information regarding what students saw as the problem: the survey's inclusion of the "transgender" category, which was "where the whole Q + A/email conflict began." The transgender option, according to this document, is a "problem" because "transgender is not a gender, and it is othering to trans people to ask them to differentiate themselves." Why, we might ask, would critics demand that agender and nonbinary be added to a survey, but transgender be removed? Moreover, it seems obvious that trans people, like all people, experience the world in relation to their gender and, further, often differentiate themselves as trans. Indeed, such positions motivate a great deal of trans studies and activism.

The circulation of the "transcription" encouraged Essig, a coauthor and the GSFS Department Chair, to contact the supervisor of both DEI staff involved with the case. In yet another meeting, this diversity officer indicated that although the survey may not have been transphobic in and of itself, if some students perceived it as transphobic, then, in essence, it was. In other words, any perception of harm is equivalent to harm itself. No evidence necessary. Throughout this series of encounters, we came to understand that we were labeled TERFs, both individually and as a department, because our academic discipline questions gender. By this logic, feminist studies faculty can never be outside the figure of the TERF.

There is much to find unnerving here—the elevation of evidence-less claims to truth, DEI staff stepping into academic affairs, and the devaluing of the expertise of feminist studies faculty among students and staff without expertise in the field. Far from simple annoyances, these elements speak to the ways in which moral panics can have real material consequences. In a moment in which Cypress College placed a faculty member "on leave" after a video went viral in which she questions a student's support of police, it is not hard to imagine this case ending in radically different ways—and especially if the department, led by its Chair, had not rallied behind its faculty. Here, we want to signal two additional issues. First, the claims that lived experience is an uncontestable form of knowledge production, which were central to non-GSFS students' claims, has been widely contested from within feminist, queer, and critical race studies (Scott, 1991; Taiwo 2020). Indeed, as Laura Briggs argues, we do not always have the tools necessary to analyze our own situations (2008). Developing a structural analysis is hard work, and it is the kind of work that happens in feminist studies. Assuming that people automatically have these tools is inaccurate, at best. At worst, this assumption is deeply anti-intellectual and reflective of the kinds of conservative impulses responsible for defunding critical studies in higher education. Second, and perhaps most bizarrely in terms of how experience as evidence circulated in these encounters, only the experiences of students who felt harmed by the survey or faculty's responses to their conservative critiques of it were taken seriously. That there were far more students passionately defending GSFS than there were critics had little impact. When non-binary and transidentified students talked about their overwhelmingly positive experiences in GSFS, they were told they were suffering from false consciousness. One of these students, a non-binary-identified gender-nonconforming GSFS major, was writing a senior thesis at the time about the gender-affirming labors that non-binary people do in intimate relationships with one another. They emailed Queers & Allies to ask the organization to circulate a call for interviewees. The group's leaders, with no training in feminist studies, told this GSFS major that their discussion of gender in their request for interviewees was problematic and they would not circulate the call. Of course, those responding knew that this student was completing their thesis under our direction, which made the intellectual work, as well as the student doing it, suspect–despite the fact that their approaches were in line with conventions in feminist, queer, and trans studies. Students' experiences only mattered insofar as they were rooted in vulnerability and perceptions of harm, as it was precisely this affective condition that allowed critiques of GSFS to persist.

As we were dealing with the ramifications of responses to our survey question, the Trans Affinity Group sent out a survey that included as the gender categories: male, female, non-binary, t-female, t-male, and other. As a reminder, the four critiques of our survey were that (1) it needed more gender categories (2) it did not include a fill-in-the-blank box and it "othered" students who had to fill in an "other" box (never mind that these positions are contradictory and that both are inaccurate) (3) it should have included the word "cis" and (4) trans is not a gender category and should not have been included. The Trans Affinity Group's survey included just one additional gender category than we did (non-binary), used the word "other" for the fill-in-the-blank box, did not include the word "cis," and included trans as a category, but in a way that was less capacious than our approach through which respondents could identify as trans and any other gender category, vs. simply t-female or t-male. In using the terms "male" and "female," the survey circulated by the Trans Affinity Group also contributes to the idea that the social condition of gender can be understood in biological terms, an idea feminist, queer, and trans studies scholars have readily critiqued. Of course, constructing survey questions around something as complex as sex/gender is really difficult and the failure of the TAG-approved survey to do anything radically different than the survey in question demonstrates this. It does not, however, indicate any transphobia.

The panic: TERFs or intersectionality?

The panic about TERFs in GSFS obscured as much as it revealed. For instance, articulating concrete steps for making the campus less transphobic was not prioritized. Perhaps more revealing, considering the survey's focus on intersectionality, is that race was brushed over in these conversations. Within our Intersectionality course, we spent the semester having complex conversations about the theory and its applications. We discussed genealogies of Black feminist thought and where intersectionality fit into these genealogies. We worked to identify the contradictory ways in which "intersectionality" discourses circulate in institutional diversity settings, activist spaces, and feminist studies. And, ultimately, through reading about what Jennifer Nash terms the "intersectionality wars," we noted the limits of commonsensical deployments of the term: that one can possess multiple marginalized identities simultaneously. Scholars writing in the veins of Black feminism and queer of color critique have cautioned against such identity-based applications of intersectionality, suggesting that the focus on individuals' race, class, gender, and other identity markers too often comes to stand in for a structural analysis of the mechanisms of racism, classism, sexism, and other forms of systemic inequities (Nash, 2008, 2019; Puar, 2007; Thomsen & Finley, 2019; Weigman, 2012).

Such texts and discussions could have helped students and DEI staff think through what it meant that Black students at the aforementioned dinner, who were connected to GSFS, remained unconvinced that the department was the problem that needed to be addressed. The Black students were not surprised, of course, that Black feminist thought was being ignored in a predominantly white and not terribly feminist institution—but the ignoring of race as part of a campaign to label feminist and lesbian scholars TERFs was an interesting sleight of hand, one that simultaneously recentered whiteness and made impossible critical discussions of intersectionality.

At precisely the time of the first meeting with the DEI staff member regarding our survey, their office was circulating a job call for an LGBTQ student affairs position that included intersectionality discourse. The call requested applicants "with an intersectional social justice lens" and with "knowledge of intersectionality and how to support students with multiple marginalized identities." Moreover, the call asks for

> applications from individuals with an understanding of the ways intersecting systems of oppression (e.g., racism, ableism, classism, heterosexism, cissexism, etc.) impact students from various underrepresented communities (e.g., students with disabilities, students of color, queer, transgender, firstgeneration, low-income, international, immigrant, undocumented, tribal and indigenous communities) and with the ability to provide culturally competent and inclusive support services.

It is not surprising that the institutional diversity office uses discourses of intersectionality, or that it does so in ways that ignore contestations around the term. What is surprising is that a posting for an "intersectional" LGBTQ student affairs position never uses the terms "woman" or "sexism," despite its long laundry lists of "intersecting systems of oppression" and members of "underrepresented communities." It is also surprising that no DEI staff attended the Beyond Intersectionality symposium, which could have informed their abilities to offer the "culturally competent and inclusive support services" they claim to provide. Arguably, if DEI staff do not recognize the category "woman" and that sexism continues to shape the lives of young women, as well as people of all genders, they are not providing "inclusive" services, just as their approaches could be more "competent" if they recognized the Black feminist genealogies out of which the terms they use emerged and the ongoing contestations around these terms. In short, we want to suggest that the anxieties driving claims that GSFS is TERFy are not disconnected from our organizing an academic conference that suggested that critical thinking around the somewhat sacred notion of "intersectionality" was crucial for developing anti-racist feminisms. The discomfort with the kinds of critical thinking that happen in feminist studies—which is at the heart of the matter—is precisely what generated attempts to discredit feminist scholars through labeling us TERFs. Of course, making feminists disappear is exactly what this moral panic over TERFs was meant to do.

Kill the feminist, kill the lesbian

The truth is that transness has been and is the object of deep hostility within some marginalized forms of feminism. Skepticism among earlier anti-trans feminists, such as Janice Raymond (1979), about transwomen being "real" women has morphed into JK Rowling's Twitter feed where she has insisted that transwomen are not women (Gardner, 2020). These ideas are, of course, deplorable, but they are also quite fringe within feminist studies and activism in the US. As trans studies scholar Grace Lavery notes, TERFs are "a minority of a minority of feminists" (Tiffany, 2020). Judith Butler recently articulated a similar point when asked about TERFs in an interview:

> I want to first question whether trans-exclusionary feminists are really the same as mainstream feminists…(M)ost feminists support trans rights and oppose all forms of transphobia. So I find it worrisome that suddenly the trans-exclusionary radical feminist position is understood as commonly accepted or even mainstream. I think it is actually a fringe movement that is seeking to speak in the name of the main-stream, and that our responsibility is to refuse to let that happen (Ferber, 2020).

Just as feminist, queer, and trans studies scholars are pushing back against the conflation of TERFs with feminists, so too are feminists beyond the academic sphere. Blogger Viv Smythe, who invented the term TERF, now says it should focus on "separatism" more than "feminism" since "(a) lot of the positions that are presented seem far too essentialist to be adequately described as feminist, let alone radical feminist" (2018).

Such conflations between the TERF and the feminist undergirded the case we examine here, a slippage that allows for "feminism"—not to mention lesbians and women—to become anachronistic. But what is really at stake in refusing to allow all feminists, feminism, and feminist studies to be made a thing of the past vis-a-vis the figure of the TERF? It is not simply that the outright dismissal of feminism's past requires a re-writing of history or that such re-writings work in the service of progress narratives (Hemmings, 2010). What is at stake in how we remember feminism, including radical feminism, is where we locate the potential for the kinds of critique, unruliness, and activities that can function as forms of social terror. Mairead Sullivan locates such potential in the radical feminist, the lesbian-as-feminist, who Sullivan notes was rarely transexclusionary. What makes the figure of the radical feminist a site of potential, Sullivan says, is that she refuses the role of the mother. To make this case, Sullivan analyzes early radical feminist texts, including Valerie Solanas' *SCUM Manifesto* (1967) and the less well-known "C.L.I.T. Papers," "to consider the spookiness, indeed the terror, of...the specter of destruction that the figure of the radical feminist contains" (2016, p. 272). Sullivan goes so far as to suggest that the radical feminist—a figure used to stand in for feminism's anachronism—is actually more destructive to the social order than the most beloved contemporary queer figures, including the sinthomosexual, the queer non-reproductive subject disinterested in the future of humanity made famous in Lee Edelman's *No Future* (2004). As Sullivan argues, "By claiming lesbianism as a structural position, rather than simply a personal identity or sexual practice, radical feminism names the threat that women's refusal of reproduction poses to the patriarchal machine, inaugurated and reinforced through the law of the heterosexual nuclear family" (p. 277). It is, as Sullivan suggests, the pairing of lesbian with feminist that strikes fear into the heart of patriarchal cultures and institutions, including ours.

An academic department composed primarily of lesbians is not in and of itself a threat to the patriarchal order, precisely because the non-feminist lesbian has been domesticated as a bride or mother. But the lesbian was once a revolutionary figure. As the Radical Lesbians famously claim in their 1970 manifesto, "A lesbian is the rage of all women condensed to the point of explosion." She was, as Valerie Solanis imagined, the kind of outsider who wanted to create a new society by cutting up men. Fifty years later, the lesbian as a radical figure is dead—in part because of the discursive conflation of radical lesbian/feminist and TERF and in part because of queer theory itself. When queer theory created the sinthomosexual as the space of non-reproductive possibilities, Sullivan notes, he was imagined as male. This figure necessarily ignores those who lived in radical and non-reproductive queer ways long before queer theory named the sinthomosexual, including radical lesbians/feminists. Scholars have explored this queer disregard for feminism, noting, that "the feminism against which queer theory defines itself is a feminism reduced almost to caricature: a feminism tied to a concern for gender, bound to a regressive and monotonous binary opposition. That reduction of feminist critique calls for analysis" (Weed & Schor, 1997, p. xi).

We, too, write against such reductions. It is, after all, the radical lesbian who refuses reproduction, disavows the child, and destroys the future. By refusing to mother students produced as fragile, and advocating instead for the radical potentials of feminist, queer, trans, and Black studies, lesbians became TERFs, feminists became TERFs, and feminist studies became TERFy. These slippages were not accidental. They represent how radical potential is conquered: through creating moral panics that can, in this case, only be solved by the DEI industry.

By constructing students as vulnerable subjects in need of protection, the diversity office set the stage for endless moral panics. The moment a faculty member, especially a woman-identified faculty member, refuses to engage in the work of "mothering," she risks becoming monstrous. And, as Sullivan urges us to see, nothing is more monstrous than the figure of the radical feminist. In the series of encounters that comprised the case study we discuss here, it became clear that the figure of the lesbian feminist refusing the needs of the child haunted our conversations. The DEI staff insisted that the professors had not taken care of the students' (read: the child's) feelings. We had refused to prioritize the feelings of students outside our department who insisted that feminist studies was a problem because we question taken-for-granted ideas about gender and sexuality. In fact, Thomsen overtly refused the role of good mother when, in one meeting, she insisted that "It is not my job to care about the feelings of every student on campus, especially those who aren't in my classes." With a look of confusion and contempt on their face, the DEI staff quickly responded, "Well, it is mine." In this moment, Thomsen found inspiration in the insights of Kyla Wazana Tompkins:

> Students come in with a lot of feelings. And of course as minoritarian teachers working in the age of the booming Student Affairs Industrial Complex, we are often expected to manage those feelings. But...managing feelings, particularly as it relates to various forms of injury IS NOT THE JOB OF THE TEACHER. As I tell my students over and over: your intuitions and feelings are what will lead you to original insight but they are not a substitute for thinking and working hard. Rather, they are the end of the psychic thread that you begin to pull at as you develop the ability to summarize and analyze the structures of thought, habits of mind, and analytic forms that undergird critical theory. What it feels like may make a bridge between you and theory and the world around us, but in my classroom we are largely going to model thinking about the last part of the tripartite clause. We are going to move from theory to the world, and not back to you...After all...the point of feminism was not to exacerbate our focus on the individual but rather to shift to structural and systemic thinking (2016).

The DEI industry and what Tompkins calls the Student Affairs Industrial Complex are, of course, close friends. Both have ignored the insights of feminist, queer, trans, and critical race studies that would complicate their assumptions. Both have also produced students as vulnerable subjects, incapable of engaging difficult subjects without trigger warnings, a survey question without intervention. In doing so, diversity officers produce the rationale for their existence.

The diversity industry will not save us

In *Diversity, Inc: The Failed Promise of a Billion-Dollar Business*, Pamela Newkirk traces the history of the diversity industry and outlines its results. Although academia, Hollywood, and corporate America have "renewed their commitment to diversity, collectively pledging billions of dollars to commission studies, set up training sessions, and hire consultants and czars to oversee diversity programs," these approaches, Newkirk says, have had little impact (2019, p. 5). She describes the outcomes of this multi-billion dollar industry as "chronically disappointing" (p. 5). Sophia Chen takes up the issue of diversity trainings, in particular, in a recent *Wired* article, in which she asks: Do they work? (2020). Her answer: "A lot of research suggests not." Chen cites sociologists Frank Dobbin and Alexandra Kalev, who analyzed three decades of data from 829 firms to argue that "the positive effects of diversity training rarely last beyond a day or two, and a number of studies suggest that it can activate bias or spark a back-lash." Considering the "toothlessness" of diversity trainings, Chen asks why the approach is so popular. Newkirk, who calls such trainings "drive-by diversity," responded: "It's easy" (Chen, 2020).

This easy approach is on full display at Middlebury, which in the last few years, has hired outside consultants to assess its diversity problems, committed additional resources to address issues of diversity (including hiring the two DEI staff involved in our case), and developed a long list of diversity workshops—despite the fact that research makes clear that the latter, in particular, do not do the work they set out to do. In Chen's critique of the diversity industry, she notes that some DEI staff continue to believe in the effectiveness of diversity training, especially if they are "ongoing" and "more than a one-off event." Chen provides as an example of this approach Columbia Professor Felicia Moore Mensah's semester-long course "designed to help K-12 teachers better support students of different racial and ethnic backgrounds" (2020).

Sustained engagement over time with critical ideas that challenge dominant ideas sounds a lot like what happens in feminist studies classrooms. Student interest in this kind of work recently has blossomed at Middlebury; we now have fifty majors or minors, triple the number from several years ago. In fact, we are one of just two Humanities programs to grow during this period, and the only program to grow to this degree, something notable at a moment when student involvement in the Humanities is waning both at Middlebury and nationwide. Despite this growth, GSFS has lost faculty lines. At this moment, the two authors of this article are the only tenure-track or tenured faculty members whose lines are primarily in GSFS.

At precisely the same time as we lost faculty lines, the College hired additional DEI staff as part of fulfilling their stated commitments to diversity efforts. How can we make sense of this stated commitment to diversity and expansion of the DEI work on campus alongside the defunding of GSFS, the very department on campus most likely to encourage critical thinking about the topics raised through the DEI machine? We want to suggest that, perhaps ironically, the increased circulation of diversity discourses, workshops, and requirements may make academic work in feminist, queer, trans, and Black studies appear less, rather than more, necessary. Put otherwise, if everyone is considered capable of doing diversity work, why do we need academic expertise? Because feminist studies is often not viewed as a discipline with discipline-specific knowledge (Soderling et al., 2018), the work that feminist studies does is often imagined as synonymous with the kind of diversity work being done in student affairs. At a public meeting, a colleague in Religious Studies suggested, for instance, that GSFS faculty could provide counseling to LGBTQ students. For some, we are too similar to DEI efforts—despite the fact that, as we have shown throughout this article, the forms of inquiry central to feminist, queer, and trans studies often run counter to those of the DEI industry.

Yet, for others, we are too threatening to these same social justice efforts. In fact, in what might seem a bizarre twist, DEI staff and TERFs are aligned in their taking aim at academic feminist studies. In an open letter in 2013, forty-eight self-identified radical feminists note that they are concerned about the rise of "gender theory" within "the academy" because, as they correctly note, feminist studies is a site for upending traditional ideas about gender ("Forbidden," 2013). While the DEI staff and a few students—bolstered by a broader multibillion dollar diversity industry—deployed the figure of the TERF to frame feminist, queer, and trans studies as anachronistic, and even a site of moral concern, actual self-identified TERFs made academic feminism itself the center of their moral panic. How ironic that real-life TERFs have a better grasp of feminist studies than do DEI staff at our own institution. The TERFs are right: What academic feminism is most guilty of is a refusal of easy answers. That this refusal could be interpreted as our not centering the child/student speaks to the degree to which our conversations were haunted by the figure of the bad mother, the lesbian, the radical feminist. Through being tethered to these ghostly figures, feminist studies professors were transmorgified into TERFs.

Such slippages aren't new. In fact, moral panics, on the left and right, often center on the child. Consider QAnon's rapidly expanding "Save the

Children" campaign. Although originally a right-wing conspiracy about a deep state pedophile ring led by Hillary Clinton, it has now convinced people from across the political spectrum that the furniture company Wayfair is selling children and that Netflix is involved in global pedophilic propaganda. This doesn't mean that child sexual abuse isn't real. It obviously is. But moral panics about non-existent global pedophile rings obscure the reality of sexual abuse, including that it primarily takes place within one's own familial networks. In much the same way, attacking lesbian feminists for being TERFs despite any evidence for such claims—other than that their expertise runs counter to more commonsensical understandings of sexuality and gender—makes it more difficult to take on the gendered ideologies that enable transphobia.

Just as we were finishing this article, the evil the DEI industry and earnest students sought to kill off returned. But this time the monster wasn't imagined TERFS. It was Peter Kreeft, an unapologetic anti-trans and anti-feminist idealogue and professor at Boston College, who was invited to speak on campus by a conservative religious student organization under the guise of the college's oft-repeated commitment to "free speech." His visit represents what we already know: transphobia is enabled by anti-feminist positions, and its eradication requires an ability to deconstruct gender ideologies. Positioning scholars who do this work as TERFs works in the service of transphobia. And this is something that should cause all of us to panic.

Acknowledgments

Special thanks to Abe Weil, CJ Jones, and four anonymous reviewers for feedback that dramatically improved our arguments. Our most profound thanks go Taite Shomo and Jules Struzyna, two former Gender, Sexuality, and Feminist Studies students whose feedback on previous drafts of this article was rooted in their weathering the storm about which we write alongside us. Their experiences defending their major inspired this article.

Disclosure of interest statement

The authors report no conflicts of interest. The authors alone are responsible for the content and writing of the paper.

References

Ahmed, S. (2007). A phenomenology of whiteness. *Feminist Theory, 8*(2), 149–168. https://doi.org/10.1177/1464700107078139

Ahmed, S. (2017). *Living a feminist life*. Duke University Press.

Briggs, L. (2008). Activisms and epistemologies: Problems for transnationalisms. *Social Text, 26*(4), 79–95. https://doi.org/10.1215/01642472-2008-012

Butler, J. (1990). *Gender trouble: Feminism and the subversion of identity*. Routledge.

Chen, S. (2020, July 14). The equity-diversity-inclusion industrial complex gets a makeover. *Wired*. https://www.wired.com/story/the-equity-diversity-inclusion-industrial-complex-gets-a-makeover/

Cohen, S. (1973). Folk Devils and Moral Panics. MacGibbon and Kee Ltd. https://read.dukeupress.edu/social-text/article-abstract/38/4%20(145)/125/167832/Thinking-with-Trans-Now?redirectedFrom=PDF

Cohen, C. (1997). Punks, bulldaggers, and welfare queens: The radical potential of queer politics?*Glq: A Journal of Lesbian and Gay Studies, 3*(4), 437–465. https://doi.org/10.1215/10642684-3-4-437

Cohen, S. (2011). *Folk devils and moral panics*. Routledge.

Edelman, L. (2004). *No future*. Duke University Press.

Eng, D., & Puar, J. (2020). Introduction: Left of queer. *Social Text, 38*(4), 1–23. (Quoting Eliza Steinbock). https://doi.org/10.1215/01642472-8680414

Enke, F. (2012). The Education of Little Cis: Cisgender and the Discipline of Opposing Bodies. Transfeminist Perspectives: In and Beyond Transgender and Gender Studies (pp. 60–77). Temple University Press.

Ferber, A. (2020, October 22). Judith Butler on the culture wars, JK Rowling and living in 'anti-intellectual' times. *New Statesman*.https://www.newstatesman.com/international/2020/09/judith-butler-culture-wars-jk-rowling-and-living-anti-intellectual-times

Forbidden discourse: The silencing of feminist criticism of 'gender'. (2013, April 12). http://meetinggroundonline.org/wp-content/uploads/2013/10/GENDER-Statement-InterActive-930.pdf

Gardner, A. (2020, October 12). A complete breakdown of the J.K. Rowling transgender comments controversy. *Glamour*. https://www.glamour.com/story/a-complete-breakdown-of-the-jk-rowling-transgender-comments-controversy

Hemmings, C. (2010). *Why stories matter: The political grammar of feminist theory*. Duke University Press.

Mitchell, G. (2016). Evangelical ecstasy meets feminist fury: Sex trafficking, moral panics, and homonationalism during global sporting events. *Glq: A Journal of Lesbian and Gay Studies, 22*(3), 325–357. https://doi.org/10.1215/10642684-3479306

Nash, J. (2008). Re-thinking intersectionality. *Feminist Review, 89*(1), 1–15. https://doi.org/10.1057/fr.2008.4

Nash, J. (2019). *Black feminism reimagined*. Duke University Press.

Newkirk, P. (2019). *Diversity, Inc.: The failed promise of a billion-dollar business*. Bold Type Books.

Puar, J. (2007). *Terrorist assemblages*. Duke University Press.

Raymond, J. (1979). *The trans sexual empire: The making of the she-male*. Beacon Press.

Rubin, G. (2006). Thinking sex: Notes for a radical theory of the politics of sexuality. In P. Aggleton & R. Parker (Eds.), *Culture, society, and sexuality* (pp. 143–178). Routledge.

Scott, J. (1991). The evidence of experience. *Critical Inquiry, 17*(4), 773–797. https://doi.org/10.1086/448612

Smythe, V. (2018, November 28). I'm credited with having coined the word 'Terf'; Here's how it happened. *The Guardian*. https://www.theguardian.com/commentisfree/2018/nov/29/im-credited-with-having-coined-the-acronym-terf-heres-how-it-happened

Soderling, S., Thomsen, C., & White, M. (2018). Critical mass, precarious value? Reflections on the gender, women's, and feminist studies Ph.D. in Austere Times. *Feminist Studies, 44*(2), 229–251. https://doi.org/10.15767/feministstudies.44.2.0229

Solanas, V. (1967). *Scum manifesto*. Olympia Press.

Sullivan, M. (2016). Kill daddy: Reproduction, futurity, and the survival of the radical feminist. *WSQ: Women's Studies Quarterly, 44*(1–2), 268–282. https://doi.org/10.1353/wsq.2016.0012

Táíwò, O. (2020). Being-in-the-room privilege: Elite capture and epistemic deference. *The Philosopher, 108*(4). https://www.thephilosopher1923.org/essay-taiwo

Tiffany, K. (2020, August 12). The secret internet of TERFs. *The Atlantic*. https://www.theatlantic.com/technology/archive/2020/12/reddit-ovarit-the-donald/617320/ (Quoting Grace Lavery).

Tompkins, K. W. (2016). We aren't here to learn what we already know. *Avidly*. https://avidly.lareviewofbooks.org/2016/09/13/we-arent-here-to-learn-what-we-know-we-already-know/

Thomsen, C., & Finley, J. (2019). On intersectionality: A review essay. *Hypatia, 34*(1), 155–160. https://doi.org/10.1111/hypa.12450

Weed, E., & Schor, N. (1997). *Feminism meets queer theory*. Indiana University Press.

Weigman, R. (2012). *Object lessons*. Duke University Press.

"Lezibian/mulezi": adoption of "globalized" lesbian identity and secondary self-labels among same-sex attracted women in Harare

Nelson Muparamoto

ABSTRACT

Drawing from ethnographic research, incorporating informal conversations, semi-structured interviews and a focus group discussion, the paper explores the subjective meanings and construction of the "lesbian" identity in a "hostile" environment among selected same-sex attracted women in Harare. While the globally circulating identity labels are loaded with historical baggage which can be limiting or confusing in non-western contexts, most of the study participants related to some of the labels that are prominent in the present-day, western-inspired global discourse on same-sex relations. Self-styling and the quest to exhibit masculine decorum was a central aspect in the narratives of most "butch" identifying women. For most butch identifying women being lesbian was closely interwoven with considerations about one's gendered self. However not all participants were comfortable with the circulating identity labels as they found them restrictive and loaded. While subjective preferences of the participants demonstrate complexity in how "lesbianism" is locally constructed and experienced, the lesbian identity is certainly not obsolete in Harare among same-sex attracted women.

Introduction

Substantial work shows that queer identities and non-heteronormative sexualities have increasingly become visible globally and Zimbabwe has witnessed an emergent queer mobilization and sexual identities politics (Muparamoto, 2020). However, post-colonial Zimbabwe has witnessed a protracted history of homophobia, vilification and marginalization toward same sex attracted individuals championed by political, religious, and indigenous pressure group leaders (Campbell, 2002; Epprecht, 1998; Muparamoto, 2020; Youde, 2017). Same sex attraction has been demonized and constructed as both "uncultural" and "unchristian." Not only have there been homophobic utterances but in some cases it translated to violent attacks and raids/intrusions on organized "queer" folks private functions and offices belonging to GALZ (Muparamoto & Moen, 2021). GALZ is the oldest LGBTI organization founded around the year 1990. Until 2013, it was known as Gays and Lesbians of Zimbabwe. The change to just GALZ was made to reflect the diverse identities which the organization represents. The homocritical narratives and struggles for recognition of gender and sexuality diverse individuals are not uniquely Zimbabwean as a number of scholars have explored how LGBTI activism in most parts of Africa occupies a complex and precarious position uncritically disparaged through the "homosexuality-is-un-African" mantra characteristic of nationalist and often anti-western rhetorics of postcolonial African leaders (Chitando & Mateveke, 2017; Currier & Migraine-George, 2017; Mateveke, 2019).

Scholarship on gender and sexuality diversity in Zimbabwe (Campbell, 2002; Epprecht, 2005, 2004, 1999, 1998; Gunda, 2010; Phillips, 2003; Shoko, 2010) has hardly focused on identity construction as much of the work either concentrated on rejecting the claim that homosexuality is foreign, the morality or immorality of homosexuality and the "homophobic" utterances of the society without delving into the lived experiences of the actors they pertain to. However, emerging scholarship (Muparamoto & Moen, 2020) has shown that notwithstanding the history of political homophobia in Zimbabwe globally circulating identity labels have been adopted by same sex attracted men in Harare. These labels are seemly popularized through processes associated with globalization, the proliferation of social media and entertainment industry depicting social and cultural identities from other contexts where queer identities are visible. Work by Altman (1997) and Kole (2007) among others has shown how images of queer sexualities and cultures based upon western-style "gayness" circulate globally.

Whilst scholarship on identity construction among gender and sexuality diverse individuals in Zimbabwe is in its infancy, focus has been on same-sex attracted men rather than same-sex attracted women which could also reflect the bias influenced by the biomedical approaches which have constructed gay men as highly vulnerable to HIV. Hildebrandt and Chua (2017) draw attention to what they call the political economy of in/visibility (political visibility), which includes being, "seen and heard by constituents whom activists represent and by state agents, and being known, recognized, tolerated and engaged by the latter to differing degrees." In Zimbabwe gay men have been included in policy and practice in HIV programming under the Global Fund Grant 2018–2020 for key populations. The predominance of the biomedical approach has marginalized same-sex attracted women as it is not centered on identity formation and identity politics. Matebeni (2008) notes that much work that is written about black lesbians often positions them as victims of violence and hate crimes, while Currier and Migraine-George (2017) attest that understandings of "African lesbian sexualities" have been affected by silence, repression and uncertainties. The paper seeks to begin to center the experiences of same-sex attracted women in Harare beyond their invisibility and victimization by focusing on identity construction. The paper explores the adoption and subjective construction of the "lesbian" category in Harare and the use and meanings of the secondary self-labels adopted by same-sex attracted women.

African queer studies

In Africa, much of the scholarship on queer African studies has remained predominantly located in South Africa (Currier & Migraine-George, 2017). A number of factors could have contributed to this skewness, such as the open official political homophobia in other countries (Zimbabwe included), the impact of the colonizers ideals on sexuality and heterosexism in the academia which marginalized queer studies. The field of queer studies has also been accused of being loaded with terminology and theoretical underpinnings that are not indigenous (Chitando and Mateveke, 2019). This has given ammunition to protagonist denouncing acceptance and tolerance of same sex relations on the basis that its "unAfrican," thus uncultural. To this end there has been a recurrent call to decolonize queer studies and abandon western concepts and categories when writing about same sex relations. It remains to be seen whether utilization of "African" concepts will contribute toward acceptance as homophobia is complexly entrenched beyond the language issue. While queer African scholarship is growing on the continent, Currier and Migraine-George (2017) bemoan that "same-sex interactions, relationships, and politics between African women have not garnered significant attention either in feminist/queer studies or in African studies and remain largely unrepresented in academic writings." Mateveke (2019) and Currier and Migraine-George (2017) among others have illustrated the uneasy and complex relationship between African feminism and African lesbian women which ranges from outright silence, timid allyship and in rare cases open support by the former toward the latter. Among other works, Reygan (2016) analysis of the Cape Town gay media also critiques the non-representation of black lesbians which is linked to the long history of lesbian invisibility in South Africa.

Methodological note

This paper builds on ethnographic research (2013–2016) focusing on the lived experiences of same-sex attracted men and women in Zimbabwe (for a detailed description of the study and methods see Muparamoto & Moen, 2020). Data was collected in Harare the capital city of Zimbabwe, where GALZ has its head office. While during fieldwork there was interaction with more than 200 same-sex attracted people, a core group of 31 study participants was recruited through purposive and snowballing sampling which was however not restricted to GALZ membership. This paper is based on interactions with 11 same-sex attracted women who were part of the core group. Most of the participants identified as "lesbian" which however did not imply uniformity in how they perceived being a lesbian. They were aged between 20 and 30 years, with most having had some level of formal schooling. 5 of the study participants were studying at local universities, while a few were employed formally and informally. Generally, the ethnic, social, religious and economic background of the participants were diverse. Some were actively religious while some had opted out of organized religion but were still spiritual (Muparamoto, 2016). At the time of data collection none of the same-sex attracted women were members of GALZ, though nearly half of them regularly attended educational and social functions organized by GALZ exposing them to LGBTI activism. However the other participants had heard about GALZ through their social networks but had never been at an event organized by GALZ or their offices. Data was collected through informal conversations, semi-structured interviews and a focus group discussion (FGD). Informal conversations referred to the casual conversations that were ongoing during participant observation. These conversations happened in "natural" settings, for example in connection with educational and social gatherings organized by GALZ (Muparamoto & Moen, 2020). 11 formal semi-structured interviews were conducted with women who are attracted to other women at venues that were perceived as safe and convenient for the participants. While each participant was interviewed once, in some cases there was additional interaction through social media platforms such as WhatsApp and Facebook messenger. Some participants who had participated in semi-structured interviews also participated in the FGD. The study protocol was reviewed and approved by the Medical Research Council of Zimbabwe.

Limitations

While the study provides a contextualized understanding of the adoption of the lesbian category to describe same sex attracted women in Harare, it also has some limitations. I am cisgender male researcher which could potentially distort my understanding of some of the issues that were pertinent to same-sex attracted women. To counter this, I deliberately had numerous discussions (member-checking) with insiders in the writeup of the doctoral thesis to ensure that I had understood the meanings. The study also relied on a small sample of purposively and snowballed urban group with exposure to differing levels of queer politics and familiarity with some western terminology. The study results could have been different had there been a deliberate approach to recruit participants through emerging transgender organizations. There is need for a broader study which captures same sex attracted women in their diversity to deepen understanding offered by this exploratory study.

Findings and discussion

Subjective identities

Multiple labels were used by same-sex attracted people (men and women) to identify themselves and their colleagues. The "lesbian category" was alive and in widespread use in Harare among the study participants. A number of secondary labels such as butch, femme, stud, futch, dyke, lipstick among others were also in use though the first two were predominant and will be discussed latter. While Muparamoto and Moen (2020) note that alongside the Anglo-Saxon labels were a number of local terms such as *ngotshani, inkotshani, stabane, ordaa, bhutsu, gumutete, ngengirosi, mwana waEliza/waEriza* which were variously used by same-sex attracted men, the same could not be said about same-sex attracted women. It was difficult to come across participants who preferred to refer to equivalent local terms except when reflecting on how the society calls them *ngochani, ngito or malele* which are derogatory/mocking. In some rare cases participants could use descriptors such as *kunge mukomana* (like a boy).

Lesbian identity

Women whose primary sexual and emotional attachments were to persons of the same gender were familiar with and had adopted the label lesbian which is in wide circulation globally. Study participants often identified themselves as lesbian, which could be pronounced as *lezibian or mulezi* in local parlance. Most participants positively constructed their subjective identities. Chibaba Tindo (21 years) affirmatively responded saying, *"I am very proud butch lesbian."* Similarly, Chibaba Nikkaz (20 years), who was recruited to be part of this study after posting details on a social media platform embraced the lesbian category.

Chibaba Nikkaz: I am a proud black lesbian, I am proud of myself

NM: You posted your details without hiding your identity on Facebook on the GALZ site, looking for a femme. If I may ask, why did you do it publicly?

Chibaba Nikkaz: I was tired of being silent about it, it's who I am, and it's all about choices. I am a proud black lesbian who wants to be happy, that's me.

Predominantly participants identified themselves as lesbians and demonstrated the permeability and porosity of borders and goes beyond the narrative of victimhood[1]. President Mugabe and his supporters had constructed and sustained a narrative that situated LGBTI persons and rights as foreign and western, which portrayed them inimical to a genuine Zimbabwean identity (Youde, 2017). Participants not only affirmed their subjective identities as "proud lesbians," but also challenged the dominant rhetoric which had not only castigated such identities but had denounced homosexual identities as antithetical to Zimbabwean identity. By drawing on being a "proud black lesbian," the participant actively challenges popular rhetoric stemming from political homophobia constructing same-sex attraction such as lesbianism as for "white" women. Additionally posting on a Facebook page with a real account/identity challenges invisibility as well as attempts to extirpate same-sex attracted women from the Zimbabwean polity by associating it with neocolonialism and colonial relics. Weeks (2007) points out that identities can be sites of contestation as they multiply points of resistance, as reflected in the use of social media in broadcasting one's sexual identity and adoption of the castigated identity.

Construction of lesbianism

When asked what it meant to be a lesbian, study participants often emphasized their emotional and physical attraction to other women. As an example, Madzimai Trish (23 years) explained
how she was attracted to women.

Madzimai Trish: Well I'm a femme lesbian

NM: What does it mean to say you are a femme lesbian?

Madzimai Trish: I am... I'm interested in girls, and...

NM: Well, I'm interested in girls too!

Madzimai Trish: (laughs) well I'm attracted to girls. I'm attracted to girls, and I'm not attracted to men. I guess that's what makes me a lesbian. Emotionally, physically, everything I'm attracted to girls... that's what makes me lesbian.

Additionally, some participants expressed how they loved other women and did not have any feelings for men in their construction of lesbianism.

.... I just like girls. Uuum my sexuality is I love girls (laughs) and men for me are just not there. (Madzimai Quality, 22 years).

In Harare a significant marker of lesbianism was that one had to show desire and attraction to women and not to men which challenged the conventional heterosexual script of a woman's desire. By constructing their sexual intimacy in this way, participants challenged heteropatriarchy and its associated conventions regulating female desire and questioning the role of the nation state in regulating the erotic spaces.

Secondary self-labels: "Butch and femme lesbian"

As indicated before several secondary self-labels were in circulation among the participants in Harare, with butch and femme being predominantly used. Despite the terms "butch" and "femme" having North American origin most study participants comfortably identified with these secondary self-labels. Inness and Lloyd (1995) attest that, "scholarship has focused on the butch-femme dyad, usually either emphasizing its historical significance for the lesbian community or decrying it as an outdated imitation of patriarchal gender roles that fails to embody feminist values." Despite contestations over the use, meaning and utility of these terms they have persisted over the years. Matebeni (2011) notes that any thesis involving lesbians which does not make reference to "butch" and "femme" is heavily criticized as these have become central terms.

Butch identities

While there is a wide range of ideas that women have about what constitutes "butchness" (Inness & Lloyd, 1995), in most studies the butch lesbian is associated with deployment and manipulation of masculine gender codes and symbols (Crawley, 2001; Inness & Lloyd, 1995). A number of participants in this study identified as butch lesbian and were more visible and accessible compared to women who identified as femme. The meaning of butch in this context was mainly constructed to refer to women who experienced sexual attraction toward other women and in most cases perceived themselves as the dominant partners. Some of the participants perceived themselves not just as women who love other women but as men in their relationships. At the time of the study, representation for the transgender community was in and probably is still in its infancy in Zimbabwe, which has also been compounded by adoption epidemiological terms such as men who have sex with men (MsM) and women who have sex with women (WsW) in HIV interventions.

Thus, while some of the narratives that follow may appear to describe transmen participants did not use transgender terminology to describe themselves.

The narratives shared by participants shows how butch identifying women appropriated masculinity to challenge the cultural scripts on being a woman, thus demonstrating how the borders, despite desired attempts to make them impermeable, can be stretched to allow agentic beings to express themselves. Sanger and Lynch (2018) in their study based in South Africa note that in generally, participants' talk revolved around gendered scripts, which were largely aligned to conventional binary notions of normative heterosexual masculinity and femininity. Whereas there has been an attack on butch identity in feminist scholarship (Crawley, 2001), as well as in this current study by some femme participants, several participants comfortably identified as butch and expected to be treated as men in their relationships with other women. Butch lesbian identity was associated with adoption of practices and behaviors that are noncompliant to expected feminine traits in their broader local cultural setting but with the adoption of behavior consistent with masculine trends.

> I see myself as man, but I know that my girl is not that and I try to meet her half-way and treat her the way she expects that girl thing... (Chibaba Thando, 30years)

Similarly, another participant laid claims on masculinity;

> Me, being a butch I really felt like yes, I'm man now, that I have achieved those things that I have. As a man I have someone who has accepted me being a butch girl attracted to other girls and somebody had accepted that, it really meant a lot to me (Chibaba Tindo)

The participants' construction of butch shows that while they linked to the heteronormative scripts, they disrupted heterosexuality by adopting subjective gendered lesbian positions. By transcending the traditional gender categories butch identifying women challenge the traditional gender distinction by appropriating masculinity which is perceived as inherently a male attribute (Levitt & Hiestand, 2004; Matebeni, 2011). Additionally, as pointed out by Sanger and Lynch (2018) inhabiting multiple spaces of marginality makes the adoption of heteronormative ways of being more desirable, highly valued and rewarded.

To further stake their claim on a butch identity which most respondents associated with being a man in the relationship some of the butch identifying women spoke about how they were involved in multiple concurrent partnerships as an attribute associated with masculinity.

Allow me to say I have watched someone I liked very much but failing to get me satisfied so I would have three or four girlfriends just like any other normal man I am normal, just like any other straight person (Chibaba Nikkaz)

Similarly, another participant shares how having multiple partners could be seen as a rite of passage for butch women.

I think that for any other lesbian it's just a time when things are just going so well you don't even care it's just all about cheating or having so many chicks (female partners), so we were just talking and she did say *"iwewe uri hure"* (you are promiscuous), "like you have got so many chicks" …. I always look at it like it was a phase I had to feel because I was so immature now it's not something that I even think of coz (because) as much as I am a 'guy' but women are so complicated so to have four is always going to bring problems, so I would like to work on myself and have one woman to please her, be a good lover, have a good home, and have a good wife but yaah. I should say most butches consider themselves as men as I have said already maybe want to have a lot of girlfriends maybe possible wives but I have passed that stage I'm all good with one (Chibaba Natsi, 26 years)

Thus, the narrative was that it was desirable and something to strive for at a certain point in time for butch identifying women to have multiple concurrent partners in authenticating their claims to masculinity. This however tends to reinforce the idea that butch lesbians fit and reinforce the traditional heterosexual masculine role characterized by less restrictions on what men can do.

Butch esthetics

Butch esthetics have considerably varied through different historical epochs. Self-styling among lesbians refers to dress, demeanor, clothing, stance, activity, eroticism and language (Matebeni, 2011). As pointed out by Matebeni (2011), clothing and appearance play dynamic functions in a black lesbian body. Most of the study participants who identified as butch were conscientious about self-styling with regards to clothing in marking and constructing a butch identity. Most participants rejected clothing styles that traditionally depicted femininity in preference to dressing constructed as masculine. Many of the butch participants indicated that they do not dress in feminine clothes, skirts and dresses were not something to be expected in their wardrobe. For instance, Chibaba Ryan said that *"No I have never worn a dress in my life, not in my wardrobe."* Clothes do constitute markers that are put in place by the society as they determine what is feminine and what is masculine. Transgressing the clothing border offered an opportunity for participants to stake their claim to a butch identity.

It's not part of my wardrobe, I don't even have a single skirt in my wardrobe although I have a twin sister who doesn't wear trousers at all, not even shorts. She

puts on dresses and skirts, but I don't have even a single skirt in my wardrobe
...... So whenever I had to go to school I had to make sure I will be putting a
little short like yaah those sports attire shorts inside, then just after we finished
school I just had to remove the dress yaah like wearing the shirt and the short.
(Chibaba Lee, 23 years).

Not only did the desire to self-style in a way that sustains masculine
decorum influence the wardrobe but also the spaces that participants could
go to by avoiding places such as "conservative churches" that required
them to dress in ways that have been constructed as feminine. "Space"
was not neutral for some participants who were conscious that people
would perceive them as contravening the hetero-gendered scripts in an
environment where this was demonized.

I used to go to church so much, I even started a choir, Youth for Christ, but I can
say now because of who we are I couldn't go because I have grown much more
older and I started dressing more like a man, and in my neighborhood there are
more whites and colored's[2] and they know somebody who dresses like this should
be gay, so they would pass out comments I don't feel comfortable (Chibaba Natsi)

The participant's reflection on race feeds into the uncritical widely circulated narrative positioning same-sex attraction as tolerable among "white"
people compared to "indigenous black Zimbabweans." However, while butch
self-styling could contribute to undesirable "gaze" in some spaces, it also
served to generate interest among potential partners. Masculine self-styling
enabled butch participants to build a desired identity in which they marked
themselves as different from other woman to draw the attention of women
(either femme or "straight" women). Participants indicated how most women
who are considered as straight get fascinated by their clothing.

Most people like my dressing *inongoita kuti vanhu vaite* attention (it's unique for a
woman and draws attention) and people start asking then some random girl comes
asking, sometimes it's just out of the blue. In the night clubs, girls invite me for
dances (Chibaba Runyararo, 28 years).

Not only was self-styling key in attracting women but also acting as a
visible marker to dissuade men who may have intentions of wooing them.
The transcript below reflects how some butch participants could tease and
ward off men who approached them given their masculine self-styling.

Like I have no problem if some man calls me. This other day I was walking from
the shops (supermarket) and this guy calls on me to wait for him I'm like *ndoto-
kumirira uum like mhanya shamari totofanba toenda* (make it snappy I'm waiting
so that we walk along), then the guy says I like you, and I'm like uum really *asi
uri ngochani kani aaaaaah chii chakunakidza pandiri takangopfeka zvakafanana step
yedu yakafanana* (are you gay, what has attracted you, isn't it I'm just dressed like
you, I walk just like you) maybe you gay or something (Chibaba Lee).

Zway and Boonzaier (2015) explore how in South Africa participants constructed positive lesbian identities through participation in embodied activities such as soccer, *pantsula* dancing and other activities. Similarly in this study, besides clothing, some of the participants also constructed a butch identity by narrating their participation in traditionally masculine sporting activities that required muscular physiological activity such as professional soccer, rugby and cricket.

Femme lesbian

Sanger and Lynch (2018) observed that in South Africa, their study participants drew on a binary logic of gender that constructed butch and femme lesbian identities as complementary. Within such a binary logic, identifying as a femme lesbian entailed association with subservience, acquiescence and responsiveness to a masculine partners' needs (Sanger & Lynch, 2018). As much as the construction of butch subcategory is complex, the femme category presents no less challenge. While it was not difficult to come across butch identifying lesbians, the same could not be said for women who identified as "femme." The few participants who embraced femme lesbian identity, were comfortable with that label and made efforts to show how consistent their lifestyles are to that identity. "*Ok I would describe myself as a femme. The one who like takes feminine roles when two women are dating*" (Madzimai Maka, 21 years). This aptly sums the narratives that were shared by the participants about how they constructed being femme.

> In the lesbian society we have the femme and we have the butch. The femme is someone like me who is the girly type if I can say the girly type of a lesbian, and the butch is the tough one, that guy-ish lesbian. That's how you can manage to differentiate between a femme and a butch. (Madzimai Trish)

Similarly, another participant shares similar concerns.

> :...I'm not butch, I'm femme because I'm female... uuum I still have that female in me that whole lady in me okay. It doesn't mean that if I want to date a girl, I want to become the man no. I'm still a girl and I still deserve, I'm still that girl. I'm still a girl but I just like girls (Madzimai Quality).

The participants constructed their femme identity by contrasting it with butch. Despite seemingly reinforcing the conventional relationship between sex and gender, femmes did challenge the meaning of and existent heterosexual script of a woman's desire. By channeling their sexual and emotional desires to other women, femmes did stretch the often-fixed link between gender and sexual orientation by being attracted to women (Eves, 2004).

Additionally, some femme identifying women perceived being butch as just imitation of men and given a choice they would not date a butch lesbian. They questioned, why one would want to be a man and act like a man? As argued by Eves (2004) the process of claiming a lesbian identity involves reflexivity and choice. The narrative by some participants was that if lesbianism is an identity of choice, why would one settle for an identity that depicts a man if she is a woman. As Madzimai Quality said:

> In Zimbabwe well, butch would be... for me honestly my argument is why would you want to be a butch? If you are going to be dressing up like a guy, the reason why I am a lesbian is I want to see you in a short skirt, wearing a dress but you are wearing jeans and timberlands.

Local labels—kunge mukomana/like a guy

When participants were asked whether there were vernacular words to depict the distinction between femme and butch in a focus group discussion. Participants referred to a descriptor that would mainly be used for butch identifying women.

> NM: I was also thinking of this distinction between butch and femme, do you have any words for that in Shona?

> Respondent 2: People usually just say *"uyu anoita kunge mukomana"* (she is just like a guy)

> Respondent 1: And also because what we are doing is already considered as English, you know there won't be terms for that because *chachirungu* (it's western), it's already British or whatever it's English or it's western. So people would not find expressions for that because it's already English.

> NM: But in Shona if you leave aside the sexuality how do you describe a woman who looks manly, are there any terms for that?

> Respondent 1: It's just tomboy, *arikuita kunge mukomana* (they look like a guy/ man)... (laughs) *arikuita kunge ngochani* (they look homosexual).

At the time of the interview, there seemed to be no word in the vernacular that could be used to distinguish between femme and butch apart from labeling women who looked masculine as being like a guy/man. While GALZ has adopted the term *Sahwira* in its publications as a local idiom to depict intimate friends (Chitando & Mateveke, 2017), among the participants it was not mentioned. Thus, while there are calls to Africanize the discourse on gender and sexuality diversity, in Zimbabwe, where antecedent "identities" may not have existed, vernacular terms may be difficult to find apart from those that described the same-sex practices albeit in a derogatory way.

Just different

Not all women who participated in the study embraced and neatly fitted into the popularized lesbian category. Some participants interrogated the categories or did cross the boundaries of the subcategories and preferred to be identified as different.

> Chibaba Ryan: I told her I'm different, I don't like it when people call me gay or lesbian, I prefer different, I don't like the labeling in it like the stereotypes with the name, so when people call me different I like it because it's so cool.
>
> NM: So if you were to say you are different on campus will people know?
>
> Chibaba Ryan: They won't, like yesterday I was in town in a mall, so I saw some girls in a mall and they were looking at me and saying wow, are you a guy? And I said no and they said, are you a lady? And I said yes I am and they said no and I just said I'm different, so they can't really tell what it means.
>
> NM: So if you were to explain to me what's inside that word, 'different'?
>
> Chibaba Ryan: Oh that word, it shows I like different things from what people call maybe normal just like different when it comes to things such as love, sex or even gender and so on.

Thus, instead of self-identifying as a lesbian, Chibaba Ryan felt that the label "different" had a better meaning than the widely accepted term "lesbian." The concern was that with labels there is always potential for stereotypes and some labels are marginalized and designate something inferior.

> Yaah the labels is what I don't like because they are stereotypes, I feel sometimes gay or lesbian is synonymous with lesser in society. It's like you are down and under there in the society, so that's what I hate. So most of the time, my girlfriend knows that I work very hard to be on top, I want high standards, I want to show the world that we are capable of doing great things, being different doesn't mean we are not capable just like straight people (Chibaba Ryan).

Jenkins (2008) notes that identity can imply social position and status. The "border wars" on sexual identity in Zimbabwe have been systematically and hierarchically structured with same-sex attracted people marginalized and considered less human by the most vocal groups (Muparamoto, 2020). Rejection of the lesbian category was thus inspired by the desire to reject the societal perceptions of classifying gender and sexuality diverse people as incapable of normal functionality.

Fluidity of identities

Hall (1996) proposes that identity should be perceived as being in a constant flux as it is never fully fledged or complete. Madzimai Maka's narrative shows how fluid identities can be as participants resist being pigeon-holed into static categories. While Madzimai Maka identified as femme for the greater part of the fieldwork, in follow up discussions the preference had shifted.

> Madzimai Maka: Haaaa but what I said in the scripts and what I identify now is different unless you want me to explain things according to those scripts (laughs)

> NM: What do you mean different. I doubt if you remember the scripts well, might as well go with the present.

> Madzimai Maka: By different I mean tt tym (that time) I identified as femme but now I identify myself as butch. I remember them so well

> NM: What a transformation, what led to that?

> Madzimai Maka: (laughs) not really a transformation (laughs) I just changed labels, but labels don't really matter...f u (if you) ever noticed my dressing had *olwez bn tt* (always been that) of a butch so haa I just thought I should just transform it and seize tu b (to be) femme

> NM: Yaa labels are socially constructed but how you feel is more important.

> Madzimai Maka: Exactly so labels distract people, so really wanna identify myself as a woman who is attracted to other women.

Consistent with Oppong's (2013) observation on the self that it can be perceived as transitory and adaptable as Madzimai Maka's subjective positions challenge primordialist assumptions on identity and shows its fluidity and malleability. The fluid nature of same-sex attractions stretches the traditional conceptualization of what women can do and can become.

Conclusion

Despite the absence of significant affirmation through supportive socio-cultural and legal structures of the lesbian identity in Zimbabwe, study participants in Harare were mostly familiar with and embraced it. Participants had the agency to go beyond popularized victimhood by "proudly" claiming and affirming their same-sex desires and identified with the globalized lesbian identity and its secondary self-labels such as butch and femme which have origins in North America.

Firstly, in the study, participants constructed lesbianism as almost exclusively the absence of sexual, emotional and physical attraction to men but desire for women. Largely, being lesbian in Harare was closely interwoven with considerations about one's gendered self particularly for butch identifying lesbians. It was common for butch identifying participants to refer to themselves as a man and embraced hegemonic masculinity. Similar to other contexts, in Harare masculine decorum and practices were central to claiming an "authentic" butch lesbian identity, which could be expressed through clothing preferences and normalizing multiple concurrent partnerships. While one could perceive the butch identity as imitating heterosexual masculinity, the identity did challenge and stretch what it means to be a woman. Femme identifying participants while expressing their same-sex desire, they largely constructed it in contrast to butch.

Secondly, while a number of participants could easily relate to the lesbian category and the associated secondary self-labels, it is of import to note that some narratives challenged and problematized this during fieldwork, as some preferred not to be identified as lesbian. Being identified with widely circulated same-sex identity labels in Zimbabwe invoked feelings of inferiority, marginality and less value, hence rejecting the lesbian label was an attempt to shrug this off. Thus, as argued by Muparamoto and Moen (2020), the dominant Anglo-American labels that circulate in a globalized world are not simply copied and pasted by people but can perhaps better be regarded as inputs in the always ongoing process people engage in of figuring out who they are in relation to local realities.

In conclusion, while there is provocative problematization of the lesbian identity as obsolete, in Harare the lesbian identity is very much alive. The stories told by study participants and the terms they use to refer to themselves and each other testify of the adoption of the globally circulated lesbian identity label and secondary self-labels among same-sex attracted women in Harare.

Notes

1. There is often told portrayal of non-gender conforming women being victims, who are castigated and go underground as if they do not have agency.
2. People of mixed race are often referred to in popular Zimbabwean lingo as coloureds.

Funding

International Association for the Study of Sexuality, Culture and Sexuality.

References

Altman, D. (1997). Global Gaze/Global Gays. *GLQ: A Journal of Lesbian and Gay Studies*, 3(4), 417–436. https://doi.org/10.1215/10642684-3-4-417

Campbell, H. (2002). *Homophobia in Zimbabwe or the politics of intolerance: Occasional paper series* (Vol. 6). Pretoria: AAPS.

Chitando, E., & Mateveke, P. (2017). Africanizing the discourse on homosexuality: Challenges and prospect. *Critical African Studies*, 9(1), 124–140. https://doi.org/10.108 0/21681392.2017.1285243

Crawley, S. L. (2001). Are butch and fem working-class and antifeminist? *Gender & Society*, 15(2), 175–196. https://doi.org/10.1177/089124301015002002

Currier, A., & Migraine-George, T. (2017). "Lesbian"/female same-sex sexualities in Africa. *Journal of Lesbian Studies*, 21(2), 133–150. https://doi.org/10.1080/10894160.2016.1146 031

Epprecht, M. (1998). The 'unsaying' of Indigenous homosexualities in Zimbabwe: Mapping a blindspot in an African masculinity. *Journal of Southern African Studies*, 24(4), 631–651. https://doi.org/10.1080/03057079808708594

Epprecht, M. (1999). The gay oral history project in Zimbabwe: Black empowerment, human rights, and the research process. *History in Africa*, 26, 25–41. https://doi. org/10.2307/3172136

Epprecht, M. (2004). *Hungochani: The history of dissident sexuality in Southern Africa*. Montreal.

Epprecht, M. (2005). Black skin, 'cowboy' masculinity: A genealogy of homophobia in the African nationalist movement in Zimbabwe to 1983. *Culture, Health & Sexuality*, 7 (3), 253–266. https://doi.org/10.1080/13691050410001730243

Eves, A. (2004). Queer theory, butch/femme identities and Lesbian space. *Sexualities*, 7(4), 480–496. https://doi.org/10.1177/1363460704047064

Gunda, M. R. (2010). *The Bible and homosexuality in Zimbabwe a socio-historical analysis of the political, cultural and Christian arguments in the homosexual public debate with special reference to the use of the Bible*. University of Bamberg Press.

Hall, S. (1996). Who needs identity? In S. Hall & P. Du Gay (Eds.), *Questions of cultural identity* (pp. 1–17). Sage.

Hildebrandt, T., & Chua, L. J. (2017). Negotiating in/visibility: The political economy of Lesbian activism and rights advocacy. *Development and Change*, 48(4), 639–662. https:// doi.org/10.1111/dech.12314

Inness, S. A., & Lloyd, M. (1995). "G.I. Joes in Barbie Land": Recontextualizing butch in twentieth-century Lesbian culture. *NWSA Journal*, 7(3), 1–23. www.jstor.org/stable/4316399

Jenkins, R. (2008). *Social identity* (3rd ed.). Routledge.

Kole, S. K. (2007). Globalizing queer? AIDS, homophobia and the politics of sexual identity in India. *Globalization and Health*, 3(8), 8–16. https://doi.org/10.1186/1744-8603-3-8

Levitt, H. M., & Hiestand, K. R. (2004). A quest for authenticity: Contemporary butch gender. *Sex Roles*, 50(9/10), 605–621. https://doi.org/10.1023/B:SERS.0000027565.59109.80

Matebeni, Z. (2008). Vela Bambhentsele: Intimacies and complexities in researching within black Lesbian groups in Johannesburg. *Feminist Africa: Researching for Life: Paradigms and Power*, 11, 89–96.

Matebeni, Z. (2011). *Exploring black Lesbian sexualities and identities in Johannesburg* [Thesis (PhD)]. University of the Witwatersrand.

Mateveke, P. (2019). "If we must be freaks, let us be freaks with a voice": Southern feminisms and LGBTI activism in Africa. *Agenda*, 33 (3), 78–86. https://doi.org/10.1080/1 0130950.2019.1685896

Muparamoto, N. (2016). Enduring and subverting homophobia: Religious experiences of same-sex loving people in Zimbabwe. In E. Chitando & A. Van Klinken (Eds.), *Christianity and controversies over homosexuality in contemporary Africa. Religion in modern Africa* (pp. 143–156). Routledge.

Muparamoto, N. (2020). LGBT individuals and the struggle against Robert Mugabe's extirpation in Zimbabwe. *Africa Review*, *13*(sup1), S1–S16. https://doi.org/10.1080/09744053.2020.1812042

Muparamoto, N., & Moen, K. (2020). Gay, ngochani, ordaa, gumutete and mwana waEriza: 'Globalised' and 'localised' identity labels among same-sex attracted men in Harare, Zimbabwe. *Culture, Health & Sexuality*. https://doi.org/10.1080/13691058.2020.1814967

Muparamoto, N., & Moen, K. (2021). Taraidiwa ["We have been raided"]: Effects of and meanings ascribed to an assault on an LGBTI function in Harare, Zimbabwe. *Journal of Homosexuality*. https://doi.org/10.1080/00918369.2021.1923280

Oppong, S. H. (2013). Religion and identity. *American International Journal of Contemporary Research*, *3*(6), 10–16.

Phillips, O. (2003). Zimbabwean law and the production of a white man's disease. In J. Weeks, J. Holland, & M. Waites (Eds.), *Sexualities and societies: A reader* (pp. 471–491). Polity Press.

Reygan, F. (2016). Black lesbian (non)representation in 'gay' media in Cape Town: Constructing a globalized white, male, affluent, gay consumer. *African Identities*, *14*(1), 85–98. https://doi.org/10.1080/14725843.2015.1100105

Sanger, N., & Lynch, I. (2018). 'You have to bow right here': Heteronormative scripts and intimate partner violence in women's same-sex relationships. *Culture, Health & Sexuality*, *20*(2), 201–217. https://doi.org/10.1080/13691058.2017.1338755

Shoko, T. (2010). "Worse than dogs and pigs?" Attitudes toward homosexual practice in Zimbabwe *Journal of Homosexuality*, *57*(5), 634–649. https://doi.org/10.1080/00918361003712087

Weeks, J. (2007). Necessary fictions: Sexual identities and the politics of diversity. In K. E. Lovaas & M. M. Jenkins (Eds.), *Sexualities and communication in everyday life: A reader* (pp. 41–53). Sage.

Youde, J. (2017). Patriotic history and anti-LGBT rhetoric in Zimbabwean politics. *Canadian Journal of African Studies / Revue Canadienne Des Études Africaines*, *51*(1), 61–79. https://doi.org/10.1080/00083968.2016.1276850

Zway, M., & Boonzaier, F. (2015). "I believe that being a lesbian is not a curse": Young black lesbian women representing their identities through photovoice. *Agenda*, *29*(1), 96–107. https://doi.org/10.1080/10130950.2015.1013784

"Erase/rewind": How transgender Twitter discourses challenge and (re)politicize lesbian identities

Lexi Webster ⓘ

ABSTRACT
Competing views on the in/compatibility of transgender status and lesbian identity is a source of conflict in the ongoing antagonism over transgender recognition. Many individuals with different transgender identities might lay claim to lesbian identity or lesbian discourse(s) more generally. However, this inclusion has been disputed in some circles insofar as it is seen to challenge or contradict characteristics of lesbianism. This paper explores how transgender discourses might challenge and (re)politicize lesbianism and lesbian identities. Given that social media platforms concentrate minority communities in one space and can serve to exacerbate antagonism over identities, I focus in this paper specifically on the Twitter context. This paper uses corpus-informed critical discourse studies to explore how cognitive models of lesbianism are articulated in transgender Twitter discourse/s. Findings indicate that transgender Twitter users (re)articulate sociohistorical narratives in lesbian discourse/s. At the same time, however, they also challenge and (re)politicize the essentialism of sex and gender in relation to lesbian identity and social practice. Hence, transgender Twitter discourse/s reflect potential explanations for contesting transinclusion in lesbianism, which may serve to reinforce transexclusionary claims for retaining lesbianism's uniqueness as a female space and experience.

Introduction

Contesting the inclusion of transgender individuals and practices within lesbianism and lesbian identities is nothing new, starting with what Halberstam (1998) called the "border wars" of butch-femme identities in the 1960s and '70s and culminating in more recent claims of there being a "postlesbianism" of too-inclusive identities (cf. Forstie, 2020). Jeffreys (1997, p. 64) also cites transgender practices of "playing with gender" as contradicting the characteristics of lesbian feminism. However, it is important to note that some feminists consider transexclusion a fringe movement within radical feminism and lesbianism (see Thomsen & Essig, 2021). Indeed, Williams (2016, p. 254) goes as far as to argue that radical feminism and lesbianism are historically transinclusive and that such inclusivity is hidden in favor of a more "popular media narrative." Most recently, such public conflicts at the intersection of transgender and lesbian identities have manifested in movements and organizations specifically intended to separate sexual identities from gender identities (e.g., the British charity and advocacy group LGB Alliance). Such movements are billed as responses to the inclusiveness of sexual identities, threats of sexual identities becoming obsolete, and an ignorance of the sex differences that underpin sexualities (LGB Alliance, 2021). Whether for or against transinclusion in lesbian spaces, including the abstract space of *identity*, arguments invariably rely on differential conceptualizations of the interrelatedness of sex, gender, and sexuality.

Antagonism is predicated on "conflict and struggle over identity" (Walton & Boon, 2014, p. 353) and is manifested in divisions between in-groups and out-groups (see Mouffe, 2013; Thomassen, 2005). The sociohistorical narrative of contesting transinclusion is therefore rooted in an antagonism over who can truly lay claim to lesbian identity and in-group status (cf. Beemyn & Eliason, 2016; Hines, 2020). What is more, there has been a recent proliferation of discourses that contest the inclusion of specific voices on given topics, to which the intersection between factions of transgender activism and lesbian feminism has been no stranger (see Hines, 2019). The argument for transinclusion within lesbian identities, discourses, and spaces is one of prioritizing gender identity and self-identification, rather than sex, as the foundation of sexual identity (see Tate, 2012; Tate & Pearson, 2016). This position argues for a de-essentialization of the relationship between assigned sex and sexuality, citing similarities in gendered self-categorization between transgender and gender-congruent women (Tate & Pearson, 2016, p. 105).[1] The argument for transexclusion, then, cites lesbianism as a uniquely female experience (Jeffreys, 2014). Hence, this position contends that the deeply interwoven and unique sociohistorical narratives, struggles, and political victories of lesbianism over patriarchal and heteronormative structures are erased—or at least diluted—by transinclusion in lesbian experience and the subsumption of lesbian experience under catch-all labels like "LGBT" and "queer" (see Morris, 2016). These polarized perspectives constitute an antagonism over the legitimacy of in-group status—and the right to a voice on such matters—based on either gender identity or sexed experience.

Social media platforms have been used as vehicles for constructing and performing identities, including gendered identities, since their inception (see, for example, boyd & Ellison, 2007). Indeed, each platform has its own restrictions, communicative functions, and normative expectations (cf. Schmidt, 2014), which influence users' identity formation and performance. Generally, Twitter "enables condensed performances of the self" to public and private audiences of various sizes (Papacharissi, 2012, p. 1990). Such performances on Twitter are driven by social identification insofar as Twitter communication is largely predicated on sharing and finding information relevant to "the people and organizations [users] care about" (Puschmann & Burgess, 2014, p. 47). However, it is prudent to note that these affordances are not inherent in the platform's capabilities, instead arising from users' engagement with them (see Tagg, 2015). Hence, the affordances of Twitter—and other social media platforms—will vary across and among user-groups. For example, Tandoc et al. (2019, p. 32) found that Singaporean social media users engage with Facebook for group-formation and -organization, whilst using Twitter for "[sharing] their rants and opinions to a smaller and selected group of friends." Contrastively, Shane-Simpson et al. (2018) found that U.S. college students use Facebook more for private social bonding with other users also known in the offline context and Twitter for more public self-disclosure. Research on transgender users' Twitter behaviors indicate similar practices, including both public self-disclosures of sexualized identities and practices (Webster, 2018a) and users sharing opinions about civil rights and personal employment issues (Webster, 2018b).

The social homophily facilitated by identity-driven social media platforms, whereby users converge with one another based on social identity and like-mindedness (Kaakinen et al., 2020), has in many cases led to antagonism between groups. On Twitter, for example, "antagonistic discourses [are] emotionally articulated ... to negotiate terms of group identities" (Evolvi, 2019, p. 389) in the same way as offline antagonistic discourses are used to construct conflict vis-à-vis groups and out-groups (see Mouffe, 2013). Indeed, Twitter has proven to be a particularly key site of antagonistic discourses between transgender and feminist groups, representing a space within which offline politics of transgender identity recognition are reflected online (see Hines, 2019). What is more, the social recognition of preferred gender identity and its underpinning regulation is reflected in Twitter's "Hateful Conduct Policy" (Twitter, 2021). Hence, Twitter is an ideal site for exploring the discourses at the intersection of transgender identity and lesbian feminism. Indeed, given their ubiquity, social media have become technologies inextricable from our daily practices and can therefore be seen as heuristics for a general understanding of social and linguistic behaviors. As such, I use Twitter-mediated discourse in this paper as a vehicle for exploring how lesbian identities and practices are articulated by transgender people in the English-speaking global West, which may contribute to an explanatory reasoning for the antagonism over transinclusion in lesbian discourses. I argue that the articulations of lesbianism and lesbian identity on transgender Twitter reflect potential explanations for the antagonism over transinclusion within lesbianism, reflecting sociohistorical narratives of conflict within lesbian feminism and subsuming lesbian experience under catch-all umbrella terminology.

Methodology

This paper uses a corpus-informed approach to critical discourse studies, which quantifies patterns of meaning in large bodies of linguistic data for subsequent in-depth qualitative analysis (Baker et al., 2008). The data analyzed in this paper comprise the Gender-Variant Online Communication (G-VOC) corpus, containing c.3,700,000 tweets (a total of 60,028,867 words) from 2,882 Twitter users. Users' data were collected from the follower lists of U.S. and U.K. transgender celebrity and charity accounts on the basis of two essential criteria: (1) the user profile was publicly accessible at the time of collection; and (2) users' biographies included specific linguistic evidence of transgender self-identification. Transgender self-identification was determined by specific linguistic identifiers indexing gender-variance (see Table 1). Following previous research, which indicates that users with different transgender identities engage in markedly different behaviors, the corpus is also divided into six sub-corpora according to users' gender-similarity based on the identifiers used in the biography (see Webster, 2018a). This distinction between groups of users may serve to illuminate potential explanations for competing understandings of gender- and sex-based identities that characterize the conflict over transgender-inclusion in the social categorization of lesbianism.

The first stage of a corpus-informed critical discourse analysis requires the use of quantitative corpus tools, which are used to identify salient topics or themes within the data (see Gabrielatos & Baker, 2008) via an analysis of keywords and collocates. Keywords are the lexemes "most indicative (or characteristic) of one corpus, as compared to another" (Rayson & Garside, 2000, p. 3), which requires a reference corpus. The reference corpus used for comparison in this thesis is a sample of 440,154,502 tweets from the Stanford Large Network Data collection corpus (Leskovec & Krevl, 2014; see also Webster, 2018b). Keyness is measured using log-likelihood ratio, an inferential statistic; the log-likelihood of a keyword must be ±3.84 in order to be deemed statistically significant at the 95th percentile or $p < 0.05$. Collocates, then, are two words within a corpus between which there is an "above-chance frequent co-occurrence" (Baker et al., 2008, p. 278). True collocates are those that score higher

Table 1. Division of G-VOC corpus into gender-based sub-corpora.

User-group	Number of users	Sub-corpus size (tokens)	Example identifiers*
Transfeminine	992	21,489,758	"mtf," "m2f," "transwoman," "transwoman"
Transgender	615	12,444,491	"trans," "transgender," "transperson"
Transmasculine	463	8,107,698	"ftm," "f2m," "transman," "transmasc," "transguy"
Non-binary	364	11,155,668	"non binary," "b," "enby"
Transvestite	277	2,809,300	"TV," "transvestite," "crossdresser," "CD," "XD"
Transsexual	171	3,021,952	"TS," "transsexual," "shemale"

*List not exhaustive, but exemplary.

than a conventional threshold of significance on at least two measures (Baker, 2014). This paper uses both mutual information (MI) and t-scores as measures of collocation. MI measures the "probability of observing [two words] together" and has a conventional significance threshold of 3 (Church & Hanks, 1990, p. 23), and t-scores are a confidence measure of the "certainty of collocations" with a conventional significance of 2 (Hunston, 2002, p. 73). As such, thecollocates analyzed in this paper are those that score higher than the conventional significance threshold for both Mutual Information (MI) and t-score.

Following quantitative analysis, the patterns of language identified are explored qualitatively as meaningful conceptualizations of the social world that are shared within an epistemic community. Thus, a qualitative approach qua sociocognitive critical discourse studies (Koller, 2012; van Dijk, 2009) is applied to the collocates of keywords in the G-VOC corpus as a means of identifying the shared cognitive models of transgender Twitter users. Topics and themes are identified in quantitative findings, which illuminate the ideas, interests, and values of the epistemic community under analysis (cf. Van Dijk, 2015). These topics and themes are constrained by the local discourse context of transgender discourse, accounting for a contextualized understanding of the cognitive models at work that take into account individuals' subjectivities and social positioning (see Webster, 2018a). This sociocognitive approach illuminates the "cognitive interface" that "[influences] social structures" (Van Dijk, 2015, p. 64), offering an initial foundation for an explanatory critique of the relations held between the social categorizations of *transgender* and *lesbian* in an age of antagonism over their interrelatedness.

Analysis

The words *lesbian, lesbians,* and *lesbianism* are each statistically significant keywords in the Gender-Variant Online Communication (G-VOC) corpus, when compared to the reference corpus of general Twitter use. The same is true for *butch*, femme*,* and *dyke** (see Table 2).[2]

Table 2. Lesbian-indexing keywords in the G-VOC corpus.

Keyword	Freq (G-VOC)	Freq (Stanford)	Log-likelihood (LL)
Butch*	918	1,021	+1280.57
Dyke*	722	2,583	+210.21
Femme*	4,512	1,975	+1168.31
Lesbian*	7673	7,225	+12965.33

When accounting for users' gender similarity, it is evident that there are both similarities and differences in the distribution of lesbian-indexing keywords across user-groups (see Table 3). Keywords *lesbian**, *butch**, and *femme** are more frequently used in all the G-VOC sub-corpora, when compared against the reference corpus, each with a statistical significance at the 99.99th percentile (or $p < 0.0001$).[3] The greater use of *dyke** is statistically significant at the 99.99th percentile in the transfeminine, transgender, transsexual, and non-binary sub-corpora. Greater use of *dyke** in the transmasculine sub-corpus is significant at the 99.9th percentile (or $p < 0.001$). The word *dyke** is statistically significantly underused at the 95th percentile (or $p < 0.05$) in the transvestite sub-corpus.

These findings indicate that multiple articulations of lesbian identity, whether self-identification or other-representations, are characteristic of all user-groups when compared to the reference corpus of general Twitter use. Regardless of whether users self-identify as lesbians, there is a clear indication that transgender users of all gender-sex configurations have assumed a position within lesbian discourses, which is a contested aspect at the intersection of lesbian and transgender identities (cf. Hines, 2019). A more detailed exploration of the collocates and concordances of keywords, taking into account users' gender-similarity, illuminate to what extent these articulations challenge or re-politicize lesbian discourses.

Lesbian*

The non-binary sub-corpus has the highest proportion of users articulating *lesbian** keywords (66%, or 241 of 364 users), followed by the transgender sub-corpus (51%, or 211 of 615 users) and the transfeminine sub-corpus (50%, or 494 of 992 users).

It may be expected that a greater proportion of transfeminine users would articulate discourses surrounding lesbianism, given the arguably inextricable relationship between womanhood and lesbianism. Indeed, the transgender sub-corpus—which includes users who explicitly self-identify as transgender but do not index either femininity or masculinity in their biographies (cf. Webster, 2018a)—is also likely to include more transfeminine than transmasculine users. That is, demographic research indicates that transfeminine identities are more prevalent than transmasculine

Table 3. Comparison of lesbian-indexing keywords between gender-based sub-corpora.

	Butch*		Dyke*		Femme*		Lesbian*	
	Freq (LL)	Prevalence (% of users)	Freq (LL)	Prevalence (% of users)	Freq (LL)	Prevalence (% of users)	Freq (LL)	Prevalence (% of users)
Transfeminine	259 (+ 370.5)	12%	294 (+ 103)	10%	1487 (+ 4403.6)	24%	2941 (+ 6172.73)	50%
Transgender	303 (+734.39)	15%	184 (+83.99)	12%	1895 (+ 7854.09)	21%	1673 (+ 3419.72)	51%
Transmasculine	133 (+ 264.96)	14%	79 (+ 13)	8%	213 (+ 361.58)	15%	1067 (+2338.8)	46%
Non-binary	190 (+ 383.63)	23%	110 (+ 18.86)	16%	586 (+1611.19)	42%	1201 (+ 2216.45)	66%
Transvestite	6 (- 0.14)	2%	10 (- 3.89)	2%	242 (+ 915.47)	20%	339 (+ 716.49)	28%
Transsexual	27 (+ 29.84)	11%	45 (+ 25.46)	11%	89 (+ 171.27)	15%	452 (+ 1117.73)	38%

identities (cf. Webster, 2018b). The prevalence of *lesbian** use among non-binary users is therefore perhaps unexpected, though non-binary individuals are included in some conceptualizations of lesbianism (see Tate & Pearson, 2016). Indeed, the prevalence of transmasculine users' discursive constructions of lesbianism (48%, or 211 of 463 users) might also be surprising. However, narratives of transmasculine experience indicate "involvement in … lesbian communities" prior to transition (Hines, 2019, p. 145) and inclusive conceptualizations of lesbianism allow that "transgender men can also lay claim to … lesbian community" (Forstie, 2020, p. 1764).

The collocates of *lesbian** provide potential explanations for the over-representation of *lesbian** in all user-groups. There is an evident consistency among user-groups in the 10 most frequent conventionally significant collocates of *lesbian** (see Table 4). Consistent themes identified across sub-corpora can be broadly conceptualized under the categories of: (1) sexuality; (2) gender; and (3) pronouns.[4] Typical examples of these collocations include strings of often—but not always—hashtagged identifiers, users subsuming lesbianism under a queer umbrella, or equating lesbian and queer identities in some way. Some examples from the data include:

#LGBT, #lesbian, #gay, #transgender
queer women, including bi and lesbian …
queer/lesbian
lesbian and queer women

The collocation of multiple identifiers may indicate multiple—both contradictory and complementary—understandings of the relationship between lesbian and other identities. For example, listing identifiers alongside one another indicates an understanding of shared interest between several social groups. This is especially the case of hashtagged exchanges, which are often used to generate conversational publics outside of personal follower/following audiences on Twitter (see Bruns & Moe, 2014). Hence, the listing of identifiers alongside one another may not signal conflated identities, but simply like-mindedness (cf. Kaakinen, 2020). On the other hand, *queer* is variably used as an overarching category subsuming non-heterosexual practice and, separately, as a term interchangeable with or alternative to *lesbian*. This may reflect arguments that lesbian experience is subsumed by—or, at least, similar to—other identity labels (cf. Morris, 2016).

The collocation of *trans* and *transgender* with *lesbian** in all sub-corpora is not surprising, given the research context. However, it does indicate a consistent and strong collocation between transgender and lesbian identities or practices within the cognitive model of transgender Twitter, regardless of gendered user-group. Indeed, there is specifically indicated a shared

Table 4. Comparison of collocates of *lesbian** between gender-based sub-corpora.

	Trans-feminine	Transgender	Trans-masculine	Non-binary	Transvestite	Transsexual
Lesbian*	I, gay, lesbian trans, lesbians you, transgender my, bisexual women, who, bi, can, love, woman	gay, transgender bisexual, LGBT I, queer, trans women, my Black, gays, bi, out, lesbian, people	gay, I, trans new, LGBT bisexual transgender, out can, novel, not, check, reads, women, couple	gay, I, trans bisexual, you not, transgender women, bi my, out, queer people, me couple	gay, LGBT lesfic, I hot, here transgender love, bisexual, more, lesbian, click, free, sexy	I, gay, trans out, you transgender, like bisexual, women hot, check, not, my, love, couples

cognitive model of contiguity between multiple non-heterosexual identities (and transgender identities), which mirrors the wider hegemonic collectivization of identities under umbrella concepts of non-normativity (cf. Webster, 2018a). This consistent frequent collocation could arguably be seen to either reject or obscure the specificities and uniqueness of lesbian experience by equating it to gay, bisexual, transgender, and/or queer experience. That is, there is indicated a shared cognitive model between transgender Twitter user-groups that lesbianism is not a uniquely female experience, but a constituent element of wider generic constellations of non-heteronormativity.

Femme* and butch*

Again, the user-group with the highest prevalence of *femme** among its users is the non-binary group (42% – or 152 of 364 users), followed by transfeminine (24% – or 243 of 992 users) and transgender (21% – or 131 of 615 users) user-groups, respectively. *Butch** is also most prevalent among non-binary users (23% – or 82 of 364 users), though much less than their use of *femme**.

The over-representation of transfemininity among transgender identities might also go some way toward explaining the greater frequency of *femme** over *butch** in all user-groups. The differential representation of *femme** and *butch** could indicate a shared cognitive model between transgender Twitter users that prizes—or, at least, highlights—feminine identities. Indeed, it may also index a shared cognitive model of transgender hyper-femininity that is a source of antagonism for some critics of transinclusion in lesbianism and feminism (cf. Berberick, 2018).

The difference in the prevalence of *butch** among all other user-groups, except the transvestite sub-corpus wherein *butch** was underused, is minimal. Nevertheless, the statistically significant use of both *butch** and *femme** in all user-groups indicates a general self-positioning of users within discourses of historically lesbian-indexing identities. That is, they are articulating their positioning in a discursive space that is contested by others (cf. Hines, 2019). The incorporation of both *butch* and *femme* identities arguably also signifies an adherence to historical distinctions between heteronormative lesbian identities (cf. Koller, 2008), which have been the source of some ideological conflict within politicized lesbian communities (cf. Halberstam, 1998). An analysis of collocates of both *femme** and *butch** offer potential explanations for and implications of the use of these historically lesbian-indexing identity markers (see Table 5).[5]

*Butch** seems to retain its specifically lesbian- and female-indexing foundations in transgender Twitter discourse, given its consistent collocation

Table 5. Comparison of collocates of *femme** and *butch** between gender-based sub-corpora.

	Transfeminine	Transgender	Transmasculine	Non-binary
Femme*	I, trans, transgender you, my, femme women	en, I, femme me, trans, you my, guise, women,	I, trans, butch, you, gay, ftm, stud, lesbian, queer, LGBT	I, trans, my, you women, femme black, queer
	genderqueer, me non-binary, queer more, like, your black	transform, butch, queer, sexy, black, tomboy	me, women, people, tomboy, femme	love, people color, like, they, we, out
Butch*	I, femme, my, trans women, lesbians	I, trans, fairy, femme, you, handsome	I, femme, lesbian stud, ftm, trans	I, trans, women butch, femme, buff
	lesbian, woman me, you, like, up, butch, stone, she	me, birthday women, stone, blues, lesbian, benefit, today, lesbians	gay, not transman, LGBT, my	stone, exist, my me, you, lesbian, blues

with *woman** and *lesbian**. That is, most collocates of *butch** fit broadly into two categories: (1) lesbianism; and (2) gender.[6] However, there is a frequent co-occurrence of *trans** and *butch** among all user-groups. As such, uses of *butch** in context include the expected phrases "butch lesbians" and "butch women" alongside another three-word phrase: "butch transwomen." The latter suggests there is an alternative use of *butch** among transgender Twitter users that is not necessarily associated with sexuality, in much the same ways as *femme** has been used in transgender discourses (cf. Webster, 2018a). Indeed, this is perhaps reflective of a re-appropriation of historically lesbian identity markers by transgender users.

Femme* also appears to have been re-contextualized in transgender Twitter discourses, albeit slightly differently. The collocation of *femme** with umbrella categories of non-normative gender and sexuality configurations, including *genderqueer, queer,* and *LGBT*, occurs among each user-group. Indeed, typical collocations in context include the identifier phrases "queer femme" and lists of identity markers similar to those in uses of *lesbian** (e.g., "genderqueer, femme, vegan, fat"). The specific collocation of queer-indexing language with *femme** indicates the categorization of *femme** as a queer, rather than specifically lesbian identity. Indeed, its general use among transgender Twitter users use is far more closely linked with gender-indexicality than with sexuality.

Subsuming historically lesbian identities under new queer categorizations is exactly what Forstie (2020) claims underpins the postlesbian fear of "too-inclusive" identities. Indeed, the co-opting of *butch* and *femme* identities corresponds with Rothblum's (2010) findings that queer identities correspond with either butch or femme identification. This may have significant implications for butch/femme distinctions that have characterized historical lesbian discourse (cf. Koller, 2008). Instead of simply reinforcing heteronormativity (cf. Beemyn & Eliason, 2016), *butch** and *femme**

Table 6. Comparison of collocates of *dyke** between gender-based sub-corpora.

	Trans-feminine	Transgender	Trans-masculine	Non-binary	Transsexual
Dyke*	*I, march, trans, out NY, Chicago, who dyke, hard they, me, like, not, watch, my*	*march, out, watch trans, dykes butch, Chicago dyke, you*	*trans via stories*	*march trans you butch, Chicago*	*pansexual quiet watch out*

identities may be seen to simply be "'playing' with gender" (Jeffreys, 1997, p. 64) under generically non-normative sexual and gendered umbrella categorizations. However, the prevalence of *femme** over *butch** is arguably a reversal of sociohistorical narratives of femme invisibility in lesbian communities (cf. Eves, 2004). This asymmetrical re-contextualization of identifiers may therefore contribute to a perception of transgender Twitter discourse(s) challenging and re-politicizing historically lesbian identities.

Dyke*

Dyke* constructions are also most prevalent among non-binary users (16% – or 57 of 364 users). This is followed by transgender (12% – or 76 of 615), transsexual (11% – or 18 of 171 users), transfeminine (10% – or 103 of 992 users), and transmasculine (8% – of 38 of 463 users) users, respectively.[7] This may indicate a problematic appropriation or use of a historically lesbophobic epithet, even if used as a reclaimed lesbian identity marker (cf. Jones, 2012), which could easily be considered a potential explanation of antagonism (cf. Mouffe, 2013; Walton & Boon, 2014). Indeed, the collocates of *dyke** may be the most directly reflective of the antagonism surrounding claims to lesbian-indexing identities out of the terms identified in the G-VOC corpus (see Table 6).

Across the transfeminine, transgender, and non-binary sub-corpora, there is collocation between *dyke** and *march*. The immediate collocation of the two is in reference to protest marches designed to highlight lesbian visibility (cf. Podmore, 2016) and challenge the "male-focused nature" of gay pride events (Currans, 2012, p. 74). Indeed, typical contexts for this collocation reflect either celebratory (e.g., "My first Dyke March") or critical (e.g., "anti-Semitic Dyke March") comments on these specific events. What is more, the collocation of *dyke** with *trans* shows a specific articulation of "Dyke Marches" being explicitly transinclusive (i.e., "Dyke & Trans March" or "Dyke/Trans March").

"Dyke Marches" have specifically been centered in conflicts at the intersection of transgender and lesbian identity (Hines, 2019). This articulation of transgender inclusion in such practices—or, at least, self-positioning in discourses surrounding them—among several user-groups with a seeming prevalence of "femme" identities (and not by the transmasculine user-group) is perhaps reflective of a contemporary re-contextualization of what *dyke* represents. From indexing a specifically lesbian identity (cf. Jones, 2012, 2014), *dyke* now encompasses a postlesbian inclusion of queer femininity (cf. Forstie, 2020). What was a radical confrontation of the heteropatriarchal hegemony and a reclamation of lesbophobic language (cf. Currans, 2012) is now deployed in a form inclusive of wider con-stellations of sexual and gendered identities. Hence, the use of *dyke** in transgender Twitter could arguably be considered demonstrative of the very erasure of the uniquely female lesbian experience (cf. Jeffreys, 2014) that the term was designed to challenge. It is, then, arguable that the shift in meaning of *dyke*—or, at least, the inclusion of transidentities within protest movements using the epithet—offers a potential explanation for explicitly transexclusionary lesbian discourses. That is, the transinclu-siveness of politicized protest leads to an equally politicized reaction of transexclusion.

Conclusion

This paper provides some preliminary evidence that transgender Twitter discourses challenge and (re)politicize lesbian identities in a way that may serve to underpin transexclusionary narratives. That is, because transgender Twitter users appear to articulate lesbian identities and lesbianism in such a way that directly mirrors the fears and issues raised by transexclusionary lesbian discourses, there is some foundational evidence that this antago-nism over lesbian identities is not made of straw. The findings of this preliminary corpus analysis indicate that lesbian identities are subsumed under wider generic constellations of non-heteronormativity, which tran-sexclusionary discourses claim contribute to lesbian erasure. Similarly, historically lesbian-indexing identities are asymmetrically re-contextualized solely as gendered, rather than sexualized, with historical discourses of femme invisibility somewhat reversed. This re-contextualization arguably reflects the hyperfemininity and heteronormativity problematized in his-torical discourses of lesbian feminism. That is, the prevalence of trans-femininity among transgender identities contributes to the asymmetrical re-contextualization of historically lesbian identities into normative markers of—largely binary and heteronormative—gender expression. Finally, radical terminology used to challenge heteropatriarchal structures of oppression in the name of uniquely female experience have been re-appropriated as inclusive of—or, at least, the *voices* of—all feminine identities, regardless of lived female experience.

However, these findings can also be interpreted through a transpositive lens wherein identities are articulated along the lines of historical inclusivity within some radical lesbian and feminist movements. That is, the prioritization of gender-driven, rather than sexed, identities may reflect a de-essentialization of biology and physiology in the construction of or claim to identity. More specifically, claims to both butch and femme identities among transgender individuals reflects a continuation—or, perhaps, evolution—of historically lesbian identities and the similarity between transgender and gender-congruent women in self-categorization, which is the basis of transinclusionary narratives. Similarly, the alignment of lesbianism among wider constellations of non-heteronormative identities and practice may reflect shared political interest and lived experience (e.g., as subjects of patriarchal oppression). This is reinforced by the inclusion of transgender voices in perhaps the most radical of feminist and lesbian spaces, which indicates a presumed intention of transgender users to engage in political practices of resistance against systemic power inequalities that negatively affect both transgender and gender-congruent lesbians.

Of course, there are limitations to the conclusions that can be drawn from this preliminary and exploratory study. Indeed, as with any study, I do not claim that the dataset used in this paper is exhaustive of all possible transgender articulations of lesbian identity and lesbianism. For example, Twitter users who identify as transgender but do not explicitly indicate as much in their biographies are not included in this dataset, which may well have some impact on the findings herein. Similarly, the very nature of social media platforms means that so-called "trolls" or fake accounts may be included in the dataset. However, it is not within my gift to determine who is and who is not truly transgender based on the language they use and there are no reliable measures as yet for identifying "trolls" via user biographies alone. As such, this paper is intended simply as an initial attempt at exploring the long-standing antagonism over transgender inclusion in lesbian discourse(s) as it relates to lesbian obsolescence. In doing so within the limited scope and scale of one paper, there are nuances of context that cannot be fully considered by the corpus-driven methods relied upon herein. Further research should explore the nuances of transgender articulations of lesbianism using more in-depth qualitative analysis of texts-in-context to identify how these articulations are manifested and legitimized discursively as representations of actors and their actions.

I do not claim to have the answers to resolving the long-standing issue of this antagonism at the intersection of lesbianism and transgender identity. However, such articulations of lesbian identities as identified in this paper may provide *either* the foundations of an explanatory reasoning for transexclusionary narratives *or* evidence of the inextricability of trans and lesbian experience, depending on the interpretation taken. They certainly have implications for the question of lesbian obsolescence, especially at the intersection between transgender and lesbian identities. Preliminary evidence points to the notion that the conceptualization of lesbianism (and, perhaps, specifically lesbian feminism) as a uniquely female experience of sexual and politicized identity is obsolete when transinclusive. However, the term *lesbian* and its associated identity markers—whether transinclusive or not—are not obsolete in the sense that they are used as heuristics for indexing both feminine and non-heterosexual identities.

Contesting transinclusion in lesbianism and lesbian identities is not likely to end anytime soon, insofar as antagonism offers no compromise and neither "side" is likely to lay down their arms. However, research that explores potential explanations for sociopolitical issues can provide the foundations for reforming the battlegrounds upon which claims to recognition are fought. Only from a thorough understanding of both sides of antagonism can change be theorized. This paper simply aims to lay one stone in the endeavor.

Notes

1. The term *cisgender* is not used in this paper, due to its contested nature.
2. The asterisks on *butch**, *femme**, and *dyke** refer to truncation, indicating the inclusion of both the singular and plural form of the terms. *Lesbian**, as it is used in the remainder of the paper, includes each *lesbian*, *lesbians*, and *lesbianism*.
3. Log-likelihood ratios of ±3.84 are significant to the 95th percentile, ratios of ±6.63 to the 99th percentile, ratios of ±10.83 to the 99.9th percentile and ratios of ±15.13 to the 99.99th percentile (see Rayson et al., 2004).
4. There is also indicated a sexualization of lesbianism in the transvestite and transsexual sub-corpora via *sexy* and *hot* (cf. Webster, 2018a), though an exploration of this phenomenon is beyond the scope of this paper.
5. There were no significant collocates for either *femme** or *butch** in the transsexual and transvestite sub-corpora.
6. Indeed, the inclusion of *stone* and *blues* as across the sub-corpora may refer to *Stone Butch Blues* (Feinberg, 1993).
7. *Dyke** is statistically significantly under-represented in the transvestite sub-corpus.

Acknowledgments

The research and data collection underpinning this publication were conducted under the auspices of Lancaster University as part of a larger-scale doctoral project, though this paper was later written whilst the author was employed at Manchester Metropolitan University.

Declaration of interest statement

The author declares that they have no known competing financial interests or personal relationships that could have appeared to influence the work reported in this paper.

Funding

The work conducted under the auspices of Lancaster University was funded by Lancaster University's Faculty of Arts and Social Sciences Postgraduate Studentship.

ORCID

Lexi Webster (iD) http://orcid.org/0000-0001-5721-8236

References

Baker, P. (2014). *Using corpora to analyze gender*. Bloomsbury.

Baker, P., Gabrielatos, C., KhosraviNik, M., Krzyżanowski, M., McEnery, T., & Wodak, R. (2008). A useful methodological synergy? Combining critical discourse analysis and corpus linguistics to examine discourses of refugees and asylum seekers in the UK press. *Discourse & Society*, *19*(3), 273–306. https://doi.org/10.1177%2F0957926508088962 https://doi.org/10.1177/0957926508088962

Beemyn, G., & Eliason, M. (2016). "The intersections of trans women and lesbian identities, communities, and movements": An introduction. *Journal of Lesbian Studies*, *20*(1), 1–7. https://doi.org/10.1080/10894160.2015.1076232

Berberick, S. N. (2018). The paradox of trans visibility: Interrogating the "Year of Trans Visibility". *Journal of Media Critiques*, *4*(13), 123–144. https://doi.org/10.17349/jmc118107

boyd, d., & Ellison, N. B. (2007). Social network sites: Definition, history and scholarship. *Journal of Computer-Mediated Communication*, *13*(1), 210–230. https://doi.org/10.1111/j.1083-6101.2007.00393.x

Bruns, A., & Moe, H. (2014). Structural layers of communication on Twitter. In K. Weller, A. Bruns, J. Burgess, M. Mahrt, & C. Puschmann (Eds.), *Twitter and society* (pp. 15–28). Peter Lang.

Church, K. W., & Hanks, P. (1990). Word association norms, mutual information, and lexicography. *Computational Linguistics*, *16*(1), 22–29. https://doi.org/10.3115/981623.981633

Currans, E. (2012). Claiming deviance and honoring community: Creating resistant spaces in US Dyke Marches. *Feminist Formations*, *24*(1), 73–101. https://www.jstor.org/stable/23275090 https://doi.org/10.1353/ff.2012.0009

Eves, A. (2004). Queer theory, butch/femme identities and lesbian space. *Sexualities*, *7*(4), 480–496. https://doi.org/10.1177/1363460704047064

Evolvi, G. (2019). #Islamexit: Inter-group antagonism on Twitter. *Information, Communication & Society*, *22*(3), 286– 401. https://doi.org/10.1080/1369118X.2017.1388427

Feinberg, L. (1993). *Stone butch blues*. Firebrand Books.

Forstie, C. (2020). Disappearing dykes? Post-lesbian discourse and shifting identities and communities. *Journal of Homosexuality*, *67*(12), 1760–1778. https://doi.org/10.1080/009 18369.2019.1613857

Gabrielatos, C., & Baker, P. (2008). Fleeing, sneaking, flooding: A corpus analysis of discursive constructions of refugees and asylum seekers in the UK press, 1996-2005. *Journal of English Linguistics*, *36*(1), 5–38. https://doi.org/10.1177/0075424207311247

Halberstam, J. (1998). *Female masculinity*. Duke University Press.

Hines, S. (2019). The feminist frontier: On trans and feminism. *Journal of Gender Studies*, *28*(2), 145–157. https://doi.org/10.1080/09589236.2017.1411791

Hines, S. (2020). Sex wars and (trans) gender panics: Identity and body politics in contemporary UK feminism. *The Sociological Review Monographs*, *68*(4), 699. https://doi. org/10.1177/0038026120934684

Hunston, S. (2002). *Corpora in applied linguistics*. Cambridge University Press.

Jeffreys, S. (1997). Transgender activism: A lesbian feminist perspective. *Journal of Lesbian Studies*, *1*(3-4), 55–74. https://doi.org/10.1300/J155v01n03_03

Jeffreys, S. (2014). *Gender hurts: A feminist analysis of the politics of transgenderism*. Routledge.

Jones, L. (2012). *Dyke/Girl: Language and identities in a lesbian group*. Palgrave Macmillan.

Jones, L. (2014). "Dolls or teddies?" Constructing lesbian identity through community-specific practice. *Journal of Language and Sexuality*, *3*(2), 161–190. https://doi. org/10.1075/jls.3.2.01jon

Kaakinen, M., Sirola, A., Savolainen, I., & Oksanen, A. (2020). Shared identity and shared information in social media: Development and validation of the identity bubble reinforcement scale. *Media Psychology*, *23*(1), 25–51. https://doi.org/10.1080/15213269.2018.1544910

Koller, V. (2008). *Lesbian discourses: Images of a community*. Routledge.

Koller, V. (2012). How to analyse collective identity in discourse – textual and contextual parameters. *Critical Approaches to Discourse Analysis across Disciplines*, *5*(2), 19–38.

Leskovec, J., & Krevl, A. (2014). *SNAP datasets: Stanford large network dataset collection*. http://snap.stanford.edu/data

LGB Alliance. (2021). *Home*. Retrieved January 14, 2021, from https://lgballiance.org.uk/

Morris, B. J. (2016). *The disappearing L: Erasure of lesbian spaces and culture*. State University of New York Press.

Mouffe, C. (2013). *Agonistics: Thinking the world politically*. Verso.

Papacharissi, Z. (2012). Without you, I'm nothing: Performances of the self on Twitter. *International Journal of Communication*, *6*, 1989–2006. https://doi.org/1932–8036/20120005

Podmore, J. (2016). Contested dyke rights to the city: Montreal's 2012 Dyke Marches in time and space. In K. Browne & E. Ferreira (Eds.), *Lesbian geographies: Gender, place and power* (pp. 71–90). Routledge.

Puschmann, C., & Burgess, J. (2014). The politics of Twitter data. In K. Weller, A. Bruns, J. Burgess, M. Mahrt, & C. Puschmann (Eds.), *Twitter and society* (pp. 43–54). Peter Lang.

Rayson, P., & Garside, R. (2000). Comparing corpora using frequency profiling. *Proceedings of the Workshop on Comparing Corpora*, Vol. *9*, 1–6. https://doi.org/10.3115/1117729.1117730

Rayson P., Berridge D., & Francis B. (2004). Extending the Cochran rule for the comparison of word frequencies between corpora. In Volume II of Purnelle G., Fairon C., & Dister A. (Eds.), *Le poids des mots: Proceedings of the 7th International Conference* on *Statistical analysis of textual data (JADT 2004), Louvain-la-Neuve, Belgium, March 10-12, 2004* (pp. 926–936). Presses universitaires de Louvain.

Rothblum, E. D. (2010). The complexity of butch and femme among sexual minority women in the 21st century. *Psychology of Sexualities Review, 1*(1), 29–42.

Schmidt, J.-H. (2014). Twitter and the rise of personal publics. In K. Weller, A. Bruns, J. Burgess, M. Mahrt, & C. Puschmann (Eds.), *Twitter and society* (pp. 3–14). Peter Lang.

Shane-Simpson, C., Manago, A., Gaggi, N., & Gillespie-Lynch, K. (2018). Why do college students prefer Facebook, Twitter, or Instagram? Site affordances, tensions between privacy and self-expression, and implications for social capital. *Computers in Human Behavior, 86,* 276–288. https://doi.org/10.1016/j.chb.2018.04.041

Tagg, C. (2015). *Exploring digital communication: Language in action.* Routledge.

Tandoc, E. C., Lou, C., & Hui Min, V. L. (2019). Platform-swinging in a poly-social-media context: How and why users navigate multiple social media platforms. *Journal of Computer-Mediated Communication, 24*(1), 21–35. https://doi.org/10.1093/jcmc/zmy022

Tate, C. C. (2012). Considering lesbian identity from a social-psychological perspective: Two different models of "being a lesbian". *Journal of Lesbian Studies, 16*(1), 17–29. https://doi.org/10.1080/10894160.2011.557639

Tate, C. C., & Pearson, M. D. (2016). Toward an inclusive model of lesbian identity development: Outlining a common and nuanced model for cis and trans women. *Journal of Lesbian Studies, 20*(1), 97–115. https://doi.org/10.1080/10894160.2015.1076237

Thomassen, L. (2005). Antagonism, hegemony and ideology after heterogeneity. *Journal of Political Ideologies, 10*(3), 289–309. https://doi.org/10.1080/13569310500244313

Thomsen, C., & Essig, L. (2021). Lesbian, feminist, TERF: A queer attack on feminist studies. *Journal of Lesbian Studies,* 1–18. https://doi.org/10.1080/10894160.2021.1950270

Twitter. (2021). *Hateful conduct policy.* Retrieved August 23, 2021, from https://help.twitter.com/en/rules-and-policies/hateful-conduct-policy

van Dijk, T. A. (2009). Critical discourse studies: A sociocognitive approach. In R. Wodak & M. Meyer (Eds.), *Methods of critical discourse analysis* (2nd ed., pp. 62–86). SAGE.

Van Dijk, T. A. (2015). Critical discourse studies: A Sociocognitive approach. In R. Wodak & M. Meyer (Eds.), *Methods of critical discourse studies* (3rd ed., pp. 62–85). Sage.

Walton, S., & Boon, B. (2014). Engaging with a Laclau & Mouffe informed discourse analysis: A proposed framework. *Qualitative Research in Organizations and Management: An International Journal, 9*(4), 351–370. https://doi.org/10.1108/QROM-10-2012-1106

Webster, L. (2018a). "I wanna be a toy": Self-sexualisation in gender-variant Twitter users' biographies. *Journal of Language and Sexuality, 7*(2), 205–236. https://doi.org/10.1075/jls.17016.web

Webster, L. (2018b). "Misery business?": The contribution of corpus-driven critical discourse analysis to understanding gender-variant Twitter users' experiences of employment. *puntOorg International Journal, 3* (1/2), 25–30. https://doi.org/10.19245/25.05.pij.3.1/2.03

Williams, C. (2016). Radical inclusion: Recounting the trans inclusive history of radical feminism. *TSQ: Transgender Studies Quarterly, 3*(1-2), 254–258. https://doi.org/10.1215/23289252-3334463

Toward a historiography of the lesbian transsexual, or the TERF's nightmare

Jules Gill-Peterson

ABSTRACT

This essay asks after the possibility of making the transsexual lesbian signify as a historical mode of sexuality, as a contribution to an anti-TERF method in trans and lesbian studies. What logics of mid twentieth century gender and sexuality are responsible for the opacity of transsexual and transvestite lesbians prior to the 1970s, despite the ample evidence that desire between femmes played a central role in trans social life? To move towards such a historiography and method, the author considers two paradigmatically difficult cases. First, Louise Lawrence, a well-known trans women in the San Francisco Bay Area who transitioned entirely do-it-yourself in 1944, and whose long term relationship with a partner, Gay Elkins, is high opaque in the archival record. Second, the essay considers the compulsory heterosexuality embedded in the medical logic of transsexuality in the 1960s, arguing that the medical ontology of the transsexual vagina was itself dependent upon the avowal of its immediate and exclusive use for penetration by straight men, making transsexual lesbians implausible despite their evident existence.

...Every

decade is a new trans moment, the

first trans literature, the first talk

show interview, the first trans billionaire,

the first transsexual polemic, the first arrival

of trans arrival.

—Amy Marvin, "The First Trans Poem"

Don't stop me if you've heard this one before; it's sort of the point. A Hollywood actor comes out as trans. A big name, too. This time, his name is Elliot Page. The Internet goes wild. Then chimes in from Twitter one "Sister Outsider" (2020) who dares to invoke Audre Lorde to say: "I find it depressing how many young lesbians now feel that, because they do not perform or feel invested in conventional femininity, they can no longer be women. And so they shift from identifying as lesbian women to straight men. Compulsory heterosexuality all over again." The Internet goes wilder. The most direct and perhaps elegantly irreverent reply to this tweet employing the same medium comes from a friend of mine (Gordon, 2020), a few hours later: "wait terfs think Elliot Page transitioned to be straight? ahahahahahaha."

I don't come with jokes to relitigate the so-called "border wars" between lesbians and trans masculine people (Gill-Peterson, 2018, pp. 167–171), about which much ink has been spilled, both in the 1990s and more recently. What draws my attention is that the contest here, the ostensible opposition between *lesbian* and *trans* is not cleanly over "gender" or "woman"—whatever the relations or differences between those might be imagined to mean—but *sexuality*. The cited critique of the trans exclusionary "radical" feminist (TERF)'s hostility to Elliot Page concerns the comedy of their mistaking a trajectory from lesbian to trans man as being a product of what Adrienne Rich (1980) first termed "compulsory heterosexuality," a term forever caught in Rich's endorsement of Janice Raymond's transphobic magnum opus, *The Transsexual Empire* (1979).[1] As countless other tweets from the day Page came out exclaimed with glee, gay men, trans and non-trans alike, were practically placing bets (Urquhart, 2020) on just how gay Page might soon announce himself to be, aesthetically and/or romantically.

If the shallow content of the ostensible schism between *lesbian* and *trans* as imagined by the trans exclusionary speaker on Twitter is not gender so much as sexuality, it suggests that their referenced problem of "the compulsory" has yet to be adequately understood. What is the difference between being "forced" to appear heterosexual and being forced to assume a legible sexual and gender identity as distinct narratives of the self? The fallacy of assuming that trans men are all straight, or that social or medical transition is inextricable from a heterosexualizing process, is only one side of the coin of this logic. It is, strictly speaking, no less presumptuous to assume that Elliot Page will turn out to be gay. What really draws my attention to him is precisely this unfinished business of the incommensurability of sexuality and gender as enmeshed zones of trans experience, desire, and sociality that routinely transgress all systems of norms designed to discipline them. The TERF arrangement of this would be that the refusal to recognize transness as real ontologizes sexuality—in this case, lesbianism—and subjects it to attack by a heterosexuality that arrives as trans masculinity. However, there are a multitude of other epistemologically normative consequences to the increasingly rigid separation of gender identity from sexual orientation (Gill-Peterson, 2018; Valentine, 2007) over the past half century. Indeed, the queer and trans taxonomies of the very same, though they arrive at different conclusions and politics by claiming Page as gay, awkwardly serve the same master discourse as the TERF: sexology's imperative to classify, sort, and separate (Amin, 2020). That is to say, the reply that trans men most certainly can be gay has to do with an ontologization of gender as distinct and autonomous from the domain of sexuality and desire. Same style, albeit different outcome.

Moreover, this essay is not about trans men. It's about the intellectual work to be done to explore a common reply to TERF anxieties that trans men will make lesbians obsolete: can we not talk instead about how so many trans women are lesbians, making transness as much an empirical *increase* to their ranks, rather than an existential threat? I submit the following hypothesis: that the trans lesbian has been made libelously implausible because the TERF historical imaginary, derived from the same sexological modernism as contemporary gay, lesbian, and trans taxonomies, has defined the historiography on this matter despite the empirical, historical reality of trans lesbians, which leads astray from sexology's boundaries. It is not helpful to rescue trans people as gay and lesbian to protect them from TERFs. The very demand to resolve narratives around *either* gender *or* sexuality, but never their obvious admixture, is a failure to think the historicity of trans people's sexualities.

Consider the predominant narrative of how *lesbian* and *trans* supposedly fell out of step. The initial feminist, queer, and trans historiography of the 1970s made Beth Elliott's harassment at the West Coast Lesbian Conference and Sandy Stone's firing from Olivia Records into something of definitive bookends for the parting ways of these two terms, a divorce that signifies the emergence of trans-exclusionary lesbianism and feminism as an enduring political problem. Only recently have historians like Finn Enke (2018) begun to question this consensus and look at the far messier enmeshment of trans women, trans lesbians, and non-trans lesbians found in the archive of these events. As Enke points out, scholars and community memory may have both acquiesced to the TERF account of the 1970s too quickly. The present writing concurs with Enke that this historiographical narrative is too simplistic and, what's more, confers far too much power on TERFs to have defined the category of lesbian. My question is somewhat different: what happened *before* 1970? The mid-century might serve to destabilize the ongoing power of TERFs in defining the category of lesbian to police womanhood—not because it proves that trans women and lesbians got along before the 1970s, but because an expanded historical frame beyond the 1970s questions the very notion that *trans* and *lesbian* have any obvious relationship, adversarial or otherwise. In the face of a resurgent TERF movement that targets both trans men and trans women for their ostensible violations of the category of lesbian today, I seek to make the trans lesbian signify some more *as a sexuality* with a traction in the mid-century different than how it has been narrated since the 1970s. This I undertake as one entry in the broader project of elaborating an anti-TERF method for trans and lesbian studies. My guiding historical question is this: what logics of gender and sexuality in this period are responsible for the presumed and actual historical opacity of trans lesbians in the mid-century, despite the ample evidence that desire between women played a central role in trans social life?

To find an answer, I will consider two paradigmatically difficult cases, which don't scale to a representative argument but instead offer provocations for a longer study of mid-century trans lesbians. First, I will turn to Louise Lawrence, a well-known trans women in the San Francisco Bay Area who transitioned in 1944. I will survey the loud archival opacity of her relationship with a long-term, live-in female partner. Strangely, Lawrence has never been read as lesbian in terms of desire, affection, or companionate life (not to mention identity), much like the transvestites of her generation who are assumed to be straight (though even their self-professed heterosexuality, as we shall see, is rather oddly gay). Second, to spin the TERF claim about Elliot Page on its head by turning to trans *women*, I will turn to the compulsory heterosexuality embedded in the medical logic of transsexuality in the 1960s to argue that the medical ontology of the transsexual vagina was dependent upon the avowal of its expedient and exclusive use for penetration by straight men. Finally, I turn to the riddle of a footnote in Esther Newton's 1972 classic ethnography of female impersonators, *Mother Camp*: a rumor about a transsexual drag performer who became, against all norms, a lesbian.

My point, then, is not to suggest that trans lesbians "have always existed" or can be counted upon like any other category. Nor am I arguing that the 1970s was the moment of split after decades in which trans women and lesbians were more porous in their relationships. Rather, I am interested in a reading practice labile enough to engage the historical opacity of trans women's desires for one another as an anti-TERF method in the practice of trans history, transgender studies, and lesbian studies. A trans lesbian reading of women serves to destabilize the libelous and alarming assumptions upon which contemporary TERF rhetoric operates in weaponizing sexuality by ontologizing it. The continued dismissal of trans women as unable to be lesbians reflects the persistence of a kind of stubbornness one might call, for dramatic effect, *Raymondian*—as Janice Raymond's *The Transsexual Empire* established the genre for TERF discourse as concerns the disqualification of the transsexual lesbian on the grounds that she is an imposter and avatar of male sexual violence.

Like the border wars, however, I have no interest in returning to Raymond's text or its legion of excellent critiques. Rather, I am stubbornly interested in the other side of its logic, or its impact through circulation: the constriction of the trans imagination. The pleasurable but vexed possibility that the trans lesbian lives hidden in plain sight decades *before* Raymond's polemic hit bookshelves is important in challenging TERFs not just on their terms, but on the internalization of their terms by trans people, trans studies, and trans-inclusive lesbian and feminist studies. What if the capacity to interpret the trans past as lesbian (where lesbian means less a consistent identity than a patterned mode of prohibited desire between women that might look other than how we define it today[2]) is limited not by a lack of evidence, but an internalization of the TERF imagination of history? If so, then the critical history of the lesbian transvestite and the lesbian transsexual carries force in the important tradition of the *Empire* striking back (Stone, 1992)—and perhaps poetically for this metaphor, from before the Empire came to power.

Her partner was gay

Louise Lawrence (b.1912), who transitioned entirely non-medically in 1944, was something of a fixture of the San Francisco Bay Area and California trans community by the 1950s. She is, for that reason, one of the rare non-transsexual women from the mid-century to occupy a significant place in trans historiography (Meyerowitz, 2002, pp. 185–187, 211, 318n74; Stryker, 2008, pp. 55–60; and Gill-Peterson, 2018, pp. 138–151, 203–206), both because of her community networks and, more centrally, her efforts to educate a generation of American sexologists, endocrinologists, surgeons, and psychiatrists who were founding the post World War II medical model of transsexuality. While Lawrence was not herself interested in medical transition or surgery, she developed a friendship with Christine Jorgensen, the most famous transsexual woman in the world in the 1950s, and cultivated relationships with major figures of the incipient trans medical and social scientific establishment, including Alfred Kinsey and Harry Benjamin (Gill-Peterson, 2018, p. 138).

What remains glaring in the archive of Lawrence's life is the rather loud case to be made that she was, in a way that we cannot precisely elucidate because of that archive's limitations, a lesbian. Or, perhaps it is better to say that transvestites like Lawrence, who did not take hormones, did not seek gender confirmation surgery, did not always live full time as women, and were often content going by their birth names and male pronouns, are excessively heterosexualized in the historical imaginary. No doubt much of this has to do with the enduring impact of the sexological pathologization of cross-dressing and transvestism as sexual fetishes (as in Cauldwell & Haldeman-Julius, 1947). Yet the published sexological and psychiatric discourses that enveloped lives like hers were pallid in comparison to the sheer lesbianic richness of their circumstances. In her unpublished autobiography, Lawrence (1951) recalls first wearing her sister's clothing as child, for something approximating erotic gratification, and that her first sexual experience at age fourteen was with a man. But explicitly sexual events occupy no especial significance in the narrative, which makes much more of her obsessive "collecting clippings from magazines, newspapers, etc., that dealt with the subjects of female impersonation" (p. 11), and how "masquerading" led to her being arrested and sent to a Juvenile Hall (p. 19). From there, Lawrence had a girlfriend in high school and married an ostensibly straight woman in the early 1930s who later died from pneumonia (p. 52), before remarrying in 1941 to a woman named Montez, who divorced her in 1944 when she decided to transition (p. 61).

The interpretive efforts required to "straighten" out the possibilities for coding these modes of desire—a young cross-dressed girl with an older man, *or* a gay initiatory experience; a straight-passing husband to a wife with a secret life, *or* a Russian doll of cloaked femme desire for another femme—only becomes more herculean after Lawrence's divorce and transition. To support herself, Lawrence took a job in 1944 as a photographer in bars full of passing sailors, service people, and working class queer men and women. This led her "to go to Broadway in the afternoons and sit in the various bars in which I worked at night and make friends with the owners, bartenders and steady customers" (p. 114). When conversations at the bar "turned toward sex...and [they] frequently did," Lawrence recalled that she "would try to kid my way out of it as quietly as possible and most of the time I succeeded" (p. 114). Tucked into this recollection is a brief hint of something more: "Whether any of these people (*there were girls as well as fellows*) knew or suspected anything about my true sex I was never certain for the subject was never brought up...I had become well established in the neighborhood and many of the 'regulars' knew me...knew me as Louise, that is" (p. 114, emphasis added). During this period and for decades afterwards, Lawrence also carried on an extensive dom/sub correspondence with other transvestites, playing out elaborate forced feminization, servant girl, and petticoat punishment fantasies through the mail. Lawrence, who was an aspiring artist, even drew her own erotic images of some of these scenes, all depicting high femmes.[3]

After spending six months in Los Angeles in 1947, Lawrence returned to San Francisco and moved in with a roommate named Donna, with whom she became close. "Our friends never seemed to think of me as anything but [Louise], a female," she explains in her autobiography, but "the fact that a number of these friends were homosexually inclined was immaterial for they never attempted to involve either Donna or myself in this activity" (no page number). These sorts of narrative disavowals, with self-aware displays of knowledge of specific forms of desire between women, ought to be contextualized in the genre and time period in which they appear. Although never published, Lawrence was writing an autobiography for which she likely had high hopes in humanizing and pressing the case of transvestite women for a public audience. Such mid-century trans autobiographies were heavily freighted with the representational burden of producing sympathetic accounts that balanced titillating glimpses into a strange world of deviance while not reinforcing the outcast status of the author. As a white, middle class woman, Lawrence lived at a great and desired distance from poorer, policed, politicized, and racialized trans people in the era.[4]

Lawrence's statements about lesbians and relationships between women are mostly consistent across the archival record of her life: while it is not hard to imagine a range of sexual or affectionate experiences hiding behind her ostensible disavowals of the same, the materials themselves cannot be made to speak any particular truth. Interestingly, however, a major segment of that archive is, as is more often the case in queer and trans history than is recognized, rather impersonal: paperwork relating to a house that Lawrence co-owned with a woman named Gay Elkins for decades beginning in the 1950s, which they managed and rented out to various tenants over the years.[5] The litany of rent receipts, work orders, business filings, tax documents, and municipal paperwork are the largest body of evidence that Elkins, a US Army nurse, was Lawrence's partner—*business* partner, that is.[6] Whether they were more than just business partners requires some attentive reading to why it would appear so opaquely.

Quite unlike a pair of entrepreneurial women who banded together purely for financial reasons, Elkins would frequently travel with Lawrence, like when the two of them made a trip to Bloomington, Indiana in 1950 to visit Kinsey and tour his facilities. As part of that trip they also stopped in Ohio, Pennsylvania, and upstate New York to visit transvestite and transsexual friends.[7] When Elkins received orders from the Army in 1952, reassigning her to Japan for several years, the two decided that Lawrence would remain in San Francisco to manage the house.[8] Five years later, however, when Elkins was reassigned to Germany, Lawrence decided to go with her. In a letter to a friend, she related that "lo and behold, I am now the proud possessor of a United States passport in the name of Louise Lawrence, with picture and all."[9] It was this passport that would drag Lawrence and Elkins' relationship into the limelight, for it led to Elkins being dishonorably discharged from the army, presumably on the grounds that she was in a homosexual relationship.[10] Apparently the State Department then reconsidered Lawrence's passport ex postfacto on the grounds that she had committed identity fraud in obtaining it as a woman. By some means this news had gotten back to the Army, where it was presumably a problem in that the State Department had, in first approving the passport, implicitly endorsed that Elkins was a homosexual. A year later, in 1958, Elkins won an appeal, allowing her to be retroactively honorably discharged with full veteran benefits. Likewise, the State Department reversed its decision and allowed Lawrence her passport as a woman, though the reasons why remain unclear. Elkins and Lawrence immediately began planning a trip to Europe, this time as civilians.[11] The effort to bureaucratically heterosexualize Lawrence and Elkins, as well as punish the latter for any whiff of lesbianism, failed.

The Cold War, McCarthyite investigation of Elkins and Lawrence is, despite its internal contradictions, the strongest case for naming their relationship as lesbian, since the US state recognized them as much in spite of itself (see Canaday, 2009 and Johnson, 2009), using the technicality of Lawrence's sex on her birth certificate as a kind of get out of jail free card for avoiding creating a precedent out of the legal appeal. Lawrence's own words remained consistently careful on the subject, although in a 1953 letter to another trans woman she relates that "for the past 5 or 6 years I have been living with a woman of my own age who is a nurse in the Army Nurse Corps with the rank of Captain." Explaining that Elkins was stationed in Japan at the time, Lawrence writes in an unmistakably romantic mid-century idiom, "I am keeping the home fires burning for her."[12]

What seems most plausible, then, is that the narrative constraints of transvestism, which equated cross-dressing without medical transition as a heterosexual fetish, and the very real and menacing politics of the Cold War closet, convinced Lawrence to keep her decades-long relationship with Elkins something of an open secret. It seemed to work, for when Susan Stryker conducted an oral history interview (1997a) with Don Lucas, who had been friendly with Lawrence and other trans women in the 1950s and 1960s, no mention was made of Elkins. When Stryker asked if Lucas had ever met "anybody male-to-female who identified themselves as a lesbian," Lucas replied immediately and definitively, "No" (p. 20). And when Stryker pressed on, asking if he remembered "talking with people about choices they made about whether they either were or weren't sexual," he also replied no (p. 20). "The sexual thing pretty much just wasn't there," he offered.

"They would talk about just the gender thing" (p. 20). When Stryker asked specifically about Lawrence, Lucas replied, "I never got any inkling that she was ever attracted to anybody sexually" (p. 20). So much for Gay Elkins. In reality, the extreme opacity of the archive around Lawrence's life is to blame here. One gay man's recollection of someone he knew decades earlier can hardly be taken as definitive on Lawrence's sexuality. To read her as lesbian in an opaque sense—which is to say, to read her as lesbian without deciding in advance that being a lesbian has to conform to a post Stonewall, out and proud model of visibility—is as far as the archive will allow. What Lawrence's sexuality meant to her, or Elkins, is irretrievable. But such a lesbian reading of Lawrence, relieved of the sexological imperative to know if "she really was or wasn't," is a far more accurate parsing of the extensive records of her and Elkins' home.

Did you hear the one about the transsexual vagina?

If the generation of midcentury transvestites like Lawrence had their desires and relationships cloaked by heterosexualizing fetish discourses and closeting regimes engendered by the Cold War, the notion of a transsexual lesbian proved even more difficult to imagine. Here, the bad faith deployment of "compulsory heterosexuality" by contemporary TERFs finds its pre 1970s undoing in a different kind of obligation: that the trans woman's vagina bear a medical ontology dependent upon penetration by a straight cis man's penis.

While avowed heterosexuality was a strict criterion for surgery in this era, the landmark clinical volume *Transsexualism and Sex Reassignment* (1969)'s chapters on care after vaginoplasty make the penetrative imperative even more insistent. An entire chapter (Thompson, 1969) is devoted to the "vaginal form" necessary postsurgery to maintain the new vagina's shape and depth. Because this dilating device, made either of "balsa wood with a foam rubber sheathing, stockinette and plastic covering," or "lucite and silastic" plastics was meant to be left in for a number of weeks, it was typically attached to a harness that held it in place at the right depth (p. 323). Smaller, less bulky version of this girdle and panty system were given to women to take home with them once discharged from the hospital, where they would have to use them potentially for months, if not indefinitely. It is here that matters begin to slide, as the author notes that because "these patients are striving to be totally feminine," the goal of the surgeon should be to provide the most "appealing" dilator possible so that she will actually use it before finding a suitable replacement (p. 324). Leo Wollman (1969), a physician in New York City who saw trans women in the 1960s, makes that "replacement" unambiguous in the following chapter, writing: "A properly directed penis in heterosexual intercourse provides the most natural means of dilation" (p. 335). (Conspicuously enough, Wollman then adds that "the physician who treats the postsurgical, sex-altered patient *should ideally be a man*" [335, emphasis added].) The vague category of female "sexual function," including the ability to orgasm exclusively from hetero-sexual penetration, was established by endocrinologist Harry Benjamin (1967, p. 119) as a major criterion for a "successful" surgery result. Benjamin attributed what he called "the *sex motive*" to this aspect of surgery: trans women, he explained, "love normal heterosexual men and want to be as normal a sexual partner to them as surgery and medicine can make them."

The worry on the other side of this insistence was that any lapsed or disingenuous heterosexual might be given to "promiscuity" and "prostitu-tion," deviant categories associated with working class and racialized trans women. In 1967, Benjamin wrote of sex work as rather sensible in its allure from the point of view of any transsexual: "How much more can femininity be confirmed," he opined rhetorically, "than by having normal, heterosexual men again and again accept her as a woman, and even pay her for sex services?" (p. 123). Here the class and labor elements of trans-sexuality come into clearer view: heterosexuality was a narrative of class escape, of cleaning up one's act and living as a wife to avoid sex work. This normative possibility in the mid-century, from the trans feminine as a social position defined primarily by criminalized sex work, to the trans-sexual as a reformed, heterosexual subject, was immensely difficult to enforce and was the source of many rifts in tight-knit communities of trans women at the time (Heaney, 2017). In another oral history interview conducted by Susan Stryker (1997b), Aleshia Brevard Crenshaw, who worked as a female impersonator before accessing surgery through Benjamin in 1962, explained a vagina as nothing less than a gentrified escape out of "scuzzy, low, dirty dives" of San Francisco's notorious Tenderloin neigh-borhood (p. 31). While performing drag at the city's famous Finocchios club in the late 1950s, Crenshaw developed a reliance on heavy prescrip-tion drugs in the nightlife scene in the Tenderloin "until I met the man of my life, Hank," who asked her to get clean (p. 31). "And I also had surgery then," she explained, "I think at least partially because of Hank, that this was what life was about—a straight man who was willing to overlook what I had" and who could be her ticket out of the life of poor trans women, street queens, and sex workers, many of whom were women of color, unlike her (p. 31). "Very strange," she said of this later in her interview, "but very telling of how our social structure works. If you want to be a woman, you better have a man in tow" (p. 31)

This new maxim, enforced through narratives of class escape and backed by a flimsy medical discourse of "natural dilation," made the lesbian transsexual nothing less than a spectacular failure of new norms of medicalization. For that reason, rumor was more often the genre in which the lesbian transsexual could appear, spectacularized and frowned upon, but a titillating possibility born of the fact that trans women most certainly did *not* actually need a straight man to maintain their vaginas. In her rich and now foundational ethnographic study of female impersonators and poor gay and trans femme people in the 1960s, *Mother Camp* (1979), Esther Newton corroborates in a footnote at one point "the provision that 'sex changes' should get out of gay life altogether and go straight" (p. 102). However, "the 'sex changes' do not always comply," she adds, recounting that some of her informants had heard of a "successful impersonator in Chicago" who had undergone gender confirmation surgery and was *still* performing as a drag queen, in flagrant violation of the industry's norms. What's more, adds Newton, "I also heard a persistent rumor that 'she' now liked to sleep with lesbians!" (p. 102).

This exclamation point from a closeted lesbian anthropologist, writing of "sex changes" and trans women using social scientific inverted commas around the pronoun "she," offers an object lesson to reading for lesbians in the pre 1970s trans past. They may have been plentiful, but they had every reason not to appear, and to closet themselves just like Newton and other non-trans lesbians in the era.

Conclusion: the emperor's new clothes

Louise Lawrence and the unnamed transsexual lesbian from *Mother Camp* are not historical evidence of the preponderance or demography of trans lesbians in the mid twentieth century, nor are they a corrective that restores lesbianness to a trans-inclusive identity. Rather, as two archival object lessons that require careful attention to regimes of opacity, closeting, and compulsory heterosexuality, they signal lesbian *as a reading practice* for the past, a way of destabilizing the historiography that fixes the relationship of *lesbian* to *trans* in the supposed conflicts of the early 1970s, as well as their sexological matrices. While *transvestite* and *transsexual woman* were matters of shifts in gender, the archive suggests that they were also matters of sexuality, of a mode of prohibited desire between women, and much richer worlds of erotics, sociality, and relationships than contemporary taxonomies separating gender and sexuality allow for—or that the most extreme misogynist theories of trans womanhood, such as sexologist Ray Blanchard's "autogynephilia" (see Moser, 2010) would dare admit.

As an anti-TERF method for reading the past, it is ultimately to the enduring, ahistorical fantasy of the always imperiled lesbian to which this essay's historical excursion is addressed. What has changed since the mid-century is that trans men and trans children, not just trans lesbians, are now construed as existential threats to a lesbian womanhood most jealously policed and guarded by white, middle-class feminists. Yet the "unlikely bedfellows" (Bey et al., 2020) of these lesbians and feminists need to be brought into sharper relief. The United Kingdom High Court's 2020 decision barring trans children under sixteen from consenting to medical treatment with puberty blockers, the result of a coordinated, years-long libel campaign by British TERFs, has joined middle-class lesbian feminists and their apparent sympathizers—including author J.K. Rowling—to white supremacist, neo-fascists. Where the TERF ostensibly worries that young lesbians like Elliot Page are transitioning to become straight men, the fascist website the *Daily Stormer* put it this way in reference to him: "F to M Transgenderism is a Plot to Exterminate the White Race by Neutralizing Our Breeding Vessels" (quoted in Burns, 2020) In such an extremist political coalition, one which trans activists warn will result in a massive onslaught of legislative prohibitions, bans, and attacks on trans people of all genders, sexualities, and ages in the coming years, the urgency of invalidating the imperiled fantasy of the lesbian has become only more urgent. As one contribution to that project, a richer reading practice for trans lesbians prior in the past serves the purpose of denuding the TERF historical imaginary, defanging the threat that they have conjured for themselves and revealing the trans-exclusionary feminist to be the wearer of something like an Emperor's new clothes.

There is nothing particularly obsolete about lesbians if we take a non-sexological, historical point of view on the interfaces of trans and lesbian life since the 1950s, which are clearly many, if not tidy or unambiguous. While Louise Lawrence or the unnamed transsexual in *Mother Camp*'s "lesbianism" doesn't resolve into the scientific clarity—and political visibility—of a post Stonewall, out and consistent identity, that enigmatic quality might be taken up as an advantage, rather than liability. In lieu of the equation of visibility with political clout, a narrative to which trans femininity is not easily conscripted, and in concert with the well-developed queer critiques of sexual visibility (Tourmaline et al., 2017), we might note that becoming more visible has made trans lesbians the targets of TERF attack, rather than emancipated.

Notes

1. Rich's term is a loaded one to invoke in 2021, for on the one hand, her notion of the "lesbian continuum" suggests a framework for the historical inquiry at hand in this essay: that what is "lesbian" is not literally genital sexual acts, but a wider social system of affectional and companionate relationships between women. Yet, at the same time, Rich's work is increasingly read in the context of her sympathy and aid

for Janice Raymond's vicious transphobic work (Ira, 2020).

2. I am guided here by work in lesbian studies that stakes its unique place in the history of sexuality, including Jagose (2002). Of signal importance are Susan Potter's (2019) recent claim that "women's same-sex desires have been rendered knowable *by being coded, paradoxically, as invisible*, impossible, or secondary to other modes of erotic life," including heterosexuality (6), such that "lesbianism in this respect is not opposed to or distinct on heterosexuality—however much their everyday instantiations make them seem so" (p. 3).

3. Some of this dom/sub correspondence can be found in the Louise Lawrence Collection, Series 1B, Box 1, Folder 6, Kinsey Institute, Bloomington, IN. The erotic drawings can be found in Louise Lawrence Collection, Series V, Box 7, Folders 1-2, Kinsey Institute, Bloomington, IN.

4. On the class, race, and bourgeois politics of midcentury trans autobiography and their lingering effects, see Aizura (2018).

5. Louise Lawrence to Wilma, January 5, 1953, Louise Lawrence Collection, Series 1B, Box 1, Folder 11.

6. These materials can be found in the Louise Lawrence Collection, Series A, Box 1, Folder 5.

7. Louise Lawrence to Alfred Kinsey, November 16, 1950, Louise Lawrence Collection, Series 1B, Box 1, Folder 1, Kinsey Institute, Bloomington, IN.

8. Louise Lawrence to Alfred Kinsey, August 11, 1952, Louise Lawrence Collection, Series 1B, Box 1, Folder 1, Kinsey Institute, Bloomington, IN.

9. Louise Lawrence to Dr. Gebhard, October 15, 1957, Louise Lawrence Collection, Series 1B, Box 1, Folder 1, Kinsey Institute, Bloomington, IN.

10. Louise Lawrence to Paul Gebhard, April 7, 1958, Louise Lawrence Collection, Series 1B, Box 1, Folder 1, Kinsey Institute, Bloomington, IN.

11. Lawrence to Gebhard, June 11, 1958, Louise Lawrence Collection, Series 1B, Box 1, Folder 1, Kinsey Institute, Bloomington, IN.

12. Lawrence to Wilma, January 5, 1953.

Disclosure statement

No potential conflict of interest was reported by the authors.

Funding

The author(s) reported there is no funding associated with the work featured in this article.

References

Aizura, A. A. (2018). *Mobile subjects: Transnational imaginaries of gender reassignment.* Duke University Press.

Amin, K. (2020). Queer taxonomies. Unpublished manuscript.

Benjamin, H. (1967). Transvestism and Transsexualism in the Male and Female. *Journal of Sex Research*, 3(2), 107–127. https://doi.org/10.1080/00224496709550519

Bey, M., Gill-Peterson, J., & Lavery, G. (2020, August 26). *The TERF industrial complex: Transphobia, feminism, and race*. The Clayman Institute for Gender Research, Stanford University.

Burns, K. (@transscribe). (2020, December 14). *Same thing*. Twitter.

Canaday, M. (2009). *The straight state: Sexuality and citizenship in twentieth-century America*. Princeton University Press.

Cauldwell, D. O., & Haldeman-Julius, E. (1947). *Confessions of a transvestist: And more than 100 other short pieces*. Kansas: Haldeman-Julius.

Enke, F. (2018). Collective memory and the transfeminist 1970s: Toward a less plausible history. *TSQ: Transgender Studies Quarterly*, 5(1), 9–29. https://doi.org/10.1215/23289252-4291502

Gill-Peterson, J. (2018). *Histories of the transgender child*. University of Minnesota Press.

Gordon, C. G. (2020, December 2). *Wait terfs think Elliot Page transitioned to be straight?* Ahahahahahaha. Twitter. (@badinfinity2).

Green, R., & Money, J. (1969). *Transsexualism and sex reassignment*. Johns Hopkins University Press.

Heaney, E. (2017). *The new woman: Literary modernism, queer theory, and the trans feminine allegory*. Northwestern University Press.

Jagose, A. (2002). *Inconsequence: Lesbian representation and the logic of sexual sequence*. Cornell University Press.

Johnson, D. K. (2009). *The lavender scare: The Cold War persecution of gays and lesbians in the federal government*. University of Chicago Press.

Lawrence, L. (1951). *Louise Lawrence Collection, Box 1, Series A, Folder 3*. Kinsey Institute.

Marvin, A. (2020). The first trans poem. In A. Abi-Karam & K. Gabriel (Eds.), *We want it all: An anthology of radical trans poetics* (pp. 26–27). Nightboat Books.

Meyerowitz, J. (2002). *How sex changed: A history of transsexuality in the United States*. Harvard University Press.

Moser, C. (2010). Blanchard's autogynephilia theory: A critique. *Journal of Homosexuality*, 57(6), 790–809. https://doi.org/10.1080/00918369.2010.486241

Newton, E. (1979). *Mother camp: Female impersonators in America* (2nd ed.). University of Chicago Press.

Potter, S. (2019). *Queer timing: The emergence of lesbian sexuality in early cinema*. University of Illinois Press.

Raymond, J. (1979). *The transsexual empire: The making of the she-male*. Beacon Press.

Rich, A. (1980). Compulsory heterosexuality and lesbian existence. *Signs: Journal of Women in Culture and Society*, 5(4), 631–660. https://doi.org/10.1086/493756

Sister Outside (@ClaireShrugged). (2020, December 2). I find it depressing how many young lesbians now feel that, because they do not perform or feel invested in conventional femininity, they can no longer be women. And so they shift from identifying as lesbian women to straight men. Compulsory heterosexuality all over again. *Twitter*.

Stone, S. (1992). The *empire* strikes back: A posttranssexual manifesto. *Camera Obscura: Feminism, Culture, and Media Studies*, 10(2), 150–176. https://doi.org/10.1215/02705346-10-2_29-150

Stryker, S. (1997a). Oral History Interview with Don Lucas. June 13. GLBT Historical Society, Audio and Video Clips and Transcripts.

Stryker, S. (1997b). Oral History Interview with Aleshia Brevard Crenshaw. August 2, GLBT Historical Society, Audio and Video and Transcripts Collection, 19, 31.

Stryker, S. (2008). *Transgender history.* Seal Press.

Thompson, P. H. (1969). Apparatus to maintain adequate vaginal size postoperatively in the male transsexual patient. In R. Green & J. Money (Eds.), *Transsexualism and sex reassignment* (pp. 323–330). Johns Hopkins University Press.

Tourmaline, Stanley, E. A., & Burton, J. (Eds.). (2017). *Trap door: Trans cultural production and the politics of visibility.* MIT Press.

Urquhart, E. (2020, December 4). No, elliot page is not 'abandoning' lesbians. *Slate.* https://slate.com/human-interest/2020/12/elliot-page-trans-lesbian-divide.html.

Valentine, D. (2007). *Imagining transgender: An ethnography of a category.* Duke University Press.

Wollman, L. (1969). Office management of the postoperative male transsexual. In R. Green & J. Money (Eds.), *Transsexualism and sex reassignment* (pp. 331–334). Johns Hopkins University Press.

Learning butch: tracing lesbian and trans becoming in the classroom

L. Helton ⓘD

ABSTRACT

In this autobiographical essay, I study the ways in which becoming a classroom teacher illuminated the school-based gender socialization that had shaped my contested understanding of myself as a girl and woman. Leaning on the work of queer theorists both within and outside of fields explicitly marked as "pedagogical," I examine the notion of the "hidden curriculum" of gender as made manifest in my first years teaching middle school English, and the transformative capacity within my students—and the learning spaces I shared with them—to deconstruct, play with, and disrupt, if not unlearn, the gender "scripts" that had bound us to the failing coda of identification linked to larger systems of oppression which the institution of school reifies. Tracing my developing self-identification as a lesbian alongside my years of feeling "just outside" of the archetype of the professional woman teacher, I explore the possibilities for the secondary classroom to playfully and rigorously trouble normative modes of categorization and identification, broadening our understanding of who school "works" for.

Hemmed in: Performing woman/teacher

What are the words you do not have yet? What do you need to say?

-Audre Lorde (1984), "The Transformation of Silence Into Language and Action"

The public world of institutional learning was a site where the body had to be erased …No one talked about the body in relation to teaching. What did one do with the body in the classroom?

-bell hooks (1994), "Eros, Eroticism, and the Pedagogical Process"

The joke I like to tell is that I got more butch each year that I taught. It's a joke because I was deeply closeted in my years as a middle school English teacher in suburban Tennessee, and because, had I heard the word "butch" whispered anywhere around me in the 7th grade hallway, it would've disturbed and terrified me, unraveling the few remaining threads of the feminine schoolteacher façade I'd carefully cultivated and was working desperately hard to protect. As it turned out, the threads would unravel on their own. I'd eventually find a way to laugh at the fact that students used to call me "Mr." behind my back, reading, as they did, something unnamable but decidedly and queerly *wrong* in my relentless decision to wear chinos to school and to sit on the backs of desk chairs, my suede desert boots propped up in front of me while I taught. The first time I called myself a lesbian was long after I'd begun sleeping with women as a teenager myself. It was through and with the teenagers in my English classroom that the *language* of lesbianism made its way to me for the first time, resituating myself in my body, in my intellect, and in my long-felt but previously unnamed desire. I once had a seventh grade student who had a steadfast habit of asking me, each time I brought her a book recommendation, "is it gay?" The question, plain and commanding in its intention, caught me by surprise the first few times she asked me. I was unused to hearing anyone ask for exactly what it was they wanted and needed out of the media they consumed; I was still operating under the assumption that to name one's queerness, and certainly to allow that to so clearly shape the stories one might be looking for, was somehow inappropriate, illicit, disallowed. It was my students' brazen claim on the words they needed—the words, as Lorde writes, that I did not yet have—that forged space in our classroom for not only their, but my, queer becoming. Becoming a teacher allowed me to become lesbian, which allowed me to become trans. There remains, for me, no way to disentangle one from the other, and, if anything, I grow increasingly allegiant to the political utility of "lesbian" as my body and expression drifts further into that terrain we might call "masculine." I want to examine in this essay, then, where and how it is that a teacher might both become and *unbecome* gender(ed) in the space of classroom teaching—and what of it, if anything, might be generated from this as praxis for developing what trans pedagogue and educational scholar Harper Keenan calls "critical trans pedagogies" (Keenan, 2017).

The teaching profession is historically, and remains, a "feminized" one (Cortina & San Román, 2006). In the socially, politically, and religiously conservative region of the American South, where I was born, raised, and have spent the majority of my teaching life, the woman schoolteacher is her own intensified archetype, and the rules that govern her existence are as unquestionably solid and confining as the four walls of her classroom. I had assiduously studied the role of "good girl" throughout my schooling, and my induction to the classroom as a teacher signaled the unexpected continuation of this lifelong course of gender study.

At the first school where I taught, a small, conservative, affluent and predominantly white private school in Alabama, I arrived to school each day in the prescribed "professional dress" for female teachers, the pencil skirt, the accompanying heels, and the gauzy silk blouses limiting my range of movement and conferring a level of delicacy in my status as a woman teacher that was not similarly imposed upon my men colleagues. My department chair and dean, both men, dressed daily in professorial pale blue Oxford shirts, khakis, a tie and jacket. They leaned back in their classroom desk chairs, their feet propped up on their heavy wooden desks, sleeves messily rolled up and ties loosened, as boys surrounded them with admiring looks and loud laughter at lunch or in between class periods. My dean, a young, handsome man who students fell over themselves to impress, had one of those plastic basketball nets attached to the back of his office door. After meeting with students for disciplinary meetings, he'd rouse laughter and goodwill by crumbling up their demerits and shooting them through the hoop before loping out of the room. Meanwhile, I tottered around on heels, my already tall frame leaving me towering over my students. The men on faculty enjoyed a level of casual, sanctified, boyish repose and rapport that I was both culturally and sartorially denied.

And yet, despite my exhaustively prepared costume, I still frequently felt as though I was falling short of the project of femininity silently outlined by the school. My colleague next door, the 7th grade History teacher, breezed into school each day in tailored satin dresses and perfectly traced eyeliner, her enormous diamond engagement ring catching the light as she wrote the day's agenda on the board in neat lines. I found myself suspended somewhere between these two colleagues of mine—the man dean and the woman history teacher—in a way that threaded my days, even the good ones, with a low thrum of distress and ill-at-easeness. I often felt as though I was playing the part of the young lady schoolteacher, like a fraud that had tricked my way to the front of the classroom each day facing seventeen sets of scrutinizing eyes. It would be several years more before I'd hear a student whisper *dyke* as they passed me in the hallway, so quietly that I'd question if I even heard it, but in my first year teaching it was already clear to me that I was neither successfully a "man," nor a "woman." I did not yet have the language of lesbianism to name this *otherness*.

Like many first-year teachers, I was young and felt certain that my students could tell as surely as I could that I was out of place. But I began to notice a pattern amongst my students' reading of me. My girl students were obsessed with the details of my personal life—most particularly, with my then-boyfriend. They wanted to know why, at 22, he hadn't proposed yet, what his work was, how many children we wanted to have. My boy students alternately chatted with me about SEC football, specifically regarding my opinions on the rivalry of the land—Auburn vs. Alabama—and muttered about me behind my back, cracking jokes about my height, my stature, the ever-so-slightly lower timbre of my voice, my readiness to serve as the volleyball coach and the faculty player on any given soccer match.

In the celebratory lead-in days to winter break, the school hosted a faculty-student basketball game. I juked the 8th grade captain of the middle school basketball team in a drive down the court, and as he sat back up from having fallen flat on his back, I watched pass across his reddened face a look that I've seen on boys' and men's faces at me for as long as I can remember: disgust, rage, surprise. His teammates laughed at him, purpling his face even further. Some of the bolder ones high-fived me, a mix of incredulity and admiration in their eyes. Even in my carefully selected wool skirts and silk blouses, I became increasingly aware that I was failing the gender assigned to me, helplessly and seemingly out of my control. In failing womanhood, in noticing myself, as Wittig writes, as "not a woman," something like masculinity frayed at the edges of my studied role, and the children in my care noticed immediately. They seemed alternately enthralled and troubled by the open secret of my lesbian gender, as I would be for years to come.

It wasn't until after I left the middle school classroom that I would "come out," but it seems to me that I was coming out in any number of other ways over the course of my five years of teaching. My first teaching post, with its gendered uniforms (for students and faculty alike), just one of the more visible ways that gender and sexuality were carefully regulated and monitored, was the first time in which I became conscious of the rigid lines of gender socialization in school. Standing at the front of the classroom in my prim little outfit, my hair expensively and regularly dyed, the angles of my hip bones poking into my waistband from any number of the diets and pricey fitness trends to which I faithfully adhered, I began to see how thoroughly I had been schooled in the gender expected of me. Of course, I don't remember being schooled in the subject of girl- and womanhood alongside my initial learning of long division and metered rhyme as a young student. It took teaching to make visible what had, for all my life, lurked just below the conscious surface for me. That is, the "hidden curriculum" (Jackson, 1968) of gender in school only became clear to me once I had a hand in writing it.

I took my first teaching job in a public school the fall after I completed my graduate studies. I cried in my car after the interview, though not for the reasons one might suspect. The end-of-day school bell had rung as I'd entered the building for my interview, and I was temporarily shocked into silence by the outpouring of color and variety that surged forth: bright blue-dyed shaved heads, glittering dresses and chunky combat boots, sparkling septum ring piercings and high laughter, singing and smudged eyeliner, plastic stick-on gemstones shimmering underneath hand-knit beanies. I remember feeling baffled at my inability to separate the "boys" from the "girls" in this new school, conditioned as I was to "read" gender clearly and distinctly—one from the purported other. Gone were the pressed chino pants and neat plaid skirts of both my own school days and of the first school where I'd taught that, allegedly, rendered the "boys" legibly different from the "girls." Before I'd even met them, my new students were rupturing what I understood to be possible in (un)gendered self-presentation, forging space in between "boy" and "girl." It was in this space that I'd come to understand myself to be a lesbian.

Where my own schooling (spent entirely in Catholic or otherwise Christian-affiliated schools) and my first year of teaching in Alabama had taught me the purported rightness and naturalness of my own white femininity—a guise that I'd never been able to make "fit" in its quiet, clean delicacy and meekness—the fine arts public magnet school where I went on to teach was filled with young dancers, artists, actors, writers and instrumentalists who experimented loudly, daily, and variously with Butler's precept of gender as *drag*. For many of them, their gender presentation each day was just another of their many bright and brilliant art projects: an opportunity to play with and explore all that the constructed continuum of gender had to offer them. One of my students, in a self-professed fit of boredom on a weekday night, shaved his head after finishing his homework, arriving to school the next morning in one of his mother's wigs. "I got bored of looking like the same person everyday," he told me at my classroom door that morning, brushing an errant platinum blonde strand away from his face. "This way," he continued, "I can look however I feel when I wake up," which would range from wigs and false eyelashes one day to his pale shorn hair and bare face the next. I felt the same rush that I saw alight in my students' faces when a difficult concept suddenly fell into place for them, finally and for the first time: the gender I was assigned at birth was, in fact, up for negotiation. And so I began to negotiate it.

(Be)coming butch: meeting my body in the classroom

I care so much abot the whord that I cant reed/it marks mye bak wen i pass

-Jos Charles (2018), *feeld*

By the fall of my fifth and final year teaching, I had slowly and quietly drifted back in the direction of a butch presentation that, upon reflection,

I'd say matched my preferred presentation as a child, before I'd learned to feel ashamed of it. I abashedly took style cues from the many butch students who moved through my classroom over the years, taking quiet note of their combat boots, their beautiful young swagger, the black denim jackets that hung around their shoulders as they took up the space I'd been taught was unbecoming as a girl. I recovered my love of boyish sneakers, boxy tee shirts, looser-fitting pants slung lower over my waist, a way of moving in my body that reminded me of pictures of myself as a kid playing soccer: hands on my hips, baggy Umbros hanging just above my knees, hair pulled back from my ruddy, serious face. I had begun to notice and reject the ways I was expected to occupy space as a woman teacher: I'd intentionally stopped crossing my legs at faculty meetings, I stood when colleagues (especially men) came into my classroom, letting my height communicate something about the newfound authority I was kindling within myself. I was curating—in my stance, arms crossing my chest as I spoke over the colleague who'd interrupted me—what lesbian novelist Alison Bechdel calls the "ownership" that signifies butchness. Each October during Spirit Week, the student council sponsored a "Dress as a Teacher" day, wherein students donned their most ridiculous wigs, pillow stomachs, and drawn-on mustaches to parody their teachers. Each year, I'd felt a curiosity I couldn't quite name stir in me to dress up as one of my beloved men colleagues, but it wasn't until my last year that I took the opportunity to actually do it.

I spent the week prior carefully culling the items needed to portray my colleague Mark, the adored 6th grade English teacher whose lanky frame, sonorous voice, and playful spirit had given me steady companionship throughout the years. The night before dress-up day, I diligently ironed the purple gingham Oxford shirt I'd taken from my then-husband's closet, and laid beside it the pair of navy chinos I often wore myself, a purple knit tie I'd borrowed from Mark, a new pair of brown lace-up wingtip shoes I'd been too afraid to wear, and the various accessories that made up Mark's daily minutiae: wire-rimmed glasses, a worn canvas-band wrist-watch which he wore with the face on the inside of his wrist, a purple lanyard holding his school ID, a purple pen to tuck behind my ear. The next morning, I pulled my hair back into a low bun and dressed myself with a delight and excitement that bewildered me in their unfamiliarity: I was writing a text, consciously, for the first time.

In her essay, "Precocious Education," queer pedagogue Deb Britzman writes, in defense of teaching from and with one's erotic, creative life force,

living creatively requires a self who is not overwhelmed with blind compliance to outside demands. One cannot live creatively if the only relationships offered are authoritarian. The self must have opportunities to make her or his own demands to live creatively, to create something more than what she or he finds in the world (Britzman, 2000, p. 48).

Looking back, I can see the entire single day that I was dressed up as my colleague Mark as my first conscious experiment in *drag*—in creating a version of myself through the vehicle of imitating Mark, patching together a butch presentation that still felt beyond my reach at the time. The dress-up day offered me an allowance for this gender transgression, this act of self-creation, that I was too afraid to enact myself in my everyday life. It was a temporary lift of the sanctioned gender "rules" that were written into any number of regulatory systems in and outside of my school, including the dress code for teachers outlined in the handbook, wherein women were encouraged to wear "Sunday dress," specified as a dress or skirt. They were rules that I had slowly discovered the joy and queer "art," as Jack Halberstam calls it, of failing, and this dress- up day was a raucous celebration of that failure (Halberstam, 2011). All day long, students laughed, wide-eyed and pointing in the hallways, at my purple pastiche of Mark, and I laughed with them in the authorized play that the day permitted, thrumming inside with the electric delight of my butchness, of how broad my shoulders felt in an Oxford shirt, how clipped and sure my shoes sounded against the hallway linoleum floors, how, for once, I felt myself lengthen into the fullness of my tall frame rather than hunching over. One of my lesbian former students, then a high schooler and one of the many queer models for me in her flannel and languid swagger, raised a pierced eyebrow upon stopping by my classroom at lunch that day. "Damn, Bullard," she said, with a laugh. "You look good in a tie."

Judith Butler famously writes in her now-foundational 1989 *Gender Trouble*, "there is no original or primary gender a drag imitates, but gender is a kind of imitation for which there is no original" (Butler, 1989). After my imitation of Mark that day in early October, it became increasingly difficult to return to my teacher wardrobe of the last few years: the bright, flowy blouses, the heat-styled hair and meticulously applied eyeliner. The exhaustion of performance was wearing on me, and I couldn't forget the potent pleasure that had coursed through me while in drag. Nor could I forget how students responded to me that day, delightedly ribbing me in a show of appreciation for the rare show of adult gender play. If we are to follow Butler's theorizing of gender as a "script," I was finding it harder to remember my lines—I couldn't locate the "original" from which I still understood myself as somehow deviating. Already I knew that rumors about my sexuality floated throughout the halls, students taking note of my persistent positioning of myself as a particularly enthusiastic queer "ally," of the rainbow flag on my wall and GLSEN "safe space" sticker on the classroom door. Somewhere in between my colleague Mark and my imitation of him hovered a butch presentation that I'd been fumbling toward for some time, accompanied as it was by a more conscious understanding of my long-present queerness, my "not womanness." My students watched in live time as I found my way, peeling back the layers of conditioned femininity in a quite visceral fashion, as my clothing, appearance, and mannerisms shifted or, rather, deepened into a brand of "female masculinity" (Halberstam, 1998) I'd been working to hold at bay for some time.

Teaching while trans: *Eros* and the trans body as revisionist text

> To write or speak *as a lesbian* appears a paradoxical appearance of this 'I,' one which feels neither true nor false [...] I will not appear at political occasions under the sign of lesbian, but that I would like to have it permanently unclear what precisely that sign signifies.
>
> -Judith Butler (1993), "Imitation and Gender Insubordination"

On a fresh bright day in late April of 2020, my girlfriend's dad rested his rough, gentle hand on my shoulder and ran clippers over my head, leaving my once curl-filled head shorn down to my scalp. New tattoos decorate new muscles along my arms, which I've attended to with as much (or more) devotion as my writing, nursing them with the same assiduous care as I might a child growing into his body for the very first time. My veins have been opened and closed and opened again to check the levels of my blood under hormone replacement therapy, which I began in September of 2020. My body is changing rapidly, quietly, deepening and darkening and expanding in the privacy of the home I share with my girlfriend—the only person able to closely witness these changes as we move through progressive stages of the social isolation we understand to be a privilege. Where my body was once hyper-visible in the role of classroom teacher—to middle schoolers and then to the undergraduate and graduate students I taught after leaving the secondary classroom—I transition now in a state of near-complete solitude, visible to others largely through the vehicle of a Zoom screen. I wonder what it will mean to emerge back into the classroom next fall in a different body, with a different voice and different lines along my face and thickened limbs.

Since leaving the secondary classroom three years ago, I have increasingly come to disidentify with the label of "woman," but have identified perhaps more strongly than ever with the label of being a "lesbian," and, more particularly, a *dyke*. I find myself here, again, taking cues from my lesbian former students, who, at first, shocked me with their playful, affectionate tossing of the pejorative word at one another. A cis boy student of mine once filed a complaint to the administration that he was told he couldn't sit at the lunch table of a girl he had a crush on because one of the girl's friends told him pointedly, "this is a table for dykes—you have the whole rest of the cafeteria." The girls were disciplined and eventually forced to share their table, and the anger they burned with at that decision has burned in me since; their being *dykes* signified not only their lesbian sexualities, but also their resolute middle fingers to all that their institution—the school—reified about gender, sexuality, marginalization and belonging. I became a girl and woman in my own school days, a lesbian while teaching in the classroom with middle schoolers, and I've become a trans dyke since leaving it. Selecting the language of being both *trans and* a *dyke* means, to me, that I carry with me the anger that those girls carried with them from the lunch table at my old school—that my marginalized identities are sites from which I can and should demand more from the institutions and academic spaces I inhabit. I choose the word "become" in all of these instances because it has been through the portal of my profession that I have come to understand the nature, as de Beauvoir writes, of my own gendered construction: the ways I was first built as a girl and woman by others, and then a lesbian and a trans person, by me. Over the course of this pandemic, out of public sight in ways I haven't been in nearly a decade (or perhaps ever), my body has borne the marks of rapid transformation as I wrestle with/in womanhood and the new ontological conundrums and dazzling entanglements of nonbinary identification and embodiment.

In "Precocious Education," Deb Britzman writes, "in bringing pedagogical content closer to pedagogical relations, education, itself a site of popular imagination, can also help the popular imagination ready itself to view knowledge as changing, as subject to revision, and as never completed" (Britzman, 2000, p. 47). If, as Britzman suggests, we are to reimagine education as a place for "troubling" knowledge rather than delivering it; for inculcating the skill of constant *revision* rather than solidification of one's interpretations and views; for the proliferation of identities rather than the consolidation of them, then how might the *body of the teacher* operate as a mentor text—a pedagogical example of craft—in such intellectual processes? What might it mean to model the queer art of self-creation through one's embodied expression, offering, in this choice, possibilities to, every day, disrupt notions of representation, expression, and knowledge formation? In short, how might asking hooks' question, "what to do with the body in the classroom?" act as a powerful antiracist, queer, and trans pedagogical tool to destabilize the "conceptual geography of normalization" (including the reproduction of "normal" gendered subjects) in which school is so toxically invested?

In the fabric of my teaching life, there is the tear of this year: before it, I was slowly, steadily, more butch in ways that once raised the eyebrows and hallway whispers of my students. Already, the school where I taught didn't know what to do with my undisciplined body that, however minutely, was transgressing norms of feminine presentation and teaching. What, then, will the classroom do with my trans body when I return, in a culture and a country that doesn't yet know what to do with trans bodies other than hurt them? What will *I* do with it? Each day, I reconsider newly my relationship to gender, to clothing, to ways of occupying space with my body. What will it mean to live trans, and hence live the daily act of revision and self- (re)creation, in an institutional space where the teacher's body is expected to remain stable, "neutral," and legible?

I introduce the problem of my trans and queer body in this essay not as any sort of monolithic representation of trans educators' experiences, even those for whom the words "butch" or "lesbian" or the poetic "transmasc" might resonate, but as a possible opening to consider the potentiality for disruption that the trans body carries in the classroom. I do not wish to romanticize this disruption, as it carries alongside it the horrifying statistics of violence against trans people—particularly trans people of color—that remind us daily of the inhumane precarity of trans embodiment and existence. However, I offer these moments of gender transgression in my own teaching life as portals for grasping the extent to which we have normalized, surveilled, and protected binaristic modes of gendered and sexual identification in and through schooling so that we might more intentionally notice and harness the pedagogical power of these moments of disruption. I do not yet have specific precepts for what trans author Diana Courvant calls a "specific trans pedagogy" (Courvant, 2012) to offer here: only the specificities of my own body in specific classrooms, and the specific ways in which I found it to be disruptive of students' (and my) ability to *know* anything definitive about gender or sexuality. I only have the knowledge that, now, that once-whispered word *dyke* is perhaps the most fitting descriptor of not only my gender and sexuality, but also of my teaching. It seems to me that the writing of the "specific trans pedagogy" for which Courvant advocates must necessarily be borne forth in this way: in the methodology of attending to the local, to the individual teacher and student body in the individual location in which they are situated; in naming the capacities for single trans disruptions in single classroom locations to act in concert with one another, tearing across the systematized "geography of normalization" that is American public school.

ORCID

L. Helton ⓘⒹ http://orcid.org/0000-0003-2669-5114

References

Britzman, D. (2000). Chapter 3: Precocious education. *Counterpoints, 118,* 33–59. Retrieved November 30, 2020, from http://www.jstor.org/stable/45136096

Butler, J. (1993). Imitation and gender insubordination. In H. Abelove, M. A. Barale, & D. M. Halperin (Eds.), *The lesbian and gay studies reader* (pp. 307–320). Routlege.

Butler, J. (1989). *Gender trouble: Feminism and the subversion of identity.* Routledge.

Charles, J. (2018). *XXXIII. Feeld* (p. 33). Milkweed Editions.

Cortina, R. & San Román, S. (2006). *Women and teaching: Global perspectives on the feminization of a profession.* Palgrave Macmillan.

Courvant, D. (2012). Strip!*The Radical Teacher, 92,* 26–34. https://doi.org/10.5406/radical-teacher.92.0026

Halberstam, J. (1998). *Female masculinity.* Duke University Press.

Halberstam, J. (2011). *The queer art of failure.* Duke University Press.

hooks, b. (1994). *Teaching to transgress: Education as the practice of freedom.* Routledge.

Jackson, P. W. (1968). *Life in classrooms.* Teachers College Press.

Keenan, H. (2017). Unscripting curriculum: Toward a critical trans pedagogy. *Harvard Educational Review, 87*(4), 538–556. https://doi.org/10.17763/1943-5045-87.4.538

Lorde, A. (1984). *Sister outsider: Essays and speeches.* Crossing Press.

Lesbian vitality: a provocation

Julie R. Enszer

ABSTRACT

Opening with a reflection on lesbian invisibility, "Lesbian Vitality: A Provocation" challenges the idea of lesbian erasure, particularly when it is used in relationship to transgender people. Arguing for a multiplicity of lesbian identities and spaces for capacious lesbian formations, the author draws from the history of the periodical *Sinister Wisdom* and her experiences editing it to call for lesbian vitality as an alternative to erasure and as a focus for lesbian and queer women's community-making and cultural production.

When I was coming out in the late 1980s, lesbians talked about "lesbian invisibility." It described a phenomenon when people, primarily heterosexual people, could not see lesbians in plain sight. While lesbians clearly could identify Emily Dickinson, Eleanor Roosevelt, Ma Rainey, Alberta Hunter, or Chevala Vargas as lesbians, many heterosexual people could not (Cook, 1992, 1999, 2016; Gomez, 2019; Gund, 2016; Hammer, 2019; Smith, 1998). When media outlets covered pride parades and did not include images of lesbians, lesbian invisibility was the reason. Rooted in a theoretical understanding of the intersection of sexism and homophobia as structural and institutional systems of oppression, the concept of lesbian invisibility galvanized activism for systemic change (Beck, 1988; Pharr, 1988). Activist formations such as the Lesbian Avengers, Dyke Marches, and lesbian health projects addressed lesbian invisibility with visibility, blatant actions of coming out, education, and speech (Baus & Friedrich, 1993; Cogswell, 2014; Currans, 2017; Schulman, 1994; Mautner Project Records). Lesbian invisibility named a condition that diminished and minimized lesbians and prompted an activist strategy to end it.

Over the past three decades, lesbians have become more visible and, this visibility corresponds with increases in civil rights and legal protections (Allen, 2019; Faderman, 2015; Hirshman, 2012). Recently, activists have used the term "lesbian erasure" in a similar fashion to lesbian invisibility: as a theoretical intervention and historical analysis to inspire activism on behalf of lesbians. Lesbians increasingly are coming to under-stand "lesbian erasure," or as my friend and colleague Bonnie Morris describes it "the disappearing L," as a phenomenon where the lesbian past and the myriad contributions of lesbians are erased, denied, or forgotten (2016). Most troubling, in some instances, cisgender lesbians attribute this lesbian erasure to other queer people, often transpeople and less frequently gay men. I challenge both the idea of lesbian erasure and its use. "Lesbian erasure" is divisive politically and intellectually unproductive. It also serves as a rhetorical strategy to obscure larger threats from catastrophic climate change to human existence. Rather than divide ourselves from one another as the isolationism of "lesbian erasure" invites, what if lesbian communities embraced ideas that nurture our myriad communal formations and our many solidarities?

The idea of "lesbian erasure" is often bolstered by the realities of era-sures of lesbians from history. Lesbian-feminist activists during the 1970s and 1980s addressed these historical oversights, discovering "lost" lesbian communities and educating lesbians about them. Lesbian photographer JEB (Biren, 1979; Joan E. Biren Papers) traveled the country piecing together lesbian herstory through photographs while simultaneously cre-ating new vibrant visual images along with a community of photographers that included Tee Corinne, Jean Weisinger, Lynda Koolish, Donna Gottschalk, and Honey Lee Cottrell among others (Bright, 2018; Honey Lee Cottrell Papers; Koolish, 2017; Tee A. Corinne Papers; Weisinger, 1996). Jeannette Howard Foster wrote a history of "sex variant women" who had been written about in literature (1956, 1975, 1984). Many women reassembled the stories of Renee Vivien, Natalie Clifford Barney, Dorothy Wilde, and other lesbians in Paris in the 1920s and the stories of black lesbians in Harlem in the 1920s (Davis, 1999; Pious, 2015; Rodriguez, 2002; Rubin, 1976; Shenkar, 2000; Souhami, 2004; Wilson, 2011). Morris's scholarship in *The Disappearing L* is a reclamation project; she documents a particular moment in lesbian culture where lesbian-feminists engaged in vibrant community building practices during the 1970s, 1980s, and 1990s that resulted in some lasting and some now shuttered institutions (2016). The stories of the lesbian-feminist movement of this period, like the stories of the lesbians in Paris and in Harlem in the '20s, capture a process of historical loss, reclamation, and retelling. This work is a gen-erative lesbian response to historical oversights and omissions—and it is a part of a human process of understanding who we are, where we have been, and how we might imagine different ways to be in the future. Yes, histories are lost in the past, and, yes, we must reclaim them, but to see historic omissions of lesbian lives as a nefarious process against lesbians instead of as a human process diminishes us all.

One contemporary use of "lesbian erasure" suggests that the expansion of identity categories, as in the growing LGBTQQIAA acronym, constricts the identity of lesbian, erasing its significance or disappearing it completely. A related idea is that the current attention to transidentities detracts from, minimizes, and delegitimizes attention and care for lesbian identities by other people in the broadly construed queer community. Neither idea is true.

Lesbian and lesbian identities always evolve and lesbians enjoy explicating different nuances of identities. Long before a codified acronym, lesbians mused about what to name ourselves and how and why. We argued; we proclaimed. Gayle Rubin, an anthropologist of sex and sexuality, explains that lesbianism is "a historically specific concatenation of same-sex desires, gender variability, forms of identity, and institutional repertoires" (Rubin, 2011, p. 18). Practically, Rubin means that lesbianism—and lesbians as embodied people—change. If I were able to time travel to the 1890s Paris, the 1920s New York, the 1950s Iowa, or the 1970s Detroit, I might still resonant with the word lesbian, but how it ordered my life, how I expressed my desires to other women, how I engaged in sex and sensuality would be different, constructed by time, place, broadly the world around me. I might call myself lesbian or gay girl or kiki or that way. In every instance, the idea of lesbian exists as an interplay of desire, gender variance, identity, and institutions. The contemporary LGBTQQIAA acronym is one instantiation of identity formations. There will be others, and this work of identity elaboration will continue as historical conditions evolve and change.

If lesbian is a slippery word then identity, and sorting who counts—and does not count—as lesbian is even more difficult. Are more or fewer women identifying with the word lesbian today? In the United States, do more women use the word lesbian today to describe their sexuality than they did in say 1990? What about 1980? In 2000? A recent Gallup poll tracks this data over the past decade, but at present there are no longitudinal studies (Jones, 2021). The appellation of identity is not well researched. How women relate to various words and identity categories changes over time. At one moment lesbian may be meaningful, relevant and energizing as a term; at other times less so. From a data perspective, it is impossible to say how many women identify as lesbians today and compare it to the past. As a result, it is also impossible to say quantitatively that "lesbian erasure" is—or is not—happening. If there is no empirical evidence of the erasure or disappearance of lesbians, why does this idea appeal to women? The concept of "lesbian erasure" is not a data-based analytic category, but a theoretical one used to galvanize action. Today it is being used in some locations to separate and alienate across generations.

Editing one of the longest-publishing lesbian literary and art journals, *Sinister Wisdom*, I talk with a wide-range of women about lesbianism and lesbian identity, and I have embraced as part of my mission with the journal to find ways for *Sinister Wisdom* to speak to new generations of lesbians. When I talk with women in the 20s about their understandings of their sexuality and sexuality orientation, we share experiences and ideas, and there are differences between us. Still, I recognize that we are both organizing our lives in some ways around the identities of lesbian and queer. The experience is similar when I talk with women in their 70s and 80s. Some think of themselves exclusively in relationship to the word gay; they identify as gay women. Others resonate with queer and queer women. Others identify exclusively as lesbian, still others primarily as feminist. We all desire other women and express that desire through our lives and identities, but with different names, different experiences, and different points of salience, building solidarity and shared visions for our future is a challenge and an energizing one.

Throughout the history of *Sinister Wisdom*, lesbian and separatism, the idea of having dedicated space for lesbians, have been expressed differently within its pages. *Sinister Wisdom* has published heterosexual cisgender female writers like Sharon Olds and Susan Brownmiller under the rubric of lesbian imagination. Trans writers Max Wolf Valerio, Pat Califia, and Red Jordan Arobateau all appear in the pages of *Sinister Wisdom*. Currently, an editorial collective is working on a forthcoming themed issue on trans-feminism. Increasingly, within the pages of the journal and in our online communications, I use language of "lesbians and queer women" to describe the audience of the journal, and I utilize gender pronouns. Some *Sinister Wisdom* readers push back on these developments. Some readers tell me vaguely that they do not like the direction the journal is headed. Some women tell me I am erasing lesbians, and some women cancel their subscriptions. Generally, negative responses are from an older group of readers, but not exclusively. The rhetoric of lesbian erasure continues to be used in a variety of lesbian communities.

Most concerning to me in conversations about "lesbian erasure" is the idea that transpeople and transactivism are responsible for erasing lesbians or disappearing lesbians. Conceptually linked to the notion that the struggle for transrights and liberation diminishes lesbian lives, and activism, this idea suggests that there are limits to rights and to liberatory space, and that if some people, in this instance transpeople, have access to an expanding set of rights and an expanding space in which to live their lives, some other group must be limited to accommodate that expansion. I reject that notion. To suggest that civil rights and liberation are limited in size and space is a conceptual error, and believing that transfolks taking up all the space for civil rights at the moment is a misunderstanding of the dynamics of social change.

We are in a moment of extraordinary activism and visibility for transpeople. These new instantiations of knowledge about gender and gender identity, brought into light by transactivisms, create new visibilities and new ways of living for lesbians and genderqueer women. To state it plainly: cisgender lesbians benefit from transactivism—and vice versa. The categories of trans and lesbian overlap—imagine a butch lesbian, transgressing gender roles, challenging conventional hegemonic masculinity and affirming lesbian desire. Trans and lesbian also reimagine one another as the writing of Leslie Feinberg and Minnie Bruce Pratt vibrantly reminds readers. The dynamics of social change and movement building must allow for both celebration and critique in ways that are thoughtful and respectful. I celebrate advances that transactivists are making, for transpeople, for lesbians, for heterosexual people, and for cisgender people. Expanding and challenging the constraints of gender have many beneficiaries. I celebrate advances that lesbians make for all people as well. The world is large and contains possibilities for us all.

Finally, part of why this idea of "lesbian erasure" is so disturbing to me is that we are actually living in a time of mass extinction on the planet. Climate change is creating the conditions of mass extinction in profound and disturbing ways; plants and animals are dying at a tremendous rate through no fault of their own. The environmental conditions of our planet are a crisis. Lesbian writers have been exploring this crisis—and other environmental crises—for decades, drawing our attention to these perilous times (Caldicott, 1978, 1984, 1992; Carson, 1962; Greenham Commons Collection; Griffin, 1978, 1992; Pettitt, 2006; Snitow, 2015). Why link lesbian lives to that rhetoric conceptually?

Rather than embracing the idea of "lesbian erasure" or the "disappearing L," I advocate lesbian vitality. Lesbian communities continue to be vibrant spaces of mutual care, concern, and activism. Rather than bemoaning losses, these questions hold my interests: What are we doing to make lesbian a vital and meaningful identity today? What signs of lesbian vitality do we see in the world? How can we nurture and expand lesbian communities? What makes lesbians vital? What makes lesbian communities vital? How can we enhance both individual lesbians and our communities?

Focusing on lesbian vitality and promulgating ideas of lesbian vitality in our myriad communities as opposed to bemoaning "lesbian erasure" or disappearance of lesbians reflects the world of lesbians that I see and interact with every day: vital lesbians engaged in making the world a better place.

References

Allen, S. (2019). *Real Queer America: LGBT stories from red states*. Little Brown & Company.

Baus, J., & S. Friedrich (Directors). (1993). *Lesbian Avengers eat fire, too. 1993*. Wolfe Video.

Beck, E. (1988). The politics of Jewish invisibility. *NWSA Journal, 1*(1), 93–102.

Biren, J. E. J. (1979). *Eye to eye*. Glad Hags Books.

Bright, D. (2018). *BRAVE, BEAUTIFUL OUTLAWS: The photographs of Donna Gottschalk*. Leslie-Lohman Museum of Gay and Lesbian Art.

Caldicott, H. (1978). *Nuclear madness*. W. W. Norton & Co.

Caldicott, H. (1984). *Missile envy*. William Morrow & Co.

Caldicott, H. (1992). *If you love this planet*. W. W. Norton & Co.

Carson, R. (1962). *Silent spring*. Houghton Mifflin.

Cogswell, K. (2014). *Eating fire: My life as a Lesbian Avenger*. University of Minnesota Press.

Cook, B. W. (1992, 1999, 2016). *Eleanor Roosevelt* (Vols. 1–3). Viking.

Currans, B. (2017). *Marching dykes, liberated sluts, and concerned mothers: Women transforming public space*. University of Illinois Press.

Davis, A. Y. (1999). *Blues legacies and black feminism: Gertrude "Ma" Rainey, Bessie Smith, and Billie Holiday*. Pantheon.

Faderman, L. (2015). *The gay revolution: The story of the struggle*. Simon & Schuster.

Foster, J. H. (1956). *Sex variant women in literature*. Vantage Press.

Foster, J. H. (1975). *Sex variant women in literature*. Diana Press.

Foster, J. H. (1984). *Sex variant women in literature*. Naiad Press.

Greenham Commons Collection, 1982-1983. Women's Library Archives. Gb 106 5gcc.

Griffin, S. (1978). *Women and nature: The roaring inside her*. Harper Perennial.

Griffin, S. (1992). *A chorus of stones: The private life of war*. Doubleday.

Gomez, J. (2019). "Leaving the Blues" TSOS.

Gund, C. (Director). (2016). *Chavela*. Aubin Pictures.

Hammer, K. A. (2019). "Just like a natural man": The B.D. styles of Gertrude "Ma" Rainey and Bessie Smith. *Journal of Lesbian Studies, 23*(2), 279–293. https://doi.org/10.1080/10894160.2019.1562284

Hirshman, L. (2012). *Victory: The triumphant gay revolution*. Harper.

Honey Lee Cottrell Papers, 1950-2015. Division of Rare and Manuscript Collections, Cornell University Library.

Joan E. Biren Papers, Sophia Smith Collection, SSC-MS-00587, Smith College Special Collections, Northampton, MA. Retrieved December 11, 2020, from https://findingaids.smith.edu/repositories/2/resources/915

Jones, J. M. (2021). *LGBT identification rises to 5.6% in latest U.S. estimate*. Retrieved May 14, 2021, from https://news.gallup.com/poll/329708/lgbt-identification-rises-latest-estimate.aspx

Koolish, L. (2017). *Lynda Koolish - A retrospective exhibit of 45 years*. Women's Museum of California.

Mautner Project Records, 1989-2010; item description, dates. MC 683, folder #. Schlesinger Library, Radcliffe Institute, Harvard University, Cambridge, MA. Retrieved December 11, 2020, from https://id.lib.harvard.edu/ead/sch01347/catalog

Morris, B. (2016). *The disappearing L: Erasure of lesbian spaces and cultures.* SUNY Press.

Pettitt, A. (2006). *Walking to Greenham: How the Peace Camp began and the Cold War ended.* Honno Press.

Pharr, S. (1988). *Homophobia: A weapon of sexism.* The Women's Project.

Pious, S. (2015). *A crown of violets.* Headmistress Press.

Rodriguez, S. (2002). *Wild heart: Natalie Clifford Barney and the decadence of literary Paris.* Ecco.

Rubin, G. (1976). *Introduction in a woman appeared to me.* Naiad Press.

Rubin, G. (2011). *Deviations.* Duke University Press.

Schulman, S. (1994). *My American history: Lesbian and gay life during the Reagan/Bush Years.* Routledge.

Shenkar, J. (2000). *Truly wild: The unsettling story of Dolly Wilde.* Basic Books.

Smith, M. N. (1998). *Open me carefully: Emily Dickinson's intimate letters to Susan Huntington Dickinson.* Paris Press.

Snitow, A. (2015). Occupying Greenham Common. In *The feminism of uncertainty: A gender diary.* Duke University Press.

Souhami, D. (2004). *Wild girls: Paris, Sappho, and art.* Orion Publishing Company.

Tee A. 1966-2003. Corinne Papers. Coll 263, Special Collections & University Archives, University of Oregon, Eugene, OR.

Weisinger, J. (1996). *Imagery: Women writers.* Aunt Lute Books.

Wilson, J. F. (2011). *Bulldaggers, pansies, and chocolate babies: Performance, race, and sexuality in the Harlem Renaissance.* University of Michigan Press.

Is lesbian identity obsolete? Some (limited) answers and further questions from a unique philology of human behavioral science perspective

Charlotte Chucky Tate

ABSTRACT
Many scholarly disciplines focusing exclusively on human behavior can and do approach philology in some form in the conduct of their analyses, especially implicitly. "Philology" is generally understood to mean a study of oral and written records, particularly in their original form to determine either their authenticity and/or their original meaning—especially at the time of their development and delivery. This present article sketches a philology of human behavioral science perspective to make explicit what is largely implicit in the conduct of the science (most notably in psychological science) to answer the provocative question of this special issue ("Is lesbian identity obsolete?"). From this new perspective, I ask and answer (to the extent possible) three interrelated questions about the current or future obsolescence of the concept "lesbian identity." The first question is whether *lesbian identity* like predecessor terms for the larger concept *will become* obsolete in the future. A second question is whether lesbian identity *should become* obsolete based on its potentially less inclusive meaning—either (a) from the origin terms that comprise it or (b) in comparison to other terms in the lexicon at present. A third question concerns whether lesbian identity may wane now (at the time of this writing) and then wax again in the future (some decade[s] later from this writing).

Inspired by the larger consideration of how scholars analyze the use of language (both historical and current), my article takes on the (provocative) question of this special issue "Is lesbian identity obsolete?" by tethering the framing of the answers provided below to understanding lesbian identity in the specific context of human behavior—and from my training as a human behavioral scientist. This admission is to explicitly note that other scholars from other disciplines could and should approach the analysis in which I am about to engage in a different manner, using different tools and methodologies.

What I am attempting in this piece is a novel project from the standpoint of human behavioral science. At the highest level of conceptual analysis, I am engaging in a philology of human behavioral science and writing from that perspective. *Philology* is generally understood to mean a study of oral and written records, particularly in their original form to determine either their authenticity and/or their original meaning—especially at the time of their development and delivery (Philology, 2020). From this understanding, a philology of human behavioral science would therefore be studying the oral and written records of the discussion of scientific concepts in their original form with an authentic characterization of their context to determine their meaning both historically and currently—yet always in the service of how the these concepts were and continue to be deployed in the field's understanding of human behavior (in all the forms of mentation, emotion, and manifest behavior). To my knowledge, this connection of philology and human behavioral science has not been attempted before. Thus, the perspective sketched in this paper will undoubtedly be seen as any variety of incomplete, especially critiqueable, or even under-informed when regarded from other scholarly disciplines that are already dealing explicitly with philology as part of their modes of scholarship or underpinning theoretical perspective. It should also be stated that working with historical documents is not the main training that most scientists (of any specific field of inquiry) receive—if that training exists at all—rendering work with historical documents a particular scholastic challenge to any professionally trained scientist. Yet, for any scholar, the problems of working with historical documents become compounded by the challenges of wading through and confronting historical bigotry toward and general de-valuing of non-privileged human lives in different epochs (and in different cultures across epochs). Focusing even more specifically on lesbian identity, all scholars must confront the heteronormativity, the gender bias against women, the erasure or undermining of trans-inclusion in lesbian communities, and the combination of any two or all three when focused on any information related to lesbians in the canonical literature of any scholarship (e.g., psychological science). Consequently, I made every attempt to foreground women's perspectives in my references, even while this will not fully address or eliminate heteronormativity (because some of the women authors are heterosexual), or gender bias against women (because, in the service of heteronormativity, women can repeat and defend patriarchal perspectives), or transnegative perspectives or blatant erasure of trans experience (because in the service of cisnormativity and/or heteronormativity, cis women can deny, denigrate, or erase trans women's and nonbinary individuals' inclusion in lesbian experience).

Given my training in psychological science, a reader might reasonably expect that I would try to initiate my answers to questions of lesbian identity with a focus on popular empirical methods of examining language use in this academic field, such as a textual analysis or, separately, a database search for the times (and locations) of the use of "lesbian identity" in the canonical literature record of psychological science. However, on principle, I will not engage in these methods of analysis. The focus of this sketch at a philology of human behavioral science is to create a meta-scientific perspective, one in which the often implicit, routine, or otherwise *informal* training, assumptions, and biases in the conduct of science by the scientists (as individuals and as a community) is the cornerstone. Thus, to engage a routine empirical analytic method such as textual analysis (qualitatively or quantitatively) or a database search for the terms "lesbian" and "lesbian identity" has the strong possibility of simply showing the consequences of implicit behavior among specific behavioral scientists, without interrogating the informal training, assumptions, and biases of human behavioral scientists writ large as they approach questions of self and identity. As an example, the severe heteronormativity of psychology's past would be recoverable by textual analysis or database searches for term use and so would later attempts to curb, challenge, or change that heteronormativity. (Confer with Hooker's own reflections on the challenges she faced within the psychological science community to do research on homosexuality from a non-mental-disorder perspective; Hooker, 1993; and summaries of this work; e.g., Boxer & Carrier, 1998). However, the larger question of how lesbian identity was, should, or could have been understood within psychological science would remain unanswered via these methods because the methods themselves are designed and deployed to capture the manifest behavior and possible motivations of the actors (that can be inferred from the manifest behavior)—not how the concept itself was being conceptualized and reconceptualized "behind the scenes," as it were, or in the discussions amongst behavioral scientists that did not make it into the canonical literature of that field.

Overview and plan of the paper

From this sketch of a philology of human behavioral science perspective, I ask and answer (the latter to the extent possible) three interrelated questions about the current or future obsolescence of the concept "lesbian identity." The first question is whether *lesbian identity* like predecessor terms for the larger concept of those individuals who identify as women and experience same-gender sexual attraction behavior *will become* obsolete in the future. The predecessor terms for this same concept that are now obsolete for scientific discussions include (but are not limited to): tribad, sapphist, female Uranian [aka *Urningin* in German], and female sexual invert. A second question is whether lesbian identity *should become* obsolete based on its potentially less inclusive meaning—either (a) from the origin terms that comprise it or (b) in comparison to other terms in the lexicon at present. This question explicitly considers whether terms like *dyke* or *queer woman* are more inclusive of a range of attraction sets that those who have been described as lesbians could experience and actually do experience. This question can be seen as parallel to whether *bisexual* is more conatively limited in its scope as compared to modern day counterparts like *pansexual* and *plurisexual*. A third question concerns whether lesbian identity may wane now (at the time of this writing) and then wax again in the future (some decade[s] later from this writing). This question explores whether the same fate that befell *dyke*—which was first deployed in a possibly negative or at least ambivalent use (see below), then deployed as an insult and therefore dis-preferred and dis-used, and then later fully reclaimed by community members (of a certain age cohort in the U.S.)—will happen to the term *lesbian* and thus the concept of *lesbian identity*.

First question: is the linguistic phrase "lesbian identity" obsolete in behavioral science?

Scholars might agree that whatever term the plurality of scientists use at a specific epoch within the science, the underlying phenomenon might be the same even if the language or linguistic conventions differ from epoch to epoch. Considering the *phenomenon* of focus, it seems clear that self-identified women (and those identified as women by others) having sexual and romantic relationships with self-identified women (and those identified as women by others) has been present in human history for all the time that we have written records (e.g. Zimmerman, 2000). Of course, this phenomenon itself needs to be further limited in its referent because, on the foregoing description, women who also had sexual and romantic relationships with self-identified men, for instance, would also be includable. Consequently, it is useful to add the caveat that these relationships under consideration would be largely or exclusively between self-identified women. This near-exclusivity recovers the present meaning of *lesbian* in U.S. culture, at least. Additionally, the specification of self-identified women allows for the inclusion of both cisgender and transgender women as the terms are presently understood in psychological science (cf. Tate & Pearson, 2016).

If a scholar examines the linguistic phrases used for this phenomenon over time, and within science and proto-scientific scholarship in Europe in the 1700s and 1800s, that scholar finds that at least seven different linguistic terms or phrases were used (and this is not an exhaustive list): (a) "tribad," (b) "lesbian," (c) "sapphist," (d) "female Uranian" [aka *Urningin*in German], (e) "female sexual invert," (f) "dyke," and (e) "female homosexual." Each term or phrase has origins in a different culture and different epochs within the same culture.

Tribads is one of the oldest terms referring to women who have sex with women, and is derived from the Greek language verb "to rub" (Zimmerman, 2000). The term persisted from ancient Greek times until the Victorian Era in Europe, around 1837 until 1901 (Zimmerman, 2000). The focus on rubbing and usually the vulval genital structures (i.e., the outer structures of the genitals, including the clitoris) may be a clue to why the term did not last much longer. Lesbian sexual practices feature many more activities in addition to rubbing (Newman, 2004). Additionally, lesbian identity is not recoverable from specific sexual practices. To understand the foregoing point, any two women can have sexual contact with each other without either identifying as a lesbian; instead, the women may each identify as any number of labels including "mostly straight" to "pansexual."

Lesbian and sapphist are both terms that, historically, refer to the poet Sappho who lived on the island of Lesbos (e.g., Zimmerman, 2000). Given that Sappho's enduring legacy for modern audiences is her love poetry to other women, it is unsurprising that these terms also become associated with love and sex between women.

Uranian (*Urning* in German) was a term first used by the German activist Karl Heinrich Ulrichs in a series of five booklets called *Forschungenüber das Räthsel der mannmännlichen Liebe* (which can be translated as "Research into the Riddle of Man-Male Love"), which are credited as being distributed between 1864–1865 (see Ulrichs 1864/1994). Within these booklets, Ulrichs provides a nonscientific analysis of the different types of men who engage in homosexual behavior based on what modern readers would understand as gender roles and gender expression. Later, Richard von Krafft-Ebing (1886/1939), a proto-psychological scholar of the time, simply referred to women with same gender attraction as female Uranians (which was *Urningin* in German). The term "female invert" comes from Havelock Ellis (1895), another proto-psychological scholar of that time, who argued that these women's gender roles were inverted, which attracted them to women instead of men (see also Johnston, 2007, Chap. 1). It should be noted that both von Krafft-Ebing and Ellis believed that same-sex attraction (as they used the term) was a neurological disorder. While neither scholar relied on more than case studies (which are known to be flawed in terms of generalizability to populations of people), their perspectives to different extents helped create the classification of homosexuality as a mental disorder by the American Psychiatric and Psychological Associations (see, e.g., Drescher, 2015; Morgan & Nerison, 1993).

The term *dyke* has disputed origins in U.S. English (Krantz, 1995). Dyke first appears to be used in the U.S. (in the form of "bulldiking") as either a pejorative term or simply as a description of behavior that was already designated as a mental disorder at the time in 1921 (Lichtenstein, 1921). Importantly, the Lichtenstein account uses bulldiking from the patient's perspective as her own words to describe her sexual contact with another woman. Other writers have also proposed that the term was not explicitly negative in different interacting communities, especially among Black women (e.g., Roberts, 1979)—even in 1921. Nonetheless, into the 1950s, the term became an insult toward lesbians (e.g., Kennedy & Davis, 2014; cf. Krantz, 1995). Yet, descriptively, since the 1990s (and possibly starting in the 1970s, see Garber, 2001, chap. 2; Stanley, 1974), the term appears to have been fully taken back in community and used as a positive label (e.g., Morris, 2016), with several events called *Dyke March* being held all over the United States and in many European cities since the early 1990s and continuing until the present day (the suspension of certain in-person marches notwithstanding during 2020 as a public health response to the global pandemic COVID-19.).

The main question for this section is why did "lesbian" remain or sustain in behavioral science as the label *de jour*? It seems clear from the foregoing paragraph that there were several candidate terms that could have remained in use. Yet, it should also be clear that some of the historical terms were characterizations of what we now call lesbian experience as either disordered, abnormal, or in need of correction—on one side—or as simply tack-on or parallel structure forms for terms already in existence to describe men's same gender attraction—on the other side (and "female homosexual" could be included in the latter connection). And, the two sides often appeared together in the human behavioral science of the past to characterize lesbian identity and lesbian experience. Psychological science, in particular, has still not fully reckoned with the abnormal and disordered perspectives regarding same-gender sexual contact and love proposed and defended by past thinkers who either founded or helped influence the field at large (cf. Drescher, 2015; Rothblum, 1994). Nonetheless, this marginalizing perspective of the past became (and continues, to some extent, to be) one of the legacies of psychological science thinking for the U.S. public, at least, and other industrialized cultures whose behavioral science follows the lead of the U.S. Thus, it may be unsurprising to note that one direct answer to why "lesbian" has remained the descriptor into the present is the U.S. social activism of the 1960s through the 1980s. For different historical and political reasons within the U.S., during the 1960s through 1980s, lesbian became the preferred political activism self-identifier (e.g., Grahn, 1984). Then, from the 1990s through the early 2000s, lesbian became the mainstay term in behavioral science research either (a) to counter the heteronormative perspectives of the 1930s-1950s and the mental disorder association of the other terms in psychological research (e.g., Uranian, invert) or (b) to use community-driven terms, or (c) some combination of both motivations. Again, the foregoing statements are trying to make explicit what is usually implicit in the training of new behavioral scientists in psychology—namely, that very few psychological scientists are aware of this history even as they conduct research on sexual orientation in all its forms. Yet, new activism in the early 2000s coupled with (and possibly based on) the resurgence of trans identities in the larger U.S. culture, and specifically within lesbian interacting community, and the subsequent transphobia, transnegativity, and transexclusion that resulted particularly within lesbian interacting community (cf. Green, 2006; Morris, 2005), might have created some unevenness in the use of "lesbian" as a scientific term. In fact, scholars from other disciplines appear to have put "lesbian" into the category of a waning term, in different ways and different places in the U.S., being eclipsed by "dyke," which was (and often is) seen as more trans-inclusive, at least politically speaking (e.g., Brown-Saracino & Ghaziani, 2009), even while the terms are often used as equivalents (e.g., Farquhar, 2000; Morris, 2016). One of the only attempts within psychological science to make the term "lesbian" inclusive of both trans women and nonbinary individuals comes from Tate (2012), who argued that there is nothing inherent in the term itself nor in its psychological referents that precludes trans women or certain nonbinary individuals (the latter being referenced with the term "genderqueer," at that time). Tate's (2012) specific use of *nonbinary individuals* is worth unpacking in further detail here for the understanding of this term itself and the implications of Tate's arguments. Consistent with a larger discussion of the different facets (or constructs) that are described using the term "gender," Tate et al. (2014) describe *nonbinary individuals* as referring to those people whose self-categorizations are not exclusively or not contrastively female or male. This *self-categorization* referent is further described by Tate et al. (2014) as one of the five separable facets of gender, and thereby not to be confused with two other separable facets (from self-categorization and each other)—namely, (a) gender roles, norms, and ideologies (viz., adherences or non-adherences to societal roles, norms, and expectations for gender groups) nor with (b) gender presentations and displays (e.g., clothing and accouterment use and nonverbal mannerisms). Consequently, nonbinary individuals for Tate (2012) and Tate et al. (2014) refer only to individuals whose demographic label or categorical core identity is not exclusively or contrastively female or male. From this understanding, Tate (2012) argues that any nonbinary individual whose self-categorization includes a female- or woman-type concept—for instance, "demi girl" (as in partly woman but not completely at core) or "gender blended" (viz., a female core identity as blended with another gender category [e.g., male]) or as one meaning of "transmasculine" (viz., in the sense that a female core identity exists for the self, but the person experiences a stronger male-type core identity)—could be included in a behavioral science classification as part of lesbian identity. As Tate (2012) describes, this is to create conceptual coherence to the category of lesbian itself, as referring most generally to individuals with some type of FEMALE core identity (in part or in whole) as being attracted to others with some type of FEMALE core identity (again, in part or in whole). Tate's (2012) other explicit statement is that individuals whose self-categorization excludes female- or woman-type concepts—for instance, "nullgender" (as in does not have a label at all) or a different use of "transmasculine" (viz., in the sense of only male-type identity with possibly another non-female-identity, such as neutrois). Finally, it is also clear from the Tate (2012) analysis—as updated by Tate et al. (2014)—that Tate's analysis *does not include* individuals who might identify as "nonbinary" as a description of their participation in gender roles or gender norms that are neither masculine nor feminine (or, separately, both simultaneously) and/or as their participation in gender performances or displays that are neither masculine nor feminine (or, separately, both simultaneously). Admittedly, the Tate perspective is not the only behavioral science perspective on this issue, with other researchers including flexible participation in masculine and feminine gender roles as well as gender presentations (in addition to or in place of core identity) as also describable as nonbinary individuals (see, e.g., Galupo et al., 2017).

Thus, a salient answer to this question within behavioral science at this moment is that *lesbian identity might become obsolete* as a scientific term because of its community ties to different forms of activism that have been associated (admittedly unevenly) with exclusionary behavior. Of course, this statement relies on the idea that the newer generation of behavioral scientists might find "dyke" or "queer woman" more appealing, in part, because it describes their own lived experiences and, in another part, because it seems to be associated with the activism of the 2010s and beyond. From a meta-scientific perspective, it should be unsurprising that behavioral scientists (like other scholars) might wish to use the terms that capture any era's zeitgeist, even while it is also true that the vacillations of community-based activism are not a necessity of behavioral science terminology. Nonetheless, one possible source of reticence for behavioral scientists to create their own neologisms and purely technical terms for social-behavioral phenomena is that the field of psychology in particular has an unfortunate history of engaging in this specific collective behavior to evaluate and marginalize underrepresented human experiences (e.g., Drescher, 2015; Rothblum, 1994), as we see from terms like "female invert." In sum, given the heteronormative, heterohegemonic, and cisnormative perspectives that have dominated the full history of academic psychology in Europe and North America for the past 125 years, the recent trend of using community-generated terms (within the past 20–30 years) for those groups marginalized by early academic psychology (e.g., Schudson et al., 2017), in particular, may continue into the future.

Yet, at the time of this writing, it would be descriptively accurate to state that lesbian is not (as in not yet) obsolete within human behavioral science to the extent that the term is still used in scientific reports, discussions, and data collection protocols. It is also accurate to state that, conditionally, *if and only if* behavioral science researchers created their own new and unique technical term for the experience currently describable as "lesbian identity", then the phrase lesbian identity itself would become obsolete—as all the predecessor terms have.

Second question: Should lesbian identity become obsolete in behavioral science?

The question of whether lesbian identity *should* become obsolete is distinguishable from the prior question (of whether the phrase will fall out of favor within interacting, marginalized communities). The question of *should* involves the consideration of whether the linguistic phrase lesbian identity is too limiting in its behavioral science reference. Using the understanding of the term as presented by Tate (e.g., Tate, 2012; Tate & Pearson, 2016), the phrase *lesbian identity* can be inclusive of cis women, trans women, and certain nonbinary individuals (see the detailed description in the section above), thereby not creating a limitation on who can be included in the phenomenon so long as the individual self-identifies as a woman exclusively (which both cis and trans women do) or in part (as certain, but not all, nonbinary individuals do). These arguments are acceptable for behavioral scientists communicating with each other, as colleagues, provided this is the consensus meaning of the term. However, the question of *should,* in this section, can also adjoin the reality that human behavioral scientists working in the area of sexuality in general have to solicit self-labels from participants about their own sexual orientation identities. A particular scenario may illustrate how much the solicitation of self-labels matters for the actual conduct of human behavioral science. Imagine that some women and nonbinary folks who otherwise could be includable in a behavioral scientist's data organization scheme as lesbians, do not select (or do not self-generate) the response "lesbian". (One underlying reason for these participants' behavior is that they might find the term "lesbian" too limiting to convey their experience.) The consequence would be that those individuals (who could otherwise be includable under an expanded definition of the term; see Tate, 2012, specifically) would not be part of that scientist's collected data for that category. Now we can see that the question of should lesbian identity become obsolete becomes more acute.

Moreover, there is already some empirical evidence that certain participants are themselves reconsidering the label of "lesbian" for the self. Specifically, these are women (cis or trans) who are in romantic and/or sexual partnerships with nonbinary individuals who do not have a core identity that includes female in any way, or, separately, in partnerships with trans men (see, e.g., Brown, 2009; Brown-Saracino & Ghaziani, 2009; Joslin-Roher & Wheeler, 2009)—even when that dating partner was, in the past, a member of "lesbian community" (Brown, 2009). Some of these women might have identified as a "lesbian" in the past (prior to these relationships) but now wonder whether another phrase such as "dyke"—and thereby "dyke identity"— and/or "queer"—and thereby "queer woman"— would be more inclusive or less limiting for the self as a label.

In this connection, the parallel argument that is already happening in human behavioral science regarding *bisexuality*, on one side, and *pansexuality* or *plurisexuality*, on another side, might be informative. The main argument for replacing bisexuality with terms like pansexual or plurisexual in behavioral science (but, of course, not limited to this field of inquiry) is that *bi*, denotatively (from its Latin meaning), indicates only 2 (e.g., Galupo, 2018). Thus, a bisexual person as a descriptor might be understood to be attracted to, in romantic and/or sexual terms, only two genders of individuals. (There is, admittedly, a double bias in the meaning of the "sexual" term. One bias is that there might be two sexes, but this bias has been thoroughly problematized in the past 25 years such that it is untenable in its strict meaning [e.g., Blackless et al., 2000; Hyde et al., 2019]. The other bias is that the meaning of "sexual" collapses the activities of the attraction and sex drive systems in behavioral science, which are considered to exist and operate somewhat separately [cf., Fisher et al., 2002], which makes room for the different types of asexuality and aromanticism [Antonsen et al., 2020]). Taking the two genders meaning, people who identify as bisexual in social life and social conversations may, in reality, be attracted to certain types of individuals who identify as nonbinary. Consequently, the tension is between the denotative meaning of the term (only or exactly 2) and the reality of how many classes of people can be functionally included in the attraction set. Because both *pan* (meaning "all" in Latin) and *pluri-* (meaning "many or multiple" in Latin) are denotatively more than 2, the necessary question has been asked whether researchers should consider rephrasing their terms when considering this phenomenal experience (e.g., Galupo, 2018). Notice that this rephrasing suggestion has three consequential foci—some of which may not be explicit in the summary of the points, but all of which I make explicit here. One focus is to capture participants who are increasingly identifying themselves as "pan" (but are includable within a larger behavioral science concept that includes bisexuality too—namely, plurisexual). A second focus is to have a debate about the usage of classification terms among human behavioral scientists themselves. A third focus is to also manage the communication of the meaning of this phenomenon to other scholars and the public—all of whom exist outside the human behavioral science field.

Based on the immediately foregoing point, we can now discuss three "responsibilities" of human behavioral scientists when dealing with language to characterize humans. One responsibility, and possibly the easiest for any scholar to understand, is to provide participants in scientific studies with an adequate linguistic representation of their experience so that they can recognize their ability to be included in the research. This responsibility necessitates tracking the language that different communities use and representing that same language to them in the collection of data. Yet, the two other responsibilities focus on communication to different audiences. A second responsibility is for human behavioral scientists to communicate with colleagues within that science. In terms of this responsibility, behavioral scientists are able to develop, deploy, and use whatever terms they wish *amongst themselves*, including ones that may have incomplete or insufficiently precise meanings. One reason that this would be descriptively true is because the specific training in behavioral science would presumably create a consensual understanding among its participants as to the "rules of use" of any phrase. (For those trained in quantitative methods within any behavioral science, the term "statistically significant" comes to mind as an easy illustration; we are responsible for formally teaching the meaning of this phrase to our students and other junior scholars continuing within the larger discipline.) In this way, that call for pansexuality and/or plurisexuality as the larger scientific term can happen completely within the human behavioral scientific community, and its pros and cons can be weighed against the use of bisexuality. Yet, a third responsibility is for human behavioral scientists to communicate their ideas to other scholars and to the public at large (including non-scholars). Thus, the fact that there is a current social movement (outside of the confines of behavioral scientists communicating with themselves) toward using the term "bi/pan" to refer to the larger interacting community is now its own consideration for behavioral scientists to communicate their studies and their findings to others outside this field. If the use of plurisexual or pansexual would be a more effective communication tool for scholars outside human behavioral science, then behavioral scientists need to seriously consider whether the possibility of easier integration with other disciplines and, separately, communication to the (non-scholarly) public would be of interest and an overall benefit for the field.

We can now focus on the three parallel considerations for lesbian identity. One consideration is: Is "lesbian" too limiting a term for the realities of how women (cis and trans) and certain nonbinary individuals who identify as lesbians experience their attractions to others in real interacting community? As described earlier in this section, there is qualitative research which suggests that some individual women do seem to struggle with using the "lesbian" term for themselves when they are dating a partner who does not identify as being a woman in any way. Thus, what is the next step for behavioral scientists regarding the use of the term "lesbian identity" for recruiting and including participants? A second consideration is: Will behavioral scientists create a consensus definition of the term amongst themselves (that is, among colleagues only) that is inclusive like the Tate (2012) definition? If behavioral scientists adopt an expansive definition as the consensus, then the term *lesbian identity* would not be too limiting. The third consideration is: What is the communication "cost" of using or not using "lesbian identity" to describe human behavioral science to other scholars and the public? One consequence, of course, could be the bifurcation of social and scientific experience using the same exact word. Specifically, if behavioral scientists decided to continue to use *lesbian identity* as the main technical term for themselves and to communicate with each other, it seems that there could come a point where these scientists would have to remind audiences that they are referring to *lesbian identity* as a technical phenomenon with a technical definition (viz., operationalization). The nonscientific use of the term would be allowable and allowed to evolve over time, especially to collect empirical data (qualitative or quantitative from human participants), but the scientific meaning would (and would have to) be relatively inalterable. At this point, behavioral scientists would find themselves in the familiar territory of being easily mis-understood when not being explicit in every single scientific communication.

Bringing all these considerations together, should a new term replace "lesbian identity" (as in should the existing term become obsolete?) to ensure that both scientific and nonscientific audiences do not create confusion during cross-talk? If the answer is *yes*, then the term should become obsolete. If the answer is either *maybe or no*, then the term should remain in use. In any event, the group of human behavioral scientists studying this phenomenon would have to come to a consensus in order for the answer to emerge.

Third question: Will lesbian identity experience a period of obsolescence in behavioral science?

This third and final question, addressable by my sketch ata philology of human behavioral science perspective, is whether "lesbian identity" will go into a period of obsolescence to be revived later in time. Admittedly, there is no good manner by which to predict the answer. Nonetheless, posing the question seems useful in the sense that it allows all scholars (including behavioral science researchers) to ponder the larger fact that some terms, phrases, and linguistic conventions show a period of waxing and then waning and then waxing again. Particular to the phenomenon currently described as lesbian identity, the term dyke has already experienced the closest fate to the description in the foregoing sentence. As noted above, "dyke" may have entered U.S. lexicon as either a community term or as an insult from heterosexual community, and then became almost exclusively an insult and pejorative term for a time in U.S. culture, only to reemerge as a community term, especially for political organizing (see, e.g., Morris, 2016). While "dyke" has not yet become the consensus term for describing lesbians in behavioral science literature, its place within popular lexicon seems well-established at least among lesbians and gay men. (Heterosexual women and men of a certain age may still believe the term to be an insult or carry negative connotations.)

While admittedly speculative, it is conceivable that lesbian identity may wane into (what may become) the "roaring 20s" of the 2000s. For all the reasons stated above, the term lesbian may be seen as too reactionary or else too focused on a particular set of political issues by the ensuing political generations of the 2020s and later (see Morris, 2016), who may then prefer the term "dyke" or some other term. In that event, "lesbian identity" might eventually fade from use, even in the human behavior scientific discourse, in part because demographic questions about sexual orientation might change to reflect the waning use of the term "lesbian" for self-categorization. Yet, just like "dyke," the historical object of "lesbian" would still be accessible to human behavior scientists via the canonical literature that they read to build continued scientific discourse and might be revived to the extent that there was a portion of its older use—including the political situatedness with the U.S. feminism of the 1970s as advancing women's rights—that become repurposed or rediscovered for the audiences of generations in the future. In the latter connection, "lesbian identity" may be reclaimed by behavioral scientists in the future after a period of dis-use because it will (once again) foreground (cis and trans) women's experiences in a manner that "dyke" might not. To clarify, in that far, imagined future, to start, the term "dyke" would likely include cis and trans women and certain nonbinary folks (with some female-type aspect to their core identities). To continue, those certain nonbinary folks might have different social and political experiences than the cis and trans women, even if both sets of individuals exist in similar social and sexual circles. Materially, one difference could be that those with a strong female core identity (viz., cis and trans women) may experience closer social and/ or political affinity to other women across sexual orientations (e.g., dyke women and heterosexual women), whereas, having a less strong (and not exclusively) female core identity (as certain nonbinary individuals have) may not create the same affinities toward the same groups across sexual orientations (e.g., nonbinary dykes may not experience an affinity toward heterosexual women). In that event, there may be an analytic need to demarcate the two groups of dykes (i.e., dyke women and dyke nonbinary folk) because there might be different concerns and awarenesses of social outcomes connected to their different senses of larger gender groups to which they belong. At that future time, "lesbian identity" might return to demarcate cis and trans women as a distinguishable subset of the larger dyke community.

Conclusions

While this article has, in the literal sense, raised more questions than it has provided definitive answers to, this may be an illustration of one of the useful functions of the sketch at a philology of human behavioral science perspective that I have developed. The questions raised may not have the traditional answer that is true for all time. Instead, these questions may provide a series of possible answers, which having been enumerated, in turn, make the reader aware of some of the underlying and yet-to-be-explicated tensions within the conduct of human behavioral science research itself. A science of human behavior is necessarily a science that has to respect four interlocking considerations that may seem outside the science, but are integral to its execution: (a) the history of any research question; (b) how that history has been mis-used, as is the case with sexual orientation minority experiences; (c) mis-use notwithstanding, how the status of the science influences nonscientific language and understandings of the social world; and, (d) finally, how the science itself must respond to the ever-evolving social communication of any human behavior phenomena via language. The over-arching question of whether lesbian identity is obsolete makes the scientists who study human behavior acutely aware of the assumptions that went before them, exist in their present-day, and will come after them—because all are necessary for an effective and responsible conduct of the science.

Disclosure statement

No potential conflict of interest was reported by the author.

Funding

The author reported there is no funding associated with the work featured in this article.

References

Antonsen, A. N., Zdaniuk, B., Yule, M., & Brotto, L. A. (2020). Ace and aro: Understanding the differences in romantic attractions among persons identifying as asexual. *Archives of Sexual Behavior*, 49(5), 1615–1630. https://doi.org/10.1007/s10508-019-01600-1

Blackless, M., Charuvastra, A., Derryck, A., Fausto-Sterling, A., Lauzanne, K., & Lee, E. (2000). How sexually dimorphic are we? Review and synthesis. *American Journal of Human Biology*, 12(2), 151–166. https://doi.org/10.1002/(SICI)1520-6300(200003/04)12:2<151::AID-AJHB1>3.0.CO;2-F

Boxer, A. M., & Carrier, J. M. (1998). Evelyn Hooker: A life remembered. *Journal of Homosexuality*, 36(1), 1–17. https://doi.org/10.1300/J082v36n01_01

Brown, N. (2009). I'm in transition too": Sexual identity renegotiation in sexual-minority women's relationships with transsexual men. *International Journal of Sexual Health*, 21(1), 61–77. https://doi.org/10.1080/19317610902720766

Brown-Saracino, J., & Ghaziani, A. (2009). The constraints of culture: Evidence from the Chicago dyke march. *Cultural Sociology*, 3(1), 51–75. https://doi.org/10.1177/1749975508100671

Drescher, J. (2015). Out of DSM: Depathologizing homosexuality. *Behavioral Sciences (Basel, Switzerland)*, 5(4), 565–575. https://doi.org/10.3390/bs5040565

Ellis, H. (1895). Sexual inversion in women. *Alienist and Neurologist, 16*, 141–158.

Farquhar, C. (2000). Lesbian" in a post-lesbian world? Policing identity, sex and image. *Sexualities*, *3*(2), 219–236. https://doi.org/10.1177/136346000003002007

Fisher, H. E., Aron, A., Mashek, D., Li, H., & Brown, L. L. (2002). Defining the brain systems of lust, romantic attraction, and attachment. *Archives of Sexual Behavior*, *31*(5), 413–419. https://doi.org/10.1023/a:1019888024255

Galupo, M. P. (2018). 4 Plurisexualidentity labels and the marking of bisexual desire. In D. Swan & S. Habibi (Eds.), *Bisexuality* (pp. 61–75). Springer. https://doi.org/10.1007/978-3-319-71535-3_4

Galupo, M. P., Pulice-Farrow, L., & Ramirez, J. L. (2017). Like a constantly flowing river": Gender identity flexibility among nonbinary transgender individuals. In J. D. Simott (Ed.), *Identity flexibility during adulthood* (pp. 163–177). Springer.

Garber, L. (2001). *Identity poetics: Race, class, and the lesbian-feminist roots of queer theory*. Columbia University Press.

Grahn, J. (1984). *Another mother tongue: Gay words, gay worlds*. Beacon Press.

Green, E. R. (2006). Debating trans inclusion in the feminist movement: A trans-positive analysis. *Journal of Lesbian Studies*, *10*(1–2), 231–248. https://doi.org/10.1300/J155v10n01_12

Hooker, E. (1993). Reflections of a 40-year exploration: A scientific view on homosexuality. *American Psychologist*, *48*(4), 450–453. https://doi.org/10.1037/0003-066X.48.4.450

Hyde, J. S., Bigler, R., Joel, D., Tate, C. C., & van Anders, S. M. (2019). The future of sex and gender in psychology: Five challenges to the gender binary. *The American Psychologist*, *74*(2), 171–193. https://doi.org/10.1037/amp0000307

Johnston, G. (2007). *The formation of 20th-century queer autobiography: Reading Vita Sackville-West, Virginia Woolf, Hilda Doolittle, and Gertrude Stein*. Palgrave Macmillan.

Joslin-Roher, E., & Wheeler, D. P. (2009). Partners in transition: The transition experience of lesbian, bisexual, and queer identified partners of transgender men. *Journal of Gay & Lesbian Social Services*, *21*(1), 30–48. https://doi.org/10.1080/10538720802494743

Kennedy, E. L., & Davis, M. D. (2014). *Boots of leather, slippers of gold: The history of a lesbian Community* (20th anniversary ed.). Routledge.

Krantz, S. E. (1995). Reconsidering the etymology of bulldike. *American Speech*, *70*(2), 217–221. https://doi.org/10.2307/455819

Lichtenstein, P. M. (1921). The 'fairy' and the lady lover. *Medical Review of Reviews*, *27*(8), 369–374.

Morgan, K. S., & Nerison, R. M. (1993). Homosexuality and psychopolitics: An historical overview. *Psychotherapy: Theory, Research, Practice, Training*, *30*(1), 133–140. https://doi.org/10.1037/0033-3204.30.1.133

Morris, B. J. (2005). Commentary: Valuing woman-only spaces. *Feminist Studies*, *31*(3), 618–630. https://doi.org/10.2307/20459054

Morris, B. J. (2016). *The disappearing L: Erasure of lesbian spaces and culture*. State University of New York Press.

Newman, F. (2004). *The whole lesbian sex book: A passionate guide for all of us* (2nd ed.). Cleis Press.

Philology. (2020). *Oxford languages dictionary via Google*. https://www.google.com/search?-client=firefox-b-1-d&q=philology

Roberts, J. R. (1979). In America they call us dykes: Notes on the etymology and use of "dyke. *Sinister Wisdom*, *9*, 2–11.

Rothblum, E. D. (1994). "I only read about myself on bathroom walls": The need for research on the mental health of lesbians and gay men. *Journal of Consulting and Clinical Psychology*, *62*(2), 213–220. https://doi.org/10.1037/0022-006X.62.2.213

Schudson, Z. C., Dibble, E. R., & van Anders, S. M. (2017). Gender/sex and sexual diversity via sexual configurations theory: Insights from a qualitative study with gender and sexual minorities. *Psychology of Sexual Orientation and Gender Diversity*, *4*(4), 422–437. https://doi.org/10.1037/sgd0000241

Stanley, J. P. (1974). When we say "out of the closets!" *College English*, *36*(3), 385–391. https://doi.org/10.2307/374858

Tate, C. C. (2012). Considering lesbian identity from a social-psychological perspective: Two different models of "being a lesbian". *Journal of Lesbian Studies*, *16*(1), 17–29.

Tate, C. C., & Pearson, M. D. (2016). Toward an inclusive model of lesbian identity development: Outlining a common and nuanced model for cis and trans women. *Journal of Lesbian Studies*, *20*(1), 97–115. https://doi.org/10.1080/10894160.2015.1076237

Tate, C. C., Youssef, C. P., & Bettergarcia, J. N. (2014). Integrating the study of transgender spectrum and cisgender experiences of self-categorization from a personality perspective. *Review of General Psychology*, *18*(4), 302–312. https://doi.org/10.1037/gpr0000019

Ulrichs, K. H. (1864/1994). *The riddle of "man-manly" love: The pioneering work on male homosexuality* (M. Lombardi-Nash, Trans.). Prometheus Books.

von Krafft-Ebing, R. (1886/1939). *Psychopathiasexualis: A medico-forensic study*. Pioneer Publications.

Zimmerman, B. (2000). *Lesbian histories and cultures: An encyclopedia* (Vol. 1, pp. 776–777). Taylor & Francis.

Willful lives: Self-determination in lesbian and trans feminisms

Kathryn J. Perkins

ABSTRACT

Challenging the determinism evident in assigning gender at birth, this commentary examines how lesbian and trans feminisms resist gender fatalism through willful self-determination. Conceptualizing gender fatalism as a prophecy and drawing on Sara Ahmed's (2016) work on gender fatalism and willfulness and Talia Mae Bettcher's (2014) work on reality enforcement, I argue that most lesbian and trans feminisms defy the fated outcomes predicted by gender assignment and coerced by the biopolitical regimes of gender enforcement. Instead, these feminisms share a common thread of self-determination that is a site for coalition building and solidarity. I echo this call for a rejection of gender fatalism and for the collective work of gender liberation through living willful lives built from self-determination through bodily, sexual, reproductive, and gender autonomy.

"Boys *will be* boys." A prophecy. Assigning gender at birth assumes so much, so much is foretold. The maintenance of the Western binary sex/gender/sexuality system is predicated on the accuracy of this prophecy, which is that those assigned male at birth *will be* masculine men who *will be* attracted to feminine women. Most lesbian and trans feminisms reject this prophecy, refusing to enlist bodies and energies to support the smooth functioning of the political regimes that enforce this gender fatalism. These feminisms evince a strong thread of self-determination, a willfulness, that pushes back against the tides of cisheteronormativity. In this article, I use Sara Ahmed's (2016) conceptualizations of gender fatalism and willfulness and Talia Mae Bettcher's (2014) conceptualization of reality enforcement to explore the principle of self-determination evident in lesbian and trans feminisms as a site of intersectional solidarity and coalition building. I end with a call to reject gender fatalism by living willful lives embracing gender liberation through defiance and autonomy.

Gender fatalism hurts. It foretells lives of gendered bodies that inevitably conform to their assignments and don't stand out or rebel. Gender fatalism is a resignation to the fate predicted by assigning gender at birth, it is an abnegation of the power to envision and construct new gender realities in favor of the reproduction of cisheteronormative gender based on its perceived inevitability (Ahmed, 2016). From mandatory legal gender registration systems to gender "reveal" parties, fatalistic gender conformity is strictly enforced through the myriad of biopolitical techniques that take aim at the body, at the level of the population and the individual. These techniques function as a "reality enforcement" system, meaning that the morally ascribed "reality" of binary sex, and thus binary gender, assignment at birth is centered to ensure that gendered presentations align with binary sexed bodies (Bettcher, 2014). Biopolitical techniques, such as genital verification, sex segregated spaces, and sex registration, function as kind of "straightening rod" to punish and circumscribe rebellious transgressive bodies (Ahmed, 2016; Bettcher, 2014). In the Western gender system, this gender apparatus polices bodies according to capitalist, colonial, and racialized norms of gender. This means that its reality enforcement regimes are inherently racist, ableist, sizeist, and classist, producing intersectional forms of gender oppression such as transmisogynoir. This term captures the specific oppression caused by the intersection of anti-Blackness, transphobia, and misogyny (Bailey & Trudy, 2018). The political regime of cisheteronormative gender, through traditional, oppositional, hetero and cis sexist ideologies, regulates every aspect of gendered embodiment including gender identity, sexual autonomy, and reproductive autonomy. The straightening rods of biopolitical violence help to incentivize internalized norms of self-governance to keep us on the narrow path of gender fatalism.

Lesbian feminisms reject being complicit in this gender fatalistic oppression of lesbians in favor of self-determination and willful resistance. As Monique Wittig (1992) argues, "man" and "woman" are political identities constructed to enforce a regime of heterosexuality. Her work demonstrates how oppositional sexism is used to construct women as being naturally inclined to be in subordinated sexual relationships with men. "By doing this, by admitting that there is a "natural" division between women and men, we naturalize history, we assume that "men" and "women" have always existed and will always exist. Not only do we naturalize history, but also consequently we naturalize the social phenomena which expresses our oppression, making change impossible (Wittig, 1992, pp. 10–11)." This gender fatalism thus helps to facilitate sexual violence and the appropriation of cis women's bodies for heterosexual reproductive labor. Ruthann Robson's (2000) work in lesbian legal theory shows how the juridical state acts as a straightening rod sanctioning and executing this violence by framing heterosexuality as natural and thus constructing lesbian lives and families as less "real," thereby depriving lesbians of reproductive autonomy.

This oppression of lesbians is compounded by the widespread and systemic lack of access to reproductive technologies, further limiting reproductive freedom. When the political category of woman is bound up in the political regime of heterogender, perhaps as Wittig argues, lesbians are not women. To be a lesbian is to reject the prophecy of gender fatalism, to exercise willful self-determination by building a life that does not conform to heteronormativity. Thus, as Cheryl Clarke (1981) argues, lesbianism is an act of resistance against coerced heterosexuality. For as Diane Richardson (2000) states, "lesbian feminists have insisted on the right to be lesbian, as a specific identity and practice, and the freedom (for all women) to be able to choose to have relationships with other women." Lesbian feminisms are willful, being a lesbian is willful. As Sara Ahmed (2016) shows, part of being a willful subject is to reject the heteronormative and determinative paths to "happiness" and forge our own paths and orientations instead, to live a willful life.

Trans feminisms shed light on the ways the gender apparatus actively tries to keep "boys *being* boys". Transphobic and transmisogynistic reality enforcement regimes seek to fulfill the prophecy of gender fatalism through deadnaming, misgendering, slurs, genital verification, and other forms of violence (Bettcher, 2014). As Emi Koyama (2003) argues in the "Transfeminist Manifesto", trans feminisms are about rejecting the cisnormative oppression of institutionalized gender systems in favor of self-determination and bodily autonomy. Trans feminist perspectives are grounded in intersectional feminisms and embrace the complexity and diversity of embodied gendered experiences (Stryker & Bettcher, 2016). For as Julia Serano (2007) shows, cis sexism is predicated on the assumed naturalness of cis genders and the "realness" of gender assignment at birth. It forecloses the possibility that boys might become girls just as hetero sexism forecloses the possibility that girls might desire to be with girls. Serrano also demonstrates how oppositional sexism naturalizes gender, facilitating the structural oppression, not just of women, but of femininities. In resistance to this determinism, trans feminisms advocate for gender autonomy in defiance of the reality enforcement regimes that constantly seek to anticipate and regulate our gender (Bettcher, 2014). Jillian Weiss (2001) elucidates how the juridical state also upholds cisnormativity through framing cis genders as natural and thus structurally denies the right to gender autonomy. This creates legal brick walls that can prevent trans people from transitioning and make it dangerous when they do. As Rachel Anne Williams (2019) argues, trans bodies can be seen as nails sticking out, gendered bodies that don't quite fit and thus are subject to the disciplinary reality enforcement regimes of the gender apparatus. To gender transition while being subject to reality enforcement regimes that cast trans bodies as either "deceivers" or "make-believers" is an act of willful and radical self-love (Bettcher, 2007). A dogged pursuit of gender euphoria in the wake of fatalistic gender prophecies. As CeCe McDonald (2017) illuminates, our lives are like blank canvases waiting for the colors of life, "and as we are the canvas, we are also the illustrator. And with every stroke of the brush, we decide how our art of life will be." Thus, trans feminisms are willful, taking up brushes to paint lives of gender liberation through self-determination and gender autonomy.

Lesbian and trans feminisms share an undercurrent of self-determination and willful rejection of gender fatalism. They indict the gender apparatus and its violent reality enforcement regimes and refuse to lend energy to continuing to propagate and enforce them. This apparatus compels our willing participation to fulfill the prophecy of gender fatalism; we have to choose to stop using our bodies as instruments of its violence by acting as straightening rods policing gender. We should instead work to build feminist safe havens as sites of embodied resistance to gendered violence and oppression. This means acknowledging the immense hurt and pain caused by trans exclusion in feminist discourses and spaces, and it means working from where we are to construct sites of intersectional solidarity, grounded in our collective rage at gender fatalism and its enforcement regimes.

Is lesbian identity obsolete? No, lesbian identities and feminisms are not antiquated; indeed, they show us how to resist and survive in our gender fatalistic world. Yet, lesbianism must be trans inclusive if it is to continue to light a way forward toward gender liberation. Trans inclusive lesbian identities and feminisms are not new; indeed, as Emma Heaney (2016) shows us, trans women and other trans feminine people have been lesbians and lesbian feminists from the early days of organized lesbian resistance in the United States. Trans/lesbian futures demand acknowledging these trans/lesbian pasts. To move forward, we need to liberate gender. Gender liberation means we embrace willful lives built from self-determination through bodily, sexual, reproductive, and gender autonomy as we work together to dismantle intersectional systems of oppression and create better futures for us all. To live a willful life means we take up CeCe McDonald's (2017) call to "not leave your canvases undone. Use every color imaginable to show who you are inside and out, for every tint and every hue counts. And as you create your picture remember you are the illustrator, so no one can create your picture but you. So make it the most precious and most beautiful picture that you can, with love, truth, and joy in every color."

Funding

The author(s) reported there is no funding associated with the work featured in this article.

References

Ahmed, S. (2016). *Living a feminist life*. Duke University Press.

Bailey, M., & Trudy. (2018). On misogynoir: Citation, erasure, and plagiarism. *Feminist Media Studies, 18*(4), 762–768. https://doi.org/10.1080/14680777.2018.1447395

Bettcher, T. M. (2007). Evil deceivers and make-believers: Transphobic violence and the politics of illusion. *Hypatia, 22* (3), 43–65. https://doi.org/10.1111/j.1527-2001.2007.tb01090.x

Bettcher, T. M. (2014). Trapped in the wrong theory: Rethinking trans oppression and resistance. *Signs: Journal of Women in Culture and Society, 39*(2), 383–406. https://doi.org/10.1086/673088

Clarke, C. (1981). Lesbianism: An act of resistance. In C. Moraga & T. C. Bambara (Eds.), *This bridge called my back: Writings by radical women of color* (pp. 128–137). Persephone Press.

Heaney, E. (2016). Women-identified women: Trans women in 1970s lesbian feminist organizing. *TSQ: Transgender Studies Quarterly, 3*(1–2), 137–145. https://doi.org/10.1215/23289252-3334295

Koyama, E. (2003). The transfeminist manifesto. In R. Dicker & A. Piepmeier (Eds.), *Catching a wave: Reclaiming feminism for the 21st century* (pp. 244–259). Northern University Press.

McDonald, C. (2017). "February 14, 2012." From "Go Beyond Our Natural Selves" The Prison Letters of CeCe McDonald. *TSQ: Transgender Studies Quarterly, 4*(2), 243–265. https://doi.org/10.1215/23289252-3815045

Richardson, D. (2000). Claiming citizenship? Sexuality, citizenship and lesbian/feminist theory. *Sexualities, 3*(2), 255–272. https://doi.org/10.1177/136346000003002009

Robson, R. (2000). Making mothers: Lesbian legal theory and the judicial construction of lesbian mothers. *Women's Rights Law Reporter, 22*, 15.

Serano, J. (2007). *Whipping girl: A transsexual woman on sexism and the scapegoating of femininity*. Seal Press.

Stryker, S., & Bettcher, T. M. (2016). Introduction trans/feminisms. *TSQ: Transgender Studies Quarterly, 3*(1-2), 5–14. https://doi.org/10.1215/23289252-3334127

Weiss, J. T. (2001). The gender caste system: Identity, privacy, and heteronormativity. *Law & Sexuality: Rev. Lesbian, Gay, Bisexual & Transgender Legal Issues, 10*, 123.

Williams, R. A. (2019). *Transgressive: A trans woman on gender, feminism, and politics*. Jessica Kingsley Publishers.

Wittig, M. (1992). *The straight mind and other essays*. Beacon Press.

Index

Note: **Bold** page numbers refer to tables and page numbers followed by "n" denote endnotes.

academic: affairs 118; elitism 19; feminism 41, 125
activism 2, 47, 85, 121, 194
aesthetic theorization 44
African American-Black 59, 69n8
African American people 25
"African lesbian sexualities" 131
African queer studies 131
Afro Mexicana women 60
Ahmed, Sara 37, 58, 112, 116, 214, 216
AIDS pandemic 95
Alexander, Jacqui 37
Amazones d'hier, lesbiennes d'aujourd'hui
    magazine 9
Amazon Quarterly 20
American Psychiatric and Psychological
    Associations 202
Amin, Kadji 49
Anglophone context 5
Anglo-Saxon labels 133
antagonism 147, 148, 149, 150, 157
anti-dance movement 34
anti-nautch movement 34
anti-queer politics 64; *see also contra-queer* politics
anti-racist feminisms 121
anti-sodomy laws 93
anti-TERF method 174
anti-trans feminists 121
Anzaldúa, Gloria 43, 65
Arnold, June 43
Arobateau, Red Jordan 193
asexuality 206
Atlantic slave trade 60
attachment genealogy 49
azaan (the Muslim call for prayer) 35

baby boomers 92–108
backward-onward community-formation 17, 22
backward-onward reflexivity 28
Bechdel, Alison 184
behavioral science 200–209, 205
Beins, Agatha 26

Ben Hagai, B. E. 2
Benjamin, Harry 173
Bettcher, Talia Mae 214
Beyond Intersectionality symposium 120
bharatanatyam (classical Indian dance) 35
biological sex 94, 104
biopolitical control 17
biopolitical techniques 215
birth-assigned sex 115
bisexuality 102, 200, 206
bisexual women 10
bismillah 36
Black feminist thought 119
black lesbian feminism 45
Black Lives Matter movement 48
Blackwell, Maylei 63
border wars 146, 165
Bornstein, Kate 96
Briggs, Laura 118
Britzman, Deb 184, 187
broader movement 112
Brownmiller, Susan 193
butch-femme identities 146
butch lesbians 155–157, 156; butch-femme
    dyad 135; butchness 135; butch subcategory,
    construction 139; butch women 156;
    incorporation of 155
Butler, Judith 46, 115, 185

Califia, Pat 193
Cantrell, Jaime 19
Cape Town gay media 131
capitalism 62
Chen, Mel 49
Chen, Sophia 124
Chicanas-Latinas: cultural connections to Mexico
    60; *Marcha* activities 59; from U.S. "*gringas*" 59
choreograph 35
cisgender 103–104, 160n1; cisgender people 96;
    paradoxical deployment 115; trans studies
    critiques 114

cisheteronormative gender 214, 215
cisnormativity 102
citizenship status 67
civil rights 148, 193–194
Clarke, Cheryl 216
class/classism 117, 120
classroom 183–186
Cliff, Michelle 20
climate change 194
Clinton, Hillary 126
clothing styles 137
Cloud, Thunder 21
coalition-building projects 57
coding process 77
cognitive interface 150
Cohen, Cathy 65, 117
Cohen, Stanley 112
Cold War 171, 172
Collective Comments 23
color: queer women of 56; U.S. queer women
   of 57, 65
COMAL March 56–57, 60, 62, 68
communicative functions 148
community-based activism 205
community conference 68
community conversation 116
community formation 20, 45
compulsory heterosexuality 33, 165, 172
conflicting mediations 10–12
contra-queer affective moment 63
contra-queer politics 64
conventional femininity 165
conventional relationship 139
Coop-femmes network 13n3
Corinne, Tee 191
corpus analysis 158
corpus-informed approach 149
Cottrell, Honey Lee 191
COVID pandemic 48
Crenshaw, Kimberlé 43
critical race theory 111
cross-border meeting 58
cross-dressing 169
cross-generational friendships 74
cross-generational theme 81
cultural anxieties 113
cultural assimilation 60
Cvetkovich, Ann 49
Cypress College 118

data collection 75; participants 75–76
depoliticization 11
Desmoines, Harriet 20
devadasis (Hindu temple dancers) 34, 35
Dickinson, Emily 190
Diversity, Equity, and Inclusion (DEI) 111, 112, 117
diversity industry 124–126

Dobbin, Frank 124
dyke 157–158, 181, 200, 202; ethics of
   antimonogamy 50; gender-based sub-corpora
   157; identity 206
Dyke Marches 157, 202
dynamic sexual orientation 99

Edelman, Lee 122
Ellis, Havelock 201
emotional attachments 133
Enke, Finn 114
Enszer, Julie 19
epistemic community 150
epistemological category 41
erotic 33; concept of 45; hysteria 112–113;
   methodology 37
Escudero-Alías, M. 2
essentialism vs. constructivism 47
"ethical response-ability" 50
ethnographic research 132
evidence-less claims 118
existential threat 166
extraordinary activism 194

Facebook 148
Feinberg, Lesley 96, 194
female-female relations 6
female-indexing foundations 155
female invert 205
female lesbian experience 158
Female Liberation Newsletter of Durham-Chapel
   Hill 20
female sexuality 61
female sex work 61
Feminary Collective 17, 21, 25, 29; academic elitism
   19; feminist politics 21; social movement 23;
   southern lesbianism 20
Feminary journal 17, 20, 22, 28
femininity 101, 103, 112, 136
feminism 121; demonization 41; identity politics
   41; marginalization 41; outright dismissal of
   121; political problem 166; and
   postmodernism 40
feminist: activism 35; communities 101; cultural
   practice 66; deviance 38; and lesbian critiques 43;
   politics 21, 65; psychologists 106; scholarship 43;
   spiritual work 37; women 40
feminist movements 7, 101, 159
feminist revolution 2
feminist theory 47
femme 155–157; identification 156; incorporation
   of 155
Fernandes, Leela 37
first-generation bisexual mujer 58
Fleetwood, Nicole 26
focus group discussion (FGD) 132
Francophone lesbian communities 5

Garber, Linda 46

gay 102; liberation movement 44, 62, 106; male-focused nature 157

gender 5, 42, 44, 46, 120, 156, 181; academic studies of 113; assignment 216; binary logic of 139; categories 100, 119; conceptions of 92; as cultural category 106; deviance 33; fluidity of 104; inclusion of 6; individual experiences of 103; internal experience 106; liberation 217; metaphysics of 115; outlaws 96; performativity 41, 115; proliferation of 96, 107; psychological frameworks 93; queer conceptualization 6; and sexuality diversity 130; similarity 151

gender-affirming labors 118

gender-based sub-corpora **152, 154**; dyke **157**; femme and butch **156**; lesbian **154**; lesbian-indexing keywords **152**

gender-congruent women 147, 159

gender fatalism 214, 216, 217; conceptualizations of 214

gender identity 43, 103, 106, 148; birth-assigned sex 115; extrinsic sense 103; intrinsic sense 103; sexual identities from 147; sexual orientation 166

gender-sex configurations 151

Gender, Sexuality, and Feminist Studies (GSFS) 115

"gender skeptical" demonstrates 112

gender theory 125

gender transgression 185

gender variance 96

Gender-Variant Online Communication (G-VOC) corpus 149, 150

geographic boundaries 22

Gill-Peterson, J. 3

Global Fund Grant 2018–2020 130

global gay identity 61

globalization 130

Golden, Carla 95

Gopinath, Gayatri 66

Gottschalk, Donna 191

Grahn, Judy 44

Gubar, Susan 41

Hall, Juvenile 169

harassment 166

Harker, Jaime 19, 21

Hateful Conduct Policy 148

Heaney, Emma 217

hetero-gendered scripts 138

heteronormative scripts 136

heteronormative social structures 10

heteronormativity 6, 43, 44, 47, 102, 103, 117, 198, 199

heterosexism 44, 61, 62, 65, 131

heterosexual audience 10

heterosexuality 33, 43, 62, 66, 94, 136, 165

heterosexualization 47

heterosexual matrix 33

heterosexual parenting 33

heterosexual women 83

hierarchical classification system 60

historical connection 77

homophobia 94, 129, 130, 131, 190

homosexuality 43, 94, 130, 199; behavior 201; identities 134; morality/immorality of 130; stigma 106

homosexuality-is-un-African 130

Hong, Grace 59

hooks, bell 43

1979 Hudood Ordinance 34

human behavioral science 197, 206; philology of 198, 209; "responsibilities" of 207

Humanities programs 124

humanity 100

human rights 62

Hunter, Alberta 190

identity-based spaces 6

identity politics 43

"Identity: Skin Blood Heart" (Pratt) 23

ideological conflict 155

immigrant rights 67

imperialism 62

inclusive community identity 104–105

Indian urban reformers 34

indigenous black Zimbabweans 138

individuality 11

informal training 199

intellectual activism 41

Internet 164, 165

Interpretive Phenomenological Analysis 97, 98

intersectionality 26, 119; identity-based applications of 119; knowledge of 120; notion of 121

intersectionality wars 119

Jagose, Annamarie 46

Jamieson, Deborah 17–18, 23, 29, 30n7

Jeffreys, Sheila 68

Kalev, Alexandra 124

kinship 18, 43, 45, 49

knowledge production 59

Koolish, Lynda 191

Koyama, Emi 216

Kreeft, Peter 126

K-12 teachers 124

The Ladder 20

Laguna, María Isabel Barranco 61

language 197, 207; codes 7; crisis 41

2006 *La reunión internacional* 58–61

de Lauretis, Teresa 46

Lavery, Grace 121

Lawrence, Louise 168, 174

legal gender registration systems 215

lesbian community 20, 44, 75, 82–84, 83, 84,
    135, 206
lesbian criticism 41
"lesbian" designation 7
lesbian erasure 191, 192; concept of 192;
    conversations about 193; idea of 194
lesbian exclusion 91
lesbian experience 147
lesbian feminism 17, 57, 64, 147, 158;
    characteristics of 146; contemporary contexts 62;
    demonization 41; marginalization 41; same-sex
    sexuality 62
lesbian feminist moments 63
Lesbian, Gay, Bisexual, Trans, and Queer
    (LGBTQ+) 58, 92; activism 130; affairs staff
    person 115; campus organizations 116;
    community 3, 76, 86; framework 75; identities
    97; identity politics 68; spaces 80; student affairs
    position 120; student organizations 116
lesbian identity 7, 10, 68, 73, 78, 93, 97, 140, 146,
    147, 156, 158, 159, 198, 199, 205, 208, 209, 210;
    concept of 93, 200; as dynamic sexual orientation
    102–103; linguistic phrase 205; narrativization
    of 93; as political category 102–103; stigma
    105–106
lesbian imagination 193
lesbian-indexing identities 151, 155, 157, 158;
    between gender-based sub-corpora 152; in
    G-VOC corpus 151
lesbian invisibility 11, 190
lesbianism 21, 33, 37, 79, 135, 140, 146, 147,
    156, 159, 192; conceptualizations of 153, 160;
    construction of 134–135; language of 180, 181;
    political victories of 147
lesbian legal theory 215
lesbian liberation movement 106
lesbian movements 94–95
"lesbian-only policy" 6
lesbian/queer landscape 73
lesbians 102, 180; antagonism 149; category
    42–43, 133, 141; communities 2–3, 17; concept
    and identity of 75, 77, 190; critical enquiries
    41; feminist communities 101; geographies 6;
    lesbian invisibility 190; non-binary sub-corpus
    151; political identity 57; prevalence of 153;
    self-determination in 214–217; self-identifying
    as 141; self-styling 137–138; and separatism 193;
    sexuality 33, 41; social categorizations of 150;
    terminology of 73; U.S. culture 200
lesbian-specific public space 74
lesbian theory 1–2
lesbian thinkers 41
The Lesbian Tide 20
lesbian tradition 78
lesbian visibility 157; importance of 80
lesbian vitality 190–194
lesbian women 1, 74

lesbofeminismo 57; Chicana-Latina participants
    58; contra-queer moment of 63; contra-queer
    politics of 68; definition of 61; idea of 64; and
    lesbian identity 68; manifestation of 61; in
    Mexico City, 2006 61–64, 68; rise and formation
    of 61; sociopolitical cultural objectives 66; U.S.
    temporal-spatial grids 65; value of 62
lesbophobic language 158
lesbo-queer communities 5, 6, 12
linguistic nationalism 7
linguistic phrase 200–205
Lorde, Audre 2, 37, 43, 164
Love, Heather 49
Lugones, María 45

Madzimai Maka case 141–142
male-focused nature 157
Manalansan, Martin 65
"Maps" issue 21, 25
Marcha Lésbica (Lesbian March) 7, 56, 58, 62;
    public demonstration 66; U.S. queer women 65
marginalization 129
masculine self-styling 138–139
masculinity 112, 136
materiality 50
maternal pedagogy 33
McDonald, CeCe 217
McKittrick, Katherine 30n6
McPherson, Tara 25
Medical Research Council of Zimbabwe 132
memory transmission 10
Menon, Madhavi 33
mental disorder 202
meta-scientific perspective 199, 204
Mexican culture 59
Mexican lesbians 56, 58; feminists 62; Reunión
    meeting 66; U.S. identity 59
millennials 92–108
misogyny 19
Mitchell, Gregory 113
mobilization 112
Montreal Gay Women conferences 7
Montreal lesbian culture 13
Montreal lesbian spaces 5
Moraga, Cherríe 43, 65
moral panics 118
Morris, Bonnie 191
Mother Camp 167, 174
mouth-to-ear technique 6
Muparamoto, N. 3
mutual information (MI) 150
My Mama's Dead Squirrel (Segrest) 24

Nash, Jennifer 45, 119
National Day of Protest in the U.S. 67
natural dilation 173
neo-liberal byproducts 68

neoliberal Islamization 33
neoliberalism 61
neo-liberal policies 66
neo-liberal processes 62
Netflix 126
The New Critical movement 24
New Criticism 24
The New Criticism 24
Newkirk, Pamela 124
Nicholson, Charlotte 20
non-Anglo-Saxon 47
non-binary group 155
nonbinary individuals 203, 204
non-binary sub-corpus 151
non-feminist lesbian 122
non-gender conforming woman 81
non-GSFS students 116, 117
non-heteronormativity 158; identities 159;
    sexualities 129
non-heterosexual: community 11; feminisms 43;
    identities 155
non-lesbian sexualities 63
non-mental-disorder perspective 199
non-normative gender 156
non-privileged human lives 198
non-trans staff person 116
normative heterosexual masculinity 136
North Carolina Literary Review 19
nullgender 204

Olds, Sharon 193
oppression, intersecting systems 120
ownership 184

Page, Elliot 164–166
panic 119
pansexuality 200, 206
pantsula dancing 139
Parker, Pat 44
peculiarity 11
personal employment issues 148
physical space 6
play dynamic functions 137
plurisexuality 200, 206
political: commitment 79; homophobia 131, 134;
    lesbian identification 10; lesbianism 5, 6; lesbian
    movements 1; situatedness 210; visibility 130
political theory 44
"political utility of queer" 48
popular media narrative 147
pornographic imagination 33
positionality concept 47
post-Civil Rights 59
postcolonial modernity 34
postidentity-politics newcomers 73
postlesbianism 146
postmodernism 40

postmodern sexual pluralism 41
poststructuralism 41
poststructuralist theories 41
post World War II 168
potential synergies 74
poverty 43
Pratt, Minnie Bruce 19, 23–24, 194
professional dress 181
pro-gay marriage 66
proud black lesbian 134
proud lesbians 134
public visibility 80
"Punks, Bulldaggers, and Welfare Queens" 117

Q + A/email conflict 117
qualitative analysis 149
qualitative thematic analysis 73
Quality, Madzimai 140
quantitative analysis 150
quantitative survey 114
The Quebec Lesbian Network 14n4
Québécois national context 7
queer 1; categorizations 156; community 104, 105;
    designation 7; female sexuality 44; femininity
    158; identity 2, 104–105, 129; lesbian 44;
    mobilization 129; non-reproductive subject 122;
    politics 117, 133; theoretical criticism 46; woman
    200, 204
Queer and Trans People of Color 115
queer attack on feminist studies 112; feminist lesbian
    scholars 113; student-as-vulnerable-child 113
Queer Critique 116
queer feminist criticism 49
queerphobia 11
Queers & Allies 115, 117
Queer Studies House 115, 116
queer theory 2, 41, 45, 47, 50, 112; activist genesis
    44; institutionalization of 41; and lesbian oblivion
    48–51; lesbian voices in 42–48

race 43, 44, 46, 119, 120
race-based critical enquiries 41
racial violence 17
racism 19, 44, 102, 112, 117, 120
radical feminism 147
radical feminist texts 122
radicalism 26
radical lesbian feminists 94
radical lesbians 122, 159
radical self-love 217
radical strategy 7
Rainey, Ma 190
Ransom, John Crowe 24
Raymondian 167
Raymond, Janice 121, 165
"reality enforcement" system 215
reflexive subjects 84–86

regionalism 20
relational theory 49
relationships 82
Religious Studies 125
reparative readings 48
reproductive technologies 216
Réseau des lesbiennes du Québec (RLQ) 11
responsibility 207
Reunión Internaciónal (International Meeting) 57
Reunión meeting 66
Rich, Adrienne 7, 20, 62, 165
Richardson, Diane 216
right-wing conspiracy 126
Robson, Ruthann 215
Rodríguez, Juana María 60
romantic relationships 200
Roosevelt, Eleanor 190
Rowling, J.K. 68
Rubin, Gayle 112, 192
Ryan, Chibaba 137, 141

"safe space" sticker 185
same-gender sexual attraction 138, 199
same-sex attracted men 132, 133
same sex attracted women 130, 131, 132, 133;
    lesbian identity 133–134; limitations 132–133;
    subjective identities 133
same-sex marriage 66, 93
same-sex sexuality 62
San Francisco Dyke March 104–105
"Save the Children" campaign 125–126
secondary self-labels: butch esthetics 137–139;
    butch identities 135–137; femme lesbian
    139–140; identities, fluidity of 141–142; local
    labels 140
Sedgwick, Eve K. 43
Segrest, Mab 19, 20
self-categorization 203, 209
self-determination 214, 215
"Self-Identify" 114
self-style, lesbians 137–138
semi-structured interviews 132
separatism 7, 121, 193
Serna, Cristina 61
sex attraction 129
sex/gender binary 94, 96
sexism 102, 103, 117, 190
sexological modernism 166
sex panic 113
sexual: abuse 126; attraction 97, 135; behavior 97;
    boundaries 81; deviance 33; diversity 12; fluidity
    6; function 173; minority women 2; partnerships
    206; violence 34
Sexual Configuration Theory 97
sexual identity 37, 66, 93, 95, 105–106, 107;
    inclusiveness of 147; politics 129

sexuality 5, 13, 42, 44, 46, 61, 65, 82, 102, 131,
    167, 181; academic studies of 113; complexity
    of 43; concept of 43, 92; configurations
    156; diversity 130; politics 67; queer
    conceptualization 6
sex with men (MsM) 135
sex with women (WsW) 135
Sinister Wisdom 20, 193
"Sister Outsider" 164
skepticism 121
Smith, Barbara 43
social-behavioral phenomena 205
social justice activism 59
social justice efforts 125
social media 130, 132, 147–148, 159
social movement 23, 208
Solanas, Valerie 122
Southern 17, 21
Southern lesbian: monolithic notions 20; reflexivity
    17–30
southernness 21
space 138
specific trans pedagogy 188
S/place 23–28, 30n6
Stanford Large Network Data collection 149
State Department 171
stigma 105–106
Stone, Sandy 96
structural analysis 118, 120
Stryker, Susan 96, 173
Student Affairs Industrial Complex 123
student-as-vulnerable-child 113
student organizations 113
Sufi and *Kathak* classical dancer 35
Sullivan, Mairead 122

tawaifs (courtesans) 34, 35
teaching profession 179–183
terminology 131
textual analysis 199
t-female/t-male 119
thematic analysis 77
theoretical thematic analysis 76
Thomsen, Carly 113
Tompkins, Kyla Wazana 123
Touching Feeling 50
transactivism 193, 194
Trans Affinity Group 115, 119
transcription 117
transexclusion 147, 203
trans-exclusionary lesbianism 166
trans exclusionary radical feminists (TERFs)
    17, 111, 112, 165; case study 113–119;
    intersectionality 119–121
trans feminine 157, 214–217; over-representation
    of 155

transgender 62, 117, 157; activism 147; frameworks 63; identity 63; inclusion 2–3; individuals and practices 146; movements 107; "playing with gender" 146; revolution 95–97; self-categorization 147; self-identification 149; social categorizations of 150; terminology 136
trans historiography 168
trans-inclusive lesbian 147, 168, 198
transmasculinity 92, 157, 204
transnegativity 203
transphobia 2, 11, 112, 203; eradication of 112
transsexual 157; lesbian 168, 172, 174; vagina 172–174
transvestism 169
Triangle community 20
Triangle region 17
Trish, Madzimai 134
t-scores 150
Twitter 148, 155, 158, 159, 164, 165; transgender 150

Ulrichs, Karl Heinrich 201
umbrella terminology 149, 155
uniformity 23
U.S.: anti-racist 65; Chicanas-Latinas 59; feminism 210; lesbian feminism 62; sexual identity 66; social activism 203

Valerio, Max Wolf 193
Van Anders, Sari 97
Van Deurs, Kady 22
Vargas, Chevala 190
vilification 129
violent attacks 130

virtual spaces 13
visibility 80
von Krafft-Ebing, Richard 201

Walters, Suzanna Danuta 41
Waugh, Patricia 40
Weisinger, Jean 191
Weiss, Jillian 216
welfare queen 117
whisper campaign 114
white Western feminism 43
Wiegman, Robyn 48
Willey, Angela 50
Williams, Keira V. 19
Williams, Rachel Anne 216
WIP Movement 26
Wittig, Monique 3, 7, 215
Wollman, Leo 172
"woman-identified-woman" 62
Women in Print Movement 26
women-loving-women 1, 17
"women of color" 59, 60
women-only spaces 6, 10
womens: heterosexual script of 139; history and culture of 78; refusal of reproduction 122; sexual agency 95; sexual deviance 11, 21; sexuality 95; sexualization of 95; struggles of 78
working-class lesbian 42
working-class queer Chicana 58

Zimbabwe: gender and sexuality 130; same-sex attracted men 132; same-sex attracted people 141; same-sex attracted women 132; sexual identity in 141

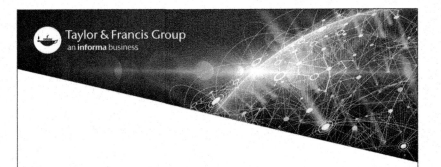